MW01120320

RACIAL CRIMINALIZATION OF MIGRANTS IN THE 21ST CENTURY

Advances in Criminology

Series Editor: David Nelken

Recent titles in the series

The full list of series titles can be found at the back of the book

Racial Criminalization of Migrants in the 21st Century

Edited by

SALVATORE PALIDDA
University of Genoa, Italy

ASHGATE

Published by
Ashgate Publishing Limited
Wey Court East
Union Road
Farnham
Surrey, GU9 7PT
England

Ashgate Publishing Company
Suite 420
101 Cherry Street
Burlington
VT 05401-4405
USA

www.ashgate.com

British Library Cataloguing in Publication Data
Racial criminalization of migrants in the 21st century. – (Advances in criminology)
   1. Racism in criminology – Europe. 2. Racism in criminology – Europe – Case studies. 3. Discrimination in criminal justice administration – Europe.
   4. Discrimination in criminal justice administration – Europe – Case studies.
   5. Equality before the law – Europe. 6. Equality before the law – Europe – Case studies. 7. Immigrants – Legal status, laws, etc. – Europe. I. Series II. Palidda, Salvatore.
   364'.086912'094–dc22

Library of Congress Cataloging-in-Publication Data
Racial criminalization of migrants in the 21st century / [edited] by Salvatore Palidda.
   p. cm.—(Advances in criminology)
  Includes index.
  ISBN 978-1-4094-0749-2 (hardback : alk. paper)—ISBN 978-1-4094-0750-8 (ebook)
  1. Crime and race—Europe. 2. Racism—Europe. 3. Immigrants—Europe.
  I. Palidda, Salvatore.

  HV6937.R33 2010
  364.3086'91094—dc22

2010034774

ISBN 9781409407492 (hbk)
ISBN 9781409407508 (ebk)

Mixed Sources
Product group from well-managed forests and other controlled sources
www.fsc.org Cert no. SA-COC-1565
© 1996 Forest Stewardship Council

Printed and bound in Great Britain by
MPG Books Ltd, Bodmin, Cornwall.

Contents

PART II   NATIONAL CASE STUDIES

PART III   PARTICULAR PRACTICES

List of Figures

List of Tables

List of Contributors

Hans-Joerg Albrecht is one of the most famous European criminologists; he is Director of the Max-Planck-Institut für Ausländisches und Internationales Strafrecht – MPIS (Freiburg im Breisgau, Germany) and author of many books.

José Ángel Brandariz García is a professor at the Facultad de Derecho of A Coruña University, Spain, and author of many essays on the topic of criminology and the sociology of law.

Fabienne Brion is a professor at the Catholic University of Louvain (Belgium) and director of the Centre de Recherches Interdisciplinaires sur la Déviance et la Pénalité. His scholarship intersects philosophy, the sociology of punishment and criminology. He is the author of many books.

Alessandro Dal Lago is Professor of the Sociology of Culture. He has been Dean of Faculty of Education at the University of Genoa, Italy, and director of many European research projects. His main publications are: *Non-Persons: The Exclusion of Migrants in a Global Society* (2009); *Mercanti d'aura. Logiche dell'arte contemporanea* (2006) and *Fuori cornice. L'arte al di là dell'arte* (with Serena Giordano) (2008); *Le nostre guerre. Filosofia e sociologia dei conflitti armati* (2010).

Alessandro De Giorgi is an Assistant Professor of Justice Studies at San José State University, USA. His research revolves around the political economy of punishment and the criminalization of migrants. He is the author of essays translated into many languages.

Cristina Fernández Bessa is a researcher at the Department: Departament de Dret Penal i Ciències Penals Department of University of Barcelona (Ub.Es), Spain. He has been an important researcher of the Spanish Team of Challenge European project.

Bernard E. Harcourt is the Julius Kreeger Professor of Law and Professor of Political Science at the University of Chicago, USA. His scholarship intersects social and political theory, the sociology of punishment, criminal law and procedure, and criminology. He is the author of many important books and the founder and editor of the journal *Carceral Notebooks*.

Yasha Maccanico is a researcher for Statewatch in the UK, after working in Spain and more recently in Italy. He has a particular expertise in the infringement of the democratic rules of state's right.

Marcello Maneri is Assistant Professor of Sociology at the University of Milano-Bicocca, Italy. He has published many essays on the media, migrations, security and war (most recently 'Peacetime war discourse: the political economy of bellicose metaphors. A success story', in Dal Lago and Palidda (eds) *Conflict, Security and the Reshaping of Society: The Civilisation of War* (2010).

Laurent Mucchielli is the Director of Research for the Centre National de la Recherche Scientifique (CNRS), lecturer at Versailles Saint-Quentin University, France, Director of the Centre de Recherches Sociologiques sur le Droit et Les Institutions Pénales (CESDIP). He is the author of many books.

Sophie Nevanen, is a research engineer at CESDIP and author of many essays with the collaboration of other CESDIP researchers.

Salvatore Palidda is Professor of Sociology at the Faculty of Education, University of Genoa, Italy. He holds a Phd in Sociology and European Studies from the Ecole des Hautes Etudes en Sciences Sociales, Paris. He has been co-director and director of several European research projects. His main books are: *Polizia postmoderna. Etnografia del nuovo controllo sociale* (2000); *Mobilità umane* (2008), and, as editor, *Délit d'immigration* (1996); (with Dal Lago) *Conflict, Security and the Reshaping of Society: The Civilisation of War* (2010).

Federico Rahola is Assistant Professor of Sociology of Cultural Processes at the University of Genoa, Italy, where he teaches Sociology of Global Processes. He is a member of the editorial board of REMHU (Brasilia), 'Etnografia e ricerca sociale' and *Conflitti globali*. He is the author of *Zone definitivamente temporanee, I luoghi dell'umanità in eccesso* (2003), *Israele come paradigma* (2008) and *Palestina annozero* (2010).

Nando Sigona is Senior Researcher at the Centre on Migration, Policy and Society (COMPAS) and Research Officer at the Refugee Studies Centre, both at the University of Oxford, UK. He also teaches Refugee Studies at Oxford Brookes University. His research interests include anthropology of migration and forced migration, ethnopolitics and migrants' claim making, and Romani studies.

Nidhi Trehan of the School of Public Policy/Political Science, University College, London, works actively in the areas of human rights and social policy as a practitioner and academic, and has published in the areas of human rights, identity politics, NGOs/social movements and migration.

Jérôme Valluy, Docteur en Science Politique (Science Po Paris), Maître de Conférences des Universités (Section 04 : science politique), Habilité à diriger des recherches-HDR (Université de Strasbourg) is Professor of Political Sociology and Public Action at the Université Panthéon-Sorbonne (Paris 1) UFR Science politique. He is the author of many books on the topic of asylum.

Acknowledgements

This book collects some contributions proposed for the workshop 'Criminalization and victimization of immigrants in Europe', organized by S. Palidda at the Dipartimento di Scienze Antropologiche of Genoa University, in the framework of Workpackage 3, 'Processes of criminalization and (de)criminalization', of the Crimprev Programme (*Assessing Deviance, Crime and Prevention in Europe* – Coordination Action – 6th FWP – Contract No. 028300 financed by the European Commission). The contribution of Mary Bosworth and Mhairi Guild, 'Governing Through Migration Control: Security and Citizenship in Britain' is published in the *British Journal of Criminology* 2008, 48, 6: 703–19 and that of Marcelo Aebi and Nathalie Delgrande, 'Les détenus étrangers en Europe: quelques considérations critiques sur les données disponibles de 1989 à 2006' in *Déviance & Société* 2009, 33, 4: 475–9. The contribution of Gabriella Petti, 'Enemies-criminals: The law and courts against global terrorism' is published in *Conflict, Security and the Reshaping of Society: The Civilization of War*, edited by Alessandro Dal Lago and Salvatore Palidda, London: Routledge, 2010, 138–50.

I would like to thank both the authors of the chapters in this book as well as the colleagues and friends who participated in workshops and debates organized in various European countries during the course of this research project. My thanks in particular go to Marcelo Aebi, Abdelahk Azamouz, Mohamed Ba, Edoardo Bazzaco, Roberto Bergalli, Didier Bigo, Hocine El Kebich, Eric Heilmann, Manuel Delgado Ruiz, Nathalie Delgrande, Silvia Finzi, Jean Pierre Garson, Jef Huysmans, René Lévy, Ainom Maricos, Gary T. Marx, Giuseppe Mosconi, Abdeljabbar Moukrim, Dalila Nadi, Mariella Pandolfi, Michel Peraldi, Antonello Petrillo, Gabriella Petti, Iñaki Rivera Beiras, Lucy Rojas, Matteo Sanfilippo, Fulvio Vassallo Paleologo, and also some friends – judges and police officers.

Chapter 1

Introduction

Salvatore Palidda

Throughout history, societies have been marked by periods of persecution and violence, at times extreme violence, directed at the 'outsider', i.e. the 'enemy of the time'.[1] But how can the intensification of the persecution of Roma people and gypsies, and of the criminalization of immigrants in present-day Europe be explained?

As the contributions collected in this volume show, it is a most elementary mechanism of social control, emerging as being useful, if not indispensable, to the solidity and/or realignment of political cohesion. The latter is in fact nourished by the fear and the insecurity attributed to such an enemy to justify practices of power that blend all sorts of prohibitionism, protectionism and authoritarianism, which also target the weaker segments of the indigenous population. The war against outsiders, against those who are different, may thus be considered one of the 'total political facts'[2] that pervades a society through discourses, rhetoric and practices that consolidate a real or supposed majority. Hence, it will be argued here, in the current racist approach that characterizes the management of societies we can find that there are overlaps with the discourses and practices applied to colonized peoples and the subordinate classes in the nineteenth and twentieth centuries.[3]

---

1   On these aspects, see my previous works in which I refer to Michel Foucault's body of thought (see especially Palidda, 2000, 2009c, 2010b, 2010c).

2   Here I recast the term 'total social fact' (*fait social total*) known as one of the most famous concepts proposed by Marcel Mauss. The notion was coined by his student Maurice Leenhardt after Durkheim's 'social fact' but in Mauss (1999 [1950], pp. 147ff.;) is cited as 'total social phenomenas'. In my interpretative perspective I prefer to speak of 'political' fact because I think that the 'war' against migrants is one of the most important aspects characterizing the political organization of the contemporary state at local, national and global level (see also Dal Lago and Palidda, 2010). The concept 'total social fact' applied to migrations is proposed by Sayad (2004, French 1999) and myself Palidda (2008a).

3   Some studies by historians and other social science researchers show that the treatment of immigrants as inferiors, and their subjection to racism and criminalization, are carried out to maintain the privileges and the dominance of the autochthonous population. For example, Italian immigrants in the United States in the nineteenth and twentieth century were among the lowest-paid workers – even paid less than blacks themselves (see also the very excellent documentary films *Pane Amaro*, by Gianfranco Norelli for RAI (see http://www.lagrandestoria.rai.it/category/0,1067207,1067034-1070313,00.html;   http://www.lagrandestoria.rai.it/category/0,1067207,1067034-1070457,00.html;   http://www.i-italy.

In other terms, the persecution of gypsies and the criminalization of migrants is currently written into a neoliberal/neoconservative political framework based on the asymmetry of power and wealth between actors that are all-powerful, and weak ones who have no rights and/or are reduced to the state of 'non-persons'.[4]

The story of the current war against immigration is intertwined with the developments in criminalization that began with the neoconservative revolution in the USA and the UK (Thatcher reached power in 1979, Reagan did so in 1981).[5] The success of this revolution continued without interruption even under 'Democratic' or 'social-democratic' administrations (Clinton, Blair, Jospin, the centre-left in Italy, and even Zapatero in Spain),[6] also because the neoconservative *discourse* (in the Foucauldian acceptation of the term) has ended up phagocytizing a sizeable share of intellectuals and leaders on the left.[7] But it is only today that the process emerges more clearly as the shift from government meant to pursue the liberal-democratic myth (as described by Foucault[8]) to neoliberal management that only pursues the *hic et nunc* prosperity of the stronger parties. The exacerbation

---

org1355/pane-amaro-quella-storia-che-ancora-non-si-conosce) and *Italians in the world* – http://vodpod.com/watch/941828-italians-in-the-world-part-1-the-beginning. Among other references in this book, see Duroselle and Serra (1978); Franzina and Stella (2002); Le Cour Graindmaison (2005); Balibar and Wallerstein (1991); Thomas (2010); Palidda (2008a).

4   The idea of nonpersons is proposed by Dal Lago (1999a) with implicit reference to H. Arendt.

5   With Thatcher and Reagan the neo-conservative management of the neo-liberal revolution in all sectors produced, in particular, the imbalance between social prevention, police prevention, prosecution, penalties, recovery or social reintegration and then the escalation of imprisonment described in the chapters of this book.

6   It is important to remember that Blair's policy may be considered as the beginning of the acceptance by the European left of neo-liberal/neoconservative thinking and practices. This is most evident in the Italian case and explains the success of Berlusconi and of the nordist party (Lega Nord) versus the former-left that has become more and more right-wing oriented.

7   In the Italian version of this book, we adopted the title 'Democratic Racism', not out of gratuitous provocation, but because the practices of racialization that are widespread in Europe today (see also Fassin, 2009) sometimes manage to affect the majority of the population, also that part of society that claims to be 'democratic' or 'on the left', the same kind of political position that supports 'humanitarian wars' to export democracy with the force of arms, and is pervaded by the urge to propagate post-modern political oxymorons. It is emblematic: sometimes such practices are hidden behind the ambiguities promoting interculturality or multiculturalism, just like it happens when the EU does, when it grants financial contributions for the day against racism, good anti-discrimination practices, or the struggle against 'human trafficking', while with its right hand spurs on and finances prohibitionism, by organizing what is in effect a war against migrations. See Fassin and Fassin (2008); Palidda (2010a).

8   In particular, see: the following volumes of his courses at the *Collège*, see Foucault (1997, 2004a, 2004b, 2008).

of criminalization, of Giuliani's 'zero tolerance' policies, or of the experiments aimed at the elimination of 'human surplus',[9] in short, of what Simon (2008) and others term the 'Crime Deal', they all reflect a management of society that a priori excludes social recovery, integration or rehabilitation, because it seeks only to 'maximize' the profits of those who are in power. Why take care of marginal people, drug addicts, the poor, deviants, and why promote the stable, peaceful and regular integration of immigrants when, today, the growth of profits can be obtained via the erosion of workers' rights, their inferiorization until they are almost reduced to a condition of neo-slavery, which also means getting rid of them at the first sign of their insubordination, when they pretend to lay claims or are too worn out, and can easily be replaced by other rightless non-persons? The government of the people taking care of its inhabitants to construct a stable, peaceful and well-regulated society in accordance with the norms of a universalistic legal order, up to the point of seeking to make everyone happy,[10] has never existed. But, since the early 1970s (i.e. since the end of second post-War new deal or – in French terms – *les Trente Glorieuses*), the political organization of the wealthy societies of the post-war period had given the impression that it was possible to aim for this prospect through the development of welfare, the softening of sentences, even of repression, democratization, and the pursuit of social balance through prevention, recovery and the widening of political participation.[11] The advent of the globalized neoconservative revolution[12] routed any such illusions, and humiliated and absorbed the intellectuals and the leaderships that once harboured them. It is hence absolutely natural that there is a rediscovery of government through manipulation of fear and of zero tolerance, which also becomes a source of consensus and profits, further diminishing the capabilities for political action by weaker parties. The careers and business deals undertaken, particularly over these last 20 years by those who have taken advantage of the new management of society

---

9   The idea of 'human surplus' or 'wasted lives' is formulated by Rahola (2003) and Bauman (2004) alluding to the condition of 'humanity in excess' as equivalent to toxic waste to be disposed of, often illegally. It then breaks the liberal-democrat myth, whereby all people must be cared after 'from cradle to grave', as described by Foucault (2004a).

10   As observed by Foucault (2004a) this was what even the thinkers on modern policing theorized, including Turquet de la Mayenne, von Justi, Delamare and also Guillauté.

11   In all the rich countries, a process of democratization and growth of welfare provision developed, although 'paternalistic' or 'pastoral' versions of the welfare state degraded it to parasitic handouts for political patronage. With the excuse of attacking these practices and excessive public indebtedness, liberalism has effectively proceeded to carry out a 'non-creative destruction', by almost entirely eliminating social prevention and integration from the array of public policies, favouring only repression and penal measures (see the chapters by De Giorgi and Palidda).

12   That is, the interweaving of financial, technological and military-policing revolutions into a political framework that becomes dominant thanks to the intensification of the asymmetries of power, strength and wealth; see Joxe (2005: 70–79, 2010).

(which has nothing to do with pastoral/paternalist or liberal-democratic notions of governmentality) are extraordinary and unprecedented in their proportions.[13] The same can be said for its victims, although today there are no longer armies shooting at impoverished crowds: to count the victims, it would be necessary to define new criteria to 'measure' the indirect or 'collateral', yet deadly, consequences of embargoes, of 'humanitarian wars', of prohibitionism against migrations and even of international aid in the event of natural catastrophes.

Thus, after the United States (Frampton, Lòpez, Simon, 2008), it appears that the Crime Deal has triumphed also in Europe, with effects that are not yet fully understood by the majority of the autochthonous people but, rather tragically, only by its victims.[14]

A Europe of States Competing in the Persecution of Gypsies and Immigrants

As shown by the copious data and information provided by the contributions gathered in this volume, since the start of the 1990s European countries have increasingly become more dogged in their persecution of gypsies (see Sigona's

---

13   According to some qualitative researches on police transformations (Jobard and Levy, 2009; Slama, 2008, Jobard and Nevanen, 2007; Mucchielli, 2008a; Bonelli, 2008; Bigo, 1996a, 2004; Ocqueteaux, 2004; Heilmann, 2007) or on what I call the 'revolution in police affairs' (Palidda, 2010c), it is useful to notice the success of some police officers with no particular professional qualities in many countries (as in the state of New York, in France, or Italy) thanks to their performances in the 'crime deal' (after Simon, 2007). As some recent revelations of more than one hundred retired New York Police Department captains and higher-ranking officers, according to two criminologists studying the department (see http://www.nytimes.com/2010/02/07/nyregion/07crime.html, and also video ABC News: interview with policeman Adil Polanco), many crime statistics during Giuliani's zero tolerance policies were falsified. In that frame, many 'democratic' or simply correctly behaved policemen have been marginalized or obliged to retire. As a matter of fact one of the consequences of the revolution in police affairs is the decline in professionalism and the incapacity of applying a pacific and regular management of social disorder. As for the crime deal, it is very interesting to note that all the business magazines or newspapers have discovered the profitable security market (intended as 'post-modern' controls or 'panopticon') in the last decade of the twentieth century and at the beginning of the twenty-first. In particular, the profits concern the extraordinary growth of video-surveillance, private polices, scanning, electronic bracelets, and other devices – more and more after the attacks of 11 September 2001 as well as the London and Madrid bombings (see Heilmann, 2007; Norris, Moran and Armstrong, 1998; Norris and Armstrong, 1999).

14   Among others and as Sayad wrote (1999/2004), Saskia Sassen also notes: 'When a state extends arbitrary powers to governors and police forces, sooner or later the latter will reach – and target – citizens. It might take that to happen in order for those in charge to shift from the *drive to control* to the *art of governing* these flows' (http://www.opendemocracy. net/saskia-sassen/immigration-control-vs-governance).

chapter) and immigrants, but also of that portion of indigenous people who are labelled as 'surplus humanity', similarly to the rubbish that one no longer knows how to dispose of (it may prove a new opportunity for recycling mafias after the experience with toxic wastes).[15]

It was more or less at the end of the famous 'Glorious Thirty Years'[16] (the decades of strong post-War growth), and particularly following the so-called oil crisis of 1973–74, that countries which were historical recipients of immigration started adopting policies to 'stop' it.[17] In reality, immigration into rich countries continued without interruption, while being in some cases still encouraged. The case of the car industry in France is emblematic, in that by persisting in exploiting the *O.S. à vie*, that is, immigrants whose skill and wage advancement was blocked, it postponed technological innovation and recruited, in particular, Moroccans through imams who were even provided places of worship in factories in order to keep them well separated from the unionized workforce.[18] It was at the end of the war in Indochina that rich countries accepted tens of thousands of *boat people*, whereas today they criminalize asylum seekers (see Valluy in this book, and also Vassallo Paleologo, 2009; Kobelinsky and Makaremi, 2009). Again in the 1970s and 1980s, hundreds of thousands of Portuguese, not yet members of

---

15　It is no exaggeration as there is very little information about the victimization, the suicides and numerous death cases of marginal persons, in particular where rich countries discharge their wastes (for example in Somalia and in the Gulf area but also near Naples, where the population revolting against the dangers for health and environment provoked by the landfill site has been considered victim of the so-called NIMBY effect – see Petrillo, 2009; see also Bauman, 2004). In the last 20 years one of the profitable activities carried out by the Italian mafia and other international entrepreneurs is precisely the disposal of toxic waste. Somali sea 'piracy' has developed just against such a phenomenon. Asked about the seizure of *Buccaneer* in 2009, Somalia's ambassador in Geneva said that 'those from Puntland are not pirates, are not criminals: they are fishermen exasperated by illegal fishing and toxic waste from the landfill continuing on our shores' (see: http://ricerca.repubblica. it/repubblica/archivio/repubblica/2009/04/15/controlleremo-il-carico-del-buccaneer. html; see also Jeffrey Gettleman's article in the *New York Times*: http://www.nytimes. com/2009/05/09/world/africa/09pirate.html).

16　The '*Trente glorieuses*' formula is frequently used by many French authors to indicate the thirty years after the Second World War: that is, a period marked by very strong economic development, that, with Polany, we can define as the 'great transformation'.

17　The so-called 'stopping migration politics' was adopted by the OECD countries in 1974 (after the oil crisis of 1973). In fact, the real stop began at the end of the 1980s and especially in the 1990s. Immigration to south Europe is more recent, i.e. in the context of the 'second great transformation' and, in particular, carried out by undocumented immigrants inserted in shadow economies. It is important to outline that most immigrants in the last 20 years have been undocumented; some of them has been regularized but probably the majority went back to their countries or elsewhere (on the Italian case, see Palidda, 2008a, 2009a and for the Spanish case, see Bergalli, 2006 and Delgado Ruiz, 2010).

18　I refer here to the research about the *O.S.* in the automobile industry (see Sayad, 2004 [1999]; see also Catani and Palidda, 1987).

the European Community, migrated to France – but also elsewhere – as did as many from the Maghreb region, Turks, Asians migrated to Germany, Belgium, Holland and other countries. In effect, coinciding with the Fall of the Berlin Wall, an increasingly overt prohibitionist shift began, which also deformed political and humanitarian asylum policy as it had been practised until then in Europe. It seemed almost as if the borders with countries 'of the South' were suddenly closed, while slowly borders opened up with the countries of the East; recall that until 1990, citizens of Maghreb countries and other countries from the South were not subject to visa requirements. It was from the start of the 1990s that European police forces started adopting racial profiling as an instrument of customary repression and control and the selection of immigrants,[19] informal but nonetheless effective, was primed to favour people coming from Eastern Europe, from Latin America, from the Philippines and some other Asian countries, to the detriment of 'Arabs' (this already before 9/11).[20] In countries with a long history of immigration, criminalization increasingly took on racist features, striking the children of immigrants first and, almost to a lesser degree, new immigrants. In countries of new immigration, there was an evident, progressive replacement of the autochthonous clients of police forces with foreigners.[21] The cases of Italy, Spain, Portugal and Greece are quite emblematic, and resemble what occurred earlier in the United States and, in part, what is also taking place in European countries where immigration   is long-standing. The combination between the near impossibility of regular immigration, and of maintaining resident status for immigrants, and the repressive clampdown targeting them, unfailingly produces an ideal payoff from a neoliberal/neoconservative point of view: on the one hand, the reproduction of irregulars, a labour force which is enslaveable because it has no rights and no possibility of accessing them (almost a sort of 'post-modern' cannon fodder); on the other, the easy stigmatization as enemy of the moment to whom responsibility for all the fears, insecurities, economic problems and social malaise caused by neoliberalism itself can be attributed. It is not a process that has been carefully planned by a 'Big Brother', but rather, of government through fear that gives rise to a veritable 'Crime Deal' in wealthy countries.

However, as we will see in the reports of Amnesty International and other NGOs (see Sigona's and Trehan's chapter), in some countries the harassment of gypsies and immigrants is worse than in others (see, in particular, the relationship between the rates of detention of foreigners and nationals). In the United States, Blacks and Latinos are imprisoned far more than WASPs (as if to confirm Huntington's theory, see Dal Lago's chapter) and there are now more than 13 million irregulars and a sizeable turnover in this category that has guaranteed the growth of the U.S.

19   On racial profiling in the United States, see Harcourt's chapter in this volume.
20   See Palidda (2009a) and Bribosia and Rea (2002).
21   See prison statistics in each chapter of this book, except for France, where there is a growth of detainees in *Illegal Immigrant Detention Centres*.

economy for at least 25 years.[22] Seemingly, there is lesser repressive doggedness in Europe, less imprisonment, less irregulars, but underground economies have developed everywhere, even in countries that deemed themselves immune to it, by exploiting both rightless foreigners or non-people and part of those autochthonous people who are discriminated against, often because they are children of immigrants. Nonetheless, in America and Europe alike, there has been a clear decrease in criminal offences, in spite of the frequent inflation of statistics by police forces and political entrepreneurs of zero tolerance.[23] In other terms, if there are more arrests while fewer crimes are being committed, this is only because the powers that be have chosen the criminalization of social problems rather than seeking to solve them, something that is certainly not done by shooting at crowds, massacring marginals and filling up prisons. But the social treatment of society's ills, worsened by neoliberal development, does not produce profits.[24]

The prohibitionist logic of 'Fortress Europe' may have caused fewer deaths among migrants who have sought to reach European borders than among those who did not leave and starved or died in wars. By now, those who migrate know they

---

22   FAIR estimates that in 2007 the illegal immigrant population was above 13 million persons. Government and academic estimates indicate that as of 2006 there were 11–12 million illegal immigrants living in the United States. The Center for Immigration Studies estimated the illegal immigrant population at 10 million as of November 2004 (see http://www.fairus.org/site/News2?page=NewsArticle&id=16859&security=1601&news_iv_ctrl=1007). But some estimates of 2008, like the one from Bear Stearns, believe the count is actually closer to a whopping 20 million (http://ohmygov.com/blogs/general_news/archive/2008/04/10/number-of-illigal-immigrants-in-u-s-may-be-closer-to-20-million.aspx). Concerning the contribution of irregular immigrants to U.S. economic growth, in particular from 1980 until the most recent economic crisis, see http://www.libraryindex.com/pages/2465/Impact-Immigration-on-Twenty-First-Century-America-CALIFORNIA-S-ROLE-IN-IMMIGRATION.html, the Rand Report of Kevin F. McCarthy and Georges Vernez (http://www.rand.org/pubs/monograph_reports/MR854.1/) and http://web.mit.edu/cis/fpi_immigration.html#V Their contribution will also probably be decisive for the overcoming of the current crisis.

23   According to the most renowned statistical institutes, since 2005 the data show crime is decreasing all over the developed world (and not just in Western Europe but also in the Balkans). Japan presents a similar situation (see Simon, 2007). Among the others, the Italian case is very emblematic: violent crimes (homicide, forcible rape, robbery and assault) as well as property crimes (burglary, larceny/theft, motor vehicle theft and arson) are in decline, in particular, from 2005 the figure for homicides is around 600 each year, while it was 2,453 in 1981 and 1,918 in 1991 (see Palidda, 2008a).

24   Between an educator who takes care of wayward teens and a CCTV camera that records their misdemeanours to later enable their arrest, administrators choose the latter even if it is not cost-effective: why spend money to prevent the youngsters from ending up in prison and becoming serial offenders? The question is then who should pay the social costs of a mode of development that produces 'surplus humanity'. On 'post-modern controls' see journals such as *Conflitti globali*, 5 (2007) and *Surveillance & Society*, http://www.surveillance-and-society.org/

are risking their lives, even after setting foot on European soil. The accounts of the living and working conditions of so-called illegals, and the appalling conditions in centres for undocumented migrants or during deportations, constitute an indelible testimony of what European democracy is capable of producing.[25] At the same time, the European Union shrouds itself in humanitarian rhetoric and lavishes with generous aid a number of NGOs that do not always make serious efforts to safeguard the fundamental rights of the weak; in fact, many of them end up embroiled in prohibitionist practices, if not in authentic wars against immigration, as happens to journalists, social scientists and other operators who are 'embedded' in theatres of war (Pandolfi and Fassin, 2008; Pandolfi, 2002).

However, there is a considerable difference between countries such as Italy, which has exacerbated a set of rules that provoke the growth of irregularity , and others who, in spite of prohibitionism, nonetheless still provide a modicum of certainty to the legal order.

Upstream from this globalized catastrophe of fundamental rights there is, firstly, the asymmetry of power and wealth between strong actors on one side, and immigrants and the indigenous weak on the other. Unfortunately, it is difficult to imagine the overcoming of this catastrophe precisely because of this asymmetry: how can immigrants and native workers themselves, who are increasingly pushed towards the condition of rightlessness, conquer bargaining power and capacity for political action? For the time being, one can only observe the unfolding dynamics, particularly at a micro sociological level. Perhaps, immigrants and the precarious and/or rightless workers are starting to experience forms and modes of public action that differ from those of the past. The high number of immigrants who have enlisted in trade unions is rather significant, but it is often a sort of tax that is due in order to have protection from employers and the state, demonstrating the extreme weakness of the condition of the foreign worker.[26]

The Contents of this Book

The first part of the book includes contributions which neatly analyse the issues concerning the discourse on migration – today characterized by prohibitionist policies and racial criminalization of migrants. Alessandro Dal Lago's contribution proposes a historical-methodological reflection showing the analogies, the

---

25   Among the many reports criticizing these conditions, we recall those by Amnesty International and other documents on various websites including http://fortresseurope. blogspot.com/2006/02/immigrants-dead-at-frontiers-of-europe_16.html

26   In Italy, there are now over 800,000 members in the different trade unions but, unfortunately, most of these memberships are a sort of mere tax paid to enjoy some safeguard or assistance, whereas the effective promotion of their trade union and political participation is rare and some trade unionists behave as much as racists as small business owners. See Palidda (2009a).

differences and the paradoxes of the theses which are used to justify discrimination and wars, theorizing conflicts among cultures. Critical analysis of racialization discourse and practices is featured also in the study presented by Fabienne Brion, with particular attention to the production of new laws: that is, cultural crimes. Marcello Maneri offers a new analysis of how the construction of prohibitionist discourse is developing into a trivialized form of racism pervading all segments of society through the influence of the media. After a short excursus on the most interesting interpretations of borders, Federico Rahola shows the 'new apparatus of capture (or detention?)' that is configured with the development of neo-liberalism ruled by neo-conservatives. In such a frame we witness the metamorphosis of the right to (political and humanitarian) asylum, transforming applicants into suspected terrorists or delinquents (see Valluy's contribution). Nando Sigona and Nidhi Trehan's chapter highlights the (re)criminalization of Roma communities: that is, the first victims of neoliberal Europe.

In the work of Delgrande and Aebi,[27] it clearly emerges that this escalating process of criminalization is generalized and effectively led by countries that, since the end of World War II, have claimed to be the most democratic in the world, either when governed by the right or by the left. Europe is now approaching the levels of 'large-scale internment' that have been experimented with by the United States, where at least a glimmer of hope can now be seen with Obama (see De Giorgi's chapter). Processing the most significant data and analysing international comparisons,[28] it is possible to see that the EU countries that imprison foreigners the most are Italy, Greece, Portugal and the Netherlands, but those that criminalize 'irregulars' the most, transforming what is an administrative offence into a criminal one, either through enforcement or legislation, are Sarkozy's France and Blair's (and Brown's) United Kingdom in particular.[29]

In Europe, it is striking that the crimes immigrants are charged with are mainly linked to the impossibility of immigrating there regularly. To this, must be added the enormous difficulties and injustices undergone to maintain a regular immigration status. In sum, these are the consequences of a prohibitionism against migrants that grants full discretion, when not free judgement, to police forces, employers and local authorities.

Beyond the small neo-Nazi groups, Germany appears as the country with less diffusion of racist criminalization practices (see Albrecht). However, even in this

27 Aebi and Delgrande are the authors of the annual Report Space (Annual Penal Statistics of the Council of Europe) see http://www.coe.int/t/e/legal_affairs/legal_co-operation/prisons_and_alternatives/Statistics_SPACE_I/List_Space_I.asp#TopOfPage

28 Following a critical analysis perspective, and hence of deconstruction of statistics deemed to be a measurement of what one wants to and is able to measure. See Kitsuse and Cicourel (1963); Robert (2005).

29 It seems unlikely that the new coalition government will change this, despite the original promise of the Liberal Democrats.

country where there are many efforts to combat racism, the trend in its favour is clearly inscribed in the Eurocentric and neo-liberal frame.

The French case is particularly emblematic. In spite of the exacerbation of repression against the *racaille* (the young 'scum' coming from the *banlieues*) and the immigrants who 'dare to seek to take advantage of the social welfare system' (see Mucchielli's and Nevanen's chapter) – an exacerbation which has helped formerly interior minister Sarkozy in the extraordinary endeavour of getting himself elected as *président de la République* – the actual number of immigrant detainees has decreased, while the internment of *clandestins* has greatly increased (see Mucchielli and Nevanen). Moreover, as noted by the most important French researchers on human and social sciences, with the creation of a Ministry of Immigration and National Identity, the Sarkozy administration destroying the entire French tradition of the struggle for universal rights for all, suggests a revaluation of colonialism and a new aggressive prohibition of migrations.[30]

The same logic has driven British governments, which, moreover, have started dabbling in the criminalization of citizens of foreign origin (Bosworth and Guild, 2008). In fact, the French and British cases show that irregular immigrants are not the only scapegoats of nativist campaigns. One could equally well say that the targets are citizens of foreign origin, and particularly those born in the country from immigrant parents, who do not accept to and cannot be treated like illegals, that is, as beings without rights who are easily forced to suffer all kinds of impositions (see Maccanico' chapter).[31]

Spain, first under Aznar and now under Zapatero, does not seem to belie the prevailing trend in Europe, because it has not entirely got rid of Francoism and because it has embarked directly on a neoliberal path of development fuelled by the underground economy, that is, off the tears and blood of *clandestinos* (see Garcia's and Fernandez's chapter).

But it is Italy that is at a vanguard of the process. Undoubtedly the country that has advanced furthest in neoconservative development, Italy has been pursuing and reproducing, for twenty years now, the transformation of immigrants into *clandestini*, both as a formidable resource for the country's economy, and as a politically profitable scapegoat for the racist nature of the right's Crime Deal, with its corollary of mayor-sheriffs of the left and the right and *homini novi* of the so-called Second and Third Republics (see Palidda's chapter). It is not by chance,

---

30   Among those researchers: M. Agier, E. Balibar, M.C. Blanc-Chaléard, L. Boltanski, M. Detienne, E. Fassin, M. Feher, F. Héritier, D. Kunth, L. Mucchielli, P. Ndiaye, G. Noiriel, M. Potte-Bonneville, R. Rechtman, S. Slama, E. Terray, T. Todorov, P. Virilio, S. Wahnich and P. Weil. See the excellent video: *Ulysse Clandestin*, available at: www.labandepassante.org/index_lbp.php. On the French case, see also E. Fassin (available at: http://www.monde-diplomatique.fr/2009/11/FASSIN/18386 - NOVEMBRE 2009).

31   On the theories of minors' juvenile deviance, see Mauger (2009).

as shown by Fulvio Vassallo Paleologo (2009), that Italy has become the first European country at war against refugees and migrants.

On the Continuum of Wars

For around two decades we have seen the proliferation of what could be called 'post-modern oxymorons': 'humanitarian war', limitations placed on freedoms in the name of security, detention centres placed beyond the jurisdiction of the laws of war, physical restraints (in other words, torture) in the name of democratic justice, and the deprivation of any legitimate status for enemies (as captured in the very broad definition of 'enemy combatants'). The kind of enemy transcends the traditional geopolitical imagination, which still provided, to a certain extent, the frame for Huntington's (1996) famous essay on the 'clash of civilizations'. The current enemy does not represent any civilization in the eyes of the liberal West but, if anything, the perversion of a religion that is easily able to penetrate the defences of 'our world'.

Migrants originating from Muslim countries in Africa and Asia are considered in the reports of various security agencies to be fertile terrain for fundamentalism and therefore terrorism (Bigo, Bonelli, Deltombe, 2009). Naturally, fighting the enemy inside complex urbanized societies with sophisticated infrastructures entails both innovative tactics and a redefinition of those liberal standards that represent the very foundation of Western societies. It might very well be argued that a continuum has been created between the global war on terrorism, war on migration and war for internal security in 'democratic' countries (Palidda, 1999; 2000; 2009a and 2009b). Amongst the most vile consequences of the prohibitionism practised in EU countries we can observe the denial of asylum to refugees coming from Afghanistan, Iraq, Palestine, Sudan and generally from all countries afflicted by war. Hundreds of people flee from massacres by the Taliban or warlords and risk their lives to reach Europe and are treated as common illegal immigrants, jailed and destined for deportation. Meanwhile, all EU and NATO countries continue to increase military expenditure.[32] They also increase the cost of enforcement against

---

32   See *SIPRY Yearbook 2010*: 192, Military Spending and Armaments, 2009, available: http://www.sipri.org/yearbook/2010/05). Military expenditure in Europe was $386 billion in 2009, an increase of 2.7 per cent in real terms over 2008. Germany budgeted €570 million for operations in Afghanistan in 2009, and France €330 million, while Italy budgeted €242 million for the first 6 months of 2009. In the global debate on measures to combat the economic crisis that exploded in 2008 due to financial speculation, no government or any parliamentary opposition of the 'democratic' countries mentioned the possibility of reducing military expenditure. All measures were to the detriment of workers and have protected banks and businesses. It is also known that the crisis will cause an increase in underground economies and will be paid for mainly by immigrants and undocumented and national less protected. According to two famous economists, Guido Rossi and Richard Posner, the dramatic character of today's situation is evident: the staff of

illegal immigration with the money coming from the payroll deductions of regular immigrants that should be allocated to integration.[33] However, the contribution to GDP of regular and irregular migrants in countries of relatively recent immigration, such as Italy, exceeds 15 per cent.[34]

The expression 'civilization of war' (Dal Lago and Palidda, 2010) allude precisely to the culture – at the same time civilian and military-police – that has been produced by Western countries in just under two decades in relation to the conflicts with those who threaten (or are presumed to threaten) Western security.

The widespread rhetoric of multiculturalism in the USA and Europe cannot hide the reality of global standardization, which is first and foremost economic and military, but which also extends to political structures and lifestyles.

The racial criminalization of migrants appears as a continuum of the war fought by each country. The internal transformation of our societies has been the full-blown institution and normalization of the 'war discourse' in its various declinations. With the concept of 'discourse', Michel Foucault (1970, English 1981) essentially alluded to the textual formations, principally written, that organize knowledge and communication in society. In contrast to the classic idea of ideology, the 'discourse' privileges structures of implicit, indirect, self-referential and procedural meanings, which subsequently tend to present themselves as 'objective', 'shared', 'necessary', 'indisputable' and so on. For Foucault, war is a regulative instrument of power relations both inside and outside society. After 11 September 2001, the discourse of war *inside* our societies has been inflected in terms of *security*: the control of foreigners, the exclusion of certain categories of 'enemies' from legal guarantees as well as limits on the freedoms of citizens. These are just the most conspicuous consequences.[35]

Immigration and Criminalization

By criminalization, what is meant here is the process leading a person or group of people to be the object, first, of repressive action by police forces, and then of judicial proceedings. In a state deemed democratic and governed by a legal order, such a process only occurs when a given person or group of people are identified as authors of criminal offences, that is, when they have contravened to one or

---

the High Authorities or the experts of the most important governments (included the Obama administration) are the same as those of the major financial speculation companies or of the military and petrol lobbies.

33   The reports of the Italian and French Court of Auditors on the expenditure of funds relating to immigration are very eloquent. See Palidda (2008a, 2009a); and D. de Blic, http://www.mouvements.asso.fr/spip.php?article26

34   See Caritas (2010) and Unioncamere (2010). In my view there is an underestimate of irregular work in the black economy.

35   Thanks to Alessandro Dal Lago for this paragraph.

more norms of the administrative, civil or criminal code, and in accordance with the rules of procedure based on the principle of the equality of all human beings before the law (and hence on the basis of indisputable evidence).

If we remove the offence of irregular immigration and other offences connected to this condition, due to prohibitionist laws that effectively make regular immigration and the maintenance of regularity impossible, other crimes attributed to foreigners 'are almost always the typical crimes of poor people' (Mucchielli and Nevanen), in short, the classic outcome of a merely repressive-penal treatment of a social issue.

Thus, some of the people who are reported, arrested, imprisoned and found guilty are effectively the authors of crimes, but it is also likely that many of the people who are charged by the police or criminal justice system have not committed any criminal offence, and also among those who have been responsible for unlawful conduct, many are victims of excessive zealousness if not abuse, harassment or even arbitrary persecution.[36]

Different authors have clearly shown how a sizeable portion of police forces do act in accordance to positive and negative stereotypes, that is, prejudices that partly correspond to social representations shared by a majority of the population, that are partly dominant in so-called public opinion, or are brandished by opinion leaders and political entrepreneurs, and thus influence the input handed down by the hierarchy of these forces.[37] It follows that the 'production' of the activity of police forces is configured as a sort of self-fulfilling and self-nourishing prophecy.[38] In supermarkets, in malls, on public transport, in the streets, in any public place, the people subjected to the most controlls are certainly those that have characteristics that are deemed typical of deviant subjects, and are hence suspected of being potential offenders.

Such negative stereotyping tends to focus on marginal subjects, youths with an attitude, clothing, behaviour and physical traits that are different from what is considered 'normal' or 'proper', and is voiced in every circumstance; these 'different' subjects constitute the great majority of people arrested, detained and

---

36   The chapters by Mucchielli and Nevanen and others include a number of bibliographic references concerning these aspects that can only be analysed through ethnographic research on police practices and on the practices of the administration of justice. In fact, it is evident that upstream from all of this lies the discretional power of police forces, that can easily translate into arbitrary discrimination which, in turn, is transferred into judicial proceedings unless the magistrates involved dispute the acts transmitted by the judicial police (a rather rare event, especially when it is a matter of people charged of minor offences for whom the trial resembles a brief moment on an assembly line). On these various aspects, see Palidda (1999, 2000, 2008a, 2010b) and Quassoli (1999).

37   In particular, I refer to Palidda (1996); Tonry (1997); Maneri (1998); Dal Lago (1999a); Quassoli (1999), Palidda (2008a, 2009a).

38   On theoretical and methodological matters pertaining to the critical deconstruction of the production of statistics, see, firstly, Kitsuse and Cicourel (1963); Robert (2005).

sentenced, and are often – obviously – marked by a high rate of repeat offences.[39] In some cases, the charges attributed to them may be made worse by a degree of arbitrariness (attempted theft can easily become attempted robbery, even in the absence of weapons or objects that may be used as such; possession of goods whose origin is not certified can turn into receipt of stolen goods; drug possession and charges of dealing may be constructed through the amount that some officers hold – unlawfully – on the side in order to 'frame' someone they never managed to 'catch'; a subject who has already been identified may be charged again with an offence that is or is not serious, if a worsening of their record as a repeat offender is sought, or if the author of that crime must be found at any cost).[40] It is also historically proven[41] that the most recent arrivals on the social scene (namely, immigrants, particularly if young and not well assimilated or not willing to put themselves in an absolutely subordinate and 'invisible' position, or even refusing to leave a so-called 'respectable' public area) are certainly those most liable to be considered inadequate, if not even undesirable or suspected as delinquents.

And it is also proven that a sizeable portion of the magistrature is not devoid of negative stereotypes, and treats 'habitual' cases concerning marginal people, repeat offenders and generally 'different' subjects in an extremely summary manner (Quassoli, 1999).

Finally, at certain junctures, a recrudescence in the criminalization of subjects that are 'other' occurs, alongside the exacerbation of fears, insecurities and responses to them. Racism reproduces itself when a novel intensification of the asymmetry between power and lack of power takes hold, up to the erosion of the democratic state's legal order. The criminalization of marginal and different people, or of the last arrivals on the social scene, takes on racist features because it reflects their stigmatization and hence the degradation and denial of their rights, leading to their super-exploitation and also pushing them towards self-elimination under the form of 'human surplus'.[42]

---

39   See the demographic prison studies in the U.S. and in Europe, among others Aebi and Delgrande (2009).

40   This is one of the usual police practices when dealing with street crime. See Palidda (2000), Brodeur (2003).

41   See Banton (1964, 1973, 1994); Bittner (1990); Palidda (1999, 2000).

42   I do not think it is necessary here to waste time criticizing the statistical analysis made by neopositivist authors who appear to adhere perfectly to the 'official thinking' prevalent in wealthy countries; perhaps without realizing it, they are siding with the Crime Deal by believing that the product of police forces is 'objective'. Such a point of view is similar to Huntington's thesis that deems non-Whites (by which he means non-WASPs) as a threat to American identity and hence to U.S. supremacy, supposedly the only guarantee of democracy and progress in the world; see Dal Lago (2006); Ciccarelli (2005); Palidda (2008a).

Polling Victimization to Exclude the Most Victimized

Since the start of the 1960s in the United States, later also in the United Kingdom, but and only over the last quarter of a century in France, periodic inquiries are carried out into so-called victimization.[43] Many experts consider these inquiries to be absolutely valid, reliable and hence scientifically unquestionable as means for looking at the actual reality of crime more closely. However, doubts concerning these new instruments of criminology appear to be just as reasonable, not just because in some cases they are telephone surveys and not face-to-face interviews, but also because 'poll-taking', which appears to be all the rage particularly in Italy, often serves to reinforce alarmism and thus the discourse on which government through fear, terror and zero tolerance is based.[44]

The composition of the sample of people heard in this sort of survey is even more questionable: the underprivileged are almost always excluded but they are the people most liable to suffer crimes against their person, impositions, abuses, violence if not even murders. In fact, who are the leading victims of these crimes, particularly in European countries, if not gypsies, 'clandestine' immigrants, the homeless, marginal people, that is, all those people who do not know how to or do not even imagine that they may have a right to have their physical integrity safeguarded? It is only in exceptional cases that police forces intervene in protection of these victims or even merely find out about the crime that they have suffered (Palidda, 2010a). Instead, it is entirely taken for granted that these victims should be excluded from the polls of victimization surveys, and this often also applies to regular immigrants themselves. Moreover, it is worth noting that studies on victimization that have so far been undertaken in Italy do not even take the victim's nationality into account.[45] In other terms, by ignoring the victimization

---

43   Among others, see Jock Young (http://www.malcolmread.co.uk/JockYoung/RISK. htm#); in which the author writes: 'Criminal victimisation studies are a useful research instrument to deal with the problem of inadequate statistics and to more accurately pinpoint problems within society. Commencing on a large scale in the United States of the 1960s they reached Britain by the late 1970s and have resulted in a series of British Crime Surveys (BCS) ... Richard Sparks and his associates, in the introduction to their pioneering British victimization study, summarized the decade of American research prior to their own with a note of jubilation: 'Within a decade ... some of the oldest problems of criminology have come at last within reach of a solution' (Young, 1977, p. 1). For France, see the chapter by Mucchielli and Nevanen. Then, see Zauberman (2009).

44   Among the many surveys that have effectively promoted the 'government of fear and zero tolerance', I point out those produced by Demos and analysed by I. Diamanti: 'In 2008, the number of Italians who believe that crime has risen decreases: it is now 81.6%, compared with 88% in 2007'. Diamanti (2007 and 2008), *Fenomenologia dell'Insicurezza*, see http://www.demos.it/a00019.php and http://www.osservatorio.it/download/10032009. la_sicurezza_in_italia.pdf

45   See the ISTAT (2004) multi-purpose survey on families, 'Sicurezza dei cittadini' Year 2002 http://www.istat.it/dati/catalogo/20040915_00/; on p.164, it is noted merely

of non-people, the rightless or 'non-existent' social subjects, these types of surveys often end up promoting the rhetoric according to which victims can only be nationals, while perpetrators can only be either gypsies or undocumented migrants.[46] Regarding acts of sexual violence or rapes, we have police statistics that are distorted to a doubly concealed degree: cases involving nationals (often relatives of the victim) are often not reported, while gypsies and illegals who are victims more often than not do not dare or do not even know how to report the crime they have suffered. However, as soon as an act of violence occurs where the perpetrator is a gipsy or an immigrant, the majority of the media does not hesitate to mention the nationality, 'ethnicity' or 'race' of the offender. Conversely, when the corpse of an immigrant woman is found, it is common for investigators and the media to talk about *in-group* crimes ('among themselves'). In such context, it is no wonder that is hard to find on the news in-depth reporting about immigrants who are murdered or have been victims of serious violence, as well as killed by accidents at work.[47]

Corruption, Abuses and Violent Acts by Police Officers and Officials

An aspect that is rather neglected in works of research about irregularity, crime and the criminalization of immigrants concerns the close connection between these facts and police practices. Individuals and groups that become preferred targets for control and repression are those that are most infiltrated by informers and informants. They are also most often subjected to blackmailing, harassment, impositions and violence by those officers-delinquents who have always inhabited police forces. But, perhaps unsurprisingly, there are no statistics on the cases of

---

that of the people rejecting the interviews there are 0.7 % of foreigners due to lack of understanding of the language... it is a telephone survey on a sample of families chosen among those that appear in directories and interviews in different languages are not envisaged, unlike happens in the face-to-face ones by INSEE in France (see the contribution by Mucchielli and Nevanen).

46   In the absence of any critical deconstruction of statistics, one inevitably reaches 'statements of fact' that claim to be 'objective' and legitimize the most horrific racist persecutions; thus, as regards sexual violence, some go so far as to state that when the authors are immigrants, 56% of the victims are Italian, and when the rapists are Italian, only 3% of the victims are of foreign origin. But how many foreign women are in the position to report they suffered a rape committed by an Italian? And in the rare cases in which this happens, are police forces as diligent as they are when dealing with Italian victims and foreign perpetrators? One does not need to have read Cicourel, Kitsuse, Garfinkel, and Robert to understand what a modicum of intellectual honesty can already allow one to discern.

47   For some information on the violence and murders committed against immigrants see http://www.terrelibere.org/, http://fortresseurope.blogspot.com/, http://www.meltingpot. org/

police corruption and abuse, as well as on the acts of violence perpetrated by police officers against gypsies, immigrants and marginal people in general (Palidda, 2010b). It is only in exceptional cases that the reality emerges about these events, either because delinquent officers have overstepped a mark, or because they have not respected pacts (as happens in the criminal underworld), or because some competitors have given them up to cover themselves, or, unfortunately less likely, because some honest police officer has managed to uncover his or her colleagues' malfeasance (Palidda, 2010b).

As pointed out by Amnesty International and associations like Statewatch, *Que fait la Police?*, the Observatori del Sistema Penal i els Drets Humans of Barcelona University and others, in the last few years, violent acts and abuses committed by the police have become frequent and are increasingly marked by racism. The French case appears to be the most serious (see http://www.amnesty.org about 'Police impunity in France'). In reality, the same type of racist police violence is customary in the other EU countries, particularly Italy, the United Kingdom, Belgium, Greece, Spain, Germany (U.S. cases of police malfeasance are better known) (see the Annual Reports of Amnesty International 2005–2009).

In several cases, history has shown[48] that it is precisely at times of police clampdowns *vis-à-vis* immigrants (that is, in periods of prohibitionism towards both emigration and immigration), that cases of police corruption and abuse increase. There are police officers and police officials who start by taking kickbacks to augment their modest salaries and soon discover that it is a veritable business to misuse the power of law enforcement (consider the case of officers who only monitor prostitutes to take money and free services off them, and the same applies to those who have preferences for certain pushers).

There is a circuit of officers, lawyers, former police officers, and all sorts of mediators who sell (even to those who do not fulfil requirements) regularizations, permit renewals, family reunions, just like visas in countries of emigration.[49]

In a period and a context in which activities that exploit the work of irregulars are widespread, the complicity of police officers in the process is quite frequent. It thus happens that small business owners and foremen (who sometimes are immigrants themselves) reach agreements with corrupt officers to turn a blind eye on undocumented workers, or intervene precisely on payday in order to cause the

---

48   See, in particular, the aforementioned *Italians in the world*, Milza (1978); Morelli (2004); Blanc-Chaléard (2000); Blanc-Chaléard, Douki, Dyonet, Millot (2001); Noiriel (1991, 2001, 2007) and the serious and important texts of Matteo Sanfilippo available at: http://www.asei.eu/

49   Some qualitative researches and the complaints of some NGOs and trade unions show that these cases occur in almost all countries of immigration, especially where the police have more discretion and are subject to fewer controls (see Amnesty International Reports of the last five years available at http://www.amnesty.org; the journal *Diritto, Immigrazione e Cittadinanza,* edited by the *Associazione per gli Studi Giuridici sull'Immigrazione (ASGI) and Magistratura Democratica, and* Palidda, 2009b).

'clandestines' to flee, so that they can divide up their wages with the site manager or employer.[50]

In the field of unlawful activities, partnerships between a delinquent immigrant and a corrupt officer are not rare, and they often develop starting from a co-operation that initially starts off 'with the best intentions' (the officer gets himself an informant for delicate inquiries).

A classic example is that of the relationship between police officers and pick-pockets on public transport vehicles: the well-inserted pick-pocket who has learnt to respect the rules of the game, and acts with dexterity and elegance, never arouses alarm and does everything he can to establish a relationship of trust with some police officer or, better still, an official; he provides all the information needed by them to arrest the new arrivals on the scene, that is, inexperienced, perhaps even violent, 'rustic' pick-pockets; in exchange, the officer turns a blind eye on the 'decent' pick-pocket/ informant.

In the field of drug dealing, instead, it is common for co-operation between the immigrant delinquent and the police officer to become a criminal partnership.[51] Among the most recent cases, it can be noticed that a foreign pusher often becomes a valuable partner for the delinquent officer: he points out the rival pushers who have acquired considerable amounts of drugs and money, and where they hide them; half of the drugs confiscated by the officer are dealt by him, while the other half is used for the judicial acts that accompany the arrest of the 'unlucky' pusher. The ideal informant-partner of the corrupt officer is precisely a young foreign pusher who often has a criminal record and is willing to co-operate unreservedly. He risks his life due to the possible revenge exacted by those he betrays. He also faces the threat of expulsion. The corrupt officer (and his colleagues who are accomplices in the same gang, as it is impossible to practise such illicit trade on one's own) may even be granted promotion for the numerous arrests and confiscations made (and the more he makes, the more he gains from them), and may even succeed in persuading a magistrate that he is an efficient and reliable police officer (or *carabiniere*).[52] This enables the officer-delinquent to eventually ask for his informant's release, in case he has been arrested by another officer, or, if he has arrested him himself, to prove him that he can dispose of this freedom as he wants and thus that he must be entirely subordinated to him (this is what

---

50   The history of immigration in the United States reveals many such cases of this phenomenon (for the Italian situation, see Franzina and Stella, 2003). See also footnote 51.

51   Bourgois (2003), Palidda (2000; 2009c, 2010b, 2010c).

52   Among recent cases, that of three officers from the Genoa drug squad who practised this kind of operative model; the same thing has been discovered in relation to some *carabinieri* in Turin and Milan, as well as police officers in other cities (from the press review filed by the Genoa Italian Team-Challenge project). In December 2008, a new judicial investigation uncovered the fact that more than twenty officers (including directors) of the Genoa state police are regular cocaine users. See Palidda (2010b).

explains the releases without expulsion of certain serial repeat offenders; in such cases, there may be a sort of pact between the judge and agent to use the pusher-informant as an infiltrated person who is especially valuable to discover drug rings). The *frame* of 'government through crime attributed to immigrants' has noticeably encouraged the proliferation of cases of officers-delinquents acting in connivance with delinquents-immigrants.

In this regard, the case of the 'Black Panda' [the popular Fiat car model] is emblematic. Criminal association, receipt of stolen goods and embezzlement, as well as episodes of violence against Italians and foreigners; these were the charges brought against seven *carabinieri* and two local police force officers of Cortenuova, a town in the province of Bergamo (Lombardy); even the *carabinieri* marshal heading the station in the nearby town of Calcio was found guilty. Every Friday night, the gang drove around in a Black Panda with a stolen licence plate to carry out their 'Negro hunt'. Apart from the beatings inflicted during the 'hard' searches for drugs, these self-appointed soldiers of ethnic cleansing did not spurn the chance to make money off with the same drug and mobile phones that they seized. They had chosen Fridays to carry out their misdeeds, so that they could make the Sunday papers. The next day, they would tell reporters of the arrests made and the 'brilliant operations against drugs' executed. As two journalists write[53], the charged officers are missed by the residents of Calcio: shortly after the arrests were made in July 2007, graffiti appeared around town. They said: 'We want our *carabinieri* back' and 'Deidda for mayor'. Deidda was the marshal of the *carabinieri* who had been nicknamed 'Herr Kommandant' by the gang. The victims of choice were clandestines, because they do not report crimes. As the investigating judge states, they acted while armed, in 'a mood of violence, collective exaltation and self-congratulation', in the small town that is run by a Lega Nord mayor. An objective of the 'big-game hunt' was also that of increasing the statistics on arrests and confiscated drugs. Deidda, who was promoted before getting caught, was obsessed 'to confiscate at least 25 kilos of drugs, so as to be able to beat his predecessor's record'. All members of the Black Panda gang were sentenced to terms of between one and six years.[54]

---

53   See Fabio Poletti, 'Dopo i raid in divisa contro gli immigrati, tutti difendono gli agenti', in *La Stampa* 9 July 2007; Cristina Marrone, 'A Bergamo sgominata la "banda" della panda nera. I raid dei carabinieri anti-immigrati', in *Il Corriere*, 29 December 2007.

54   Eight people were sentenced, eight were sent to trial, three agreed to plea bargains, and two were acquitted. All the sentences were for between one and six years of imprisonment. The offences punished were: misuse of office, bodily harm, misuse of authority, criminal association, purloining the victims' money and mobile phones, sale of a kilo of hashish. The group's leader, a former commander of the carabinieri station of Calcio (Bergamo), was sentenced to five years and two months, the captain was sentenced to three years and eight months, for the sale of a kilo of hashish and for attempted extortion (see Palidda 2008a and 2010a).

PART I
General Overview

Chapter 2
A Review of the Principal European Countries

Salvatore Palidda

In the course of the last two decades the number of arrests, imprisonments and detention of aliens and citizens of foreign origin, has gone up considerably in all European countries, both of old and new immigration, as well as in North America, Australia, Japan and recently even in countries that function as emigration and transit countries. This phenomenon has attracted the interest, not only of criminologists, but also of scholars from other social sciences. The aim of our work is to bring together some of the most qualified and experienced scholars in this field, in order to make an appraisal of the state of knowledge existing in this area and suggest avenues for further research.

By the criminalization of migrants, we mean all the discourses,[1] facts and practices made by the police, judicial authorities, but also local governments, media, and a part of the population that hold immigrants/aliens responsible for a large share of criminal offences. Thus it is evident that the problem has to be seen in a polysemic context as we are dealing with a *total social phenomenon* (Sayad, 1999; Palidda, 2008a), which does not concern only immigrants/aliens or deviants, but also takes into account the many salient political and cultural characteristics of the situations affecting both the societies of provenance and destination, as well as those between the two poles. As highlighted in a number of papers presented at the workshop and printed here, the criminalization of aliens feeds on several elements and inputs found in specific local, national and international conditions. Immigration policies as well as trends in repression and punishment that find expression in police and judicial practices are applicable to both aliens and native people. In other words, the treatment of immigrants/aliens has a *mirror function* (Sayad, 1999) in the sense that it anticipates or falls in line with how the treatment of natives evolves. Thus, it is obvious that the criminalization of aliens must be analysed in relation to the criminalization of nationals.

From an empirical point of view, the study of this subject concerns police actions and their 'output' (i.e. controls, complaints, arrests), judicial actions (arraignment, imprisonment, convictions etc.), but also those aspects which come under administrative law with regard to asylum seekers and illegals.

---

1   Here we refer to the meaning of 'discourse' as proposed by Michel Foucault (1966, 1969, 1970).

Thus the aim of our deliberations is not to establish whether aliens are 'more criminal' than nationals, but to understand how statistics, discourses and practices correspond – or do not correspond – to this assertion which is quite common today.

One of the most elementary pieces of evidence demonstrating the falsity of the campaigns of criminalization of immigrants is to note that there is no arithmetic relationship between the trend of crimes and the increase of immigrants. If there was a correlation such crimes would have had to increase by at least 5 or 10 times in the past 20 years. However, even where there has been a decrease in crime, there has been an increase in arrests and detention of foreign and national or citizens of foreign origin. And, as in the past, the latest arrivals on the social scene almost always end up being the most affected by the practices of racist criminalization and self-criminalization. As in Germany during the 1960s (when the Italians were accused of being the most criminal before that role passed to the Turks), in Italy at first it was the turn of the North Africans, then of the Albanians, then of the Romanians and now of part of the so called Latin youth gangs.

By victimization we mean the fact that immigrants/aliens are themselves victims of acts committed by nationals in the host country, by police agents, as well as by their compatriots. Now, except for France, which has conducted victimization surveys on a population sample comprising aliens and face-to-face interviews, we do not have data and comprehensive analyses on the victimization of immigrants/aliens, in spite of the fact that selective studies and a considerable amount of reliable information attest to the seriousness of the situation. In Italy, such surveys are conducted over the phone; interviewees are selected from names listed in the telephone directory, which tends to exclude aliens and Romanis, and even more so illegal immigrants.

From a methodological point of view, it should be mentioned that although the participants in the workshop had different approaches, they all made a multidisciplinary effort, since the subject required an interpretative and analytical perspective that was at the same time diachronic and synchronic, micro and macro, as well as comparative in nature.

Difficulties of Statistical Comparison

Marcelo Aebi and Nathalie Delgrande have shown that the statistical representation of the criminalization of immigrants/aliens in international comparisons is complicated by the fact that the definition of immigrant, alien and hence national, varies from country to country and, in particular, has changed most in countries once belonging to the USSR. Similarly, the status of nationals in countries that have joined the European Union has changed over time. These authors, along with others, thus stress that such problem of definition affects the interpretation of statistics, for it forms the basis for the definition of numerous offences and hence of the imprisonment of foreigners (especially in the case of illegal immigration, which can vary from administrative infringement to penal offence). Similarly, very often foreigners cannot take advantage of sanctions that are alternative to imprisonment, and are subjected to several varieties of what we call *double punishment*[2] (Sayad, 1999).

From a comparative perspective, despite statistical difficulties, it appears just as important to take into account not only prison data, but also data from detention centres, which in many countries have acquired considerable weight.

As Olivier Clochard (2010) shows, in the 27 states of the European Union the number of administrative detention centres for migrants classified as 'illegal' is estimated at about 250 (in 2009). As a matter of fact, there are no official data at European level. Even the total capacity of such centres is undetermined. We have detailed information on just 150 of them, i.e. about 32,000 places. According to many testimonies and investigations conducted by several NGOs (including Amnesty International and the European Committee against Torture) migrants who pass through all prisons and centres for expulsion (which some countries call also 'reception centres for refugees') are much more than that. In 2006, the phenomenon involved less than 1,000 people in Hungary and Latvia, while in France alone there were over 45,000 foreign 'detainees' and the same in Greece (see Migreurop, 2009).

These places of detention of migrants are located in police stations, sometimes in prisons (Germany, Cyprus, Ireland) and – in several Central European countries – even in old Soviet army barracks. Further south, there are camps made of tents or makeshift buildings (Spain, Greece, Italy, Malta). There, the material conditions are very poor. Elsewhere, some newly built facilities offer better housing conditions, but their security management increases the criminalization of migrants. Cases of self-harm and suicide are frequent as well as riots and escape attempts.

The period of detention varies from one country to another (from 15–30 days to 18 months). In these cenres families are locked up with young children, all those deemed 'vulnerable' can now be held, including, increasingly, asylum seekers, although their status should be protected (see Morice and Rodier, 2010).

Having said that, foreign prisoners are still a minority amongst those interned in penal institutions in the European Union countries, but, from 1989 to 2008, their percentage has increased everywhere. In 2006, they constituted more than 20 per cent of the total inmate population, with significant differences between Eastern and Western Europe. In the Eastern European countries, the average was less than 5 per cent, whereas in Western Europe countries it climbed to 37 pere cent (but there were also other differences amongst the latter) (see after Table 2.1).

After a re-examination of the key EU and US data (Palidda; De Giorgi), we can make the following observations:

---

2   By 'double punishment' we mean the fact of being subjected to penal sanctions and administrative measures for the same offence. A typical case is the administrative expulsion of an alien after he has served a sentence.

1. European countries with the largest number of foreign inmates are Germany, Spain and Italy, followed by France and the UK. Amongst the countries listed in the Table below (which include the principal 'old' and recent immigration countries), these countries have 75% of total foreign inmates.

2. If we look at the detention rate of aliens (i.e. number of inmates for 100,000 legal immigrants, i.e. foreigners with a residence permit), we notice that the highest rates can be found in Portugal, Netherlands, Italy and Greece, followed by Spain, Belgium and Austria. With regard to the ratio between the detention rate of alien males and national males aged between 15 and 65, we note that the highest ratio is to be found in Greece, Netherlands, Italy, Portugal and Switzerland, followed by Belgium and Austria.

3. The detention rate in the United States (where blacks are taken into custody seven times more, and latinos three times more, than whites) is 11 times higher than in Norway and Finland, 10 times more than in Denmark and Ireland, 9 times higher than Sweden and Switzerland, 8 times higher than Belgium, Greece, France and Germany, 7 times more than the Netherlands, Italy and Austria, 6 times higher than Portugal, and 5 times higher than Spain and the UK. Romania, it should be pointed out, has the highest custody rate (1,000 out of 100,000 people are inmates, mostly nationals) as compared to the United States, where the rate is 756.

4. France is the only country where a decrease in the number of foreign inmates has been registered. However, this data conflicts with the sharp increase in the number of internees held in detention centres. In addition, according to some reports, a large number if not the majority of French citizens held in prison are in reality young people who are children of immigrants.

5. A rise in the criminalization of aliens (and also of nationals) does not seem to correspond to a rise in crime: on the contrary, we note that the decrease in felonies and misdemeanours often corresponds to a rise in the number of aliens (and nationals) who are arrested or imprisoned.

For the Italian case, we have managed to provide a more detailed analysis by calculating imprisonment rates for men over 18, for aliens with residence permits, as well as reliable estimates of the number of illegal immigrants, and also of individuals born abroad and those born in each Italian province. This enables us to understand, amongst other things, the similarities between the criminalization of foreigners and that of individuals born in the most heavily stigmatized regions of Italy, those affected by the Mafia.

Table 2.1   Detention in the main European countries

Country	Total inmates	Total foreign inmates	% foreigners over total inmates	Foreigners rate x 100,000 foreigners	Ratio of foreigners rate/ national rate
Old immigration countries					
England and Wales	77,982	10,879	14.0	318	2
France	57,876	11,436	19.8	326	3
Germany	79,146	21,263	26.9	292	3
Netherlands	16,331	5,339	32.7	772	8
Belgium	9,971	4,148	41.6	461	5
Switzerland	5,888	4,062	69.0	263	7
Austria	8,780	3,768	42.9	463	5
Scandinavian	Countries				
Denmark	3,759	710	18.9	263	3
Finland	3,714	300	8.1	263	3
Norway	3,164	576	18.2	259	3
South European	Countries				
Italy	59,523	19,836	33.3	743	7
Spain	64,120	20,018	31.2	500	3
Portugal	12,636	2,552	20.2	925	7
Greece	10,113	5,902	58.4	668	12

Source: Reworking of the author from data in Aebi and Delgrande (2009) and Eurostat data on population and immigrants.

Public Policies on Migration in Europe

In countries where prohibitionist policies (very restrictive or 'zero immigration') *vis-à-vis* immigration have weakened the judicial security of aliens, increased the powers of the police and therefore their discretionary treatment of aliens, the number of illegals is likely to have increased. On the other hand, even in countries where prohibitionism has become stricter, but the rule of law and due process continue to function, the increment in the detention of foreigners has been much less, except perhaps in detention centres (this is true of France, as described by Mucchielli and Nevanen, but also of other 'old' migration countries).

The correlation between surges of xenophobia and the criminalization of aliens holds everywhere, not only with regard to the hostility towards Romanis, but also in numerous opinion polls and media analyses as proposed by Maneri and mentioned in several other chapters.

There is another correlation that would be useful to explore in the future, namely the correlation between the size of the informal economy,[3] the rate of irregularity and the rate of imprisonment of foreigners. It is obvious that in countries where clandestine labour is most widespread, the number of illegals and foreign inmates is greater. And this happens even where the ruling government adopts a policy of maximum severity against illegal immigration.

As data presented in this book show, the increase in the criminalization of aliens (and especially imprisonment) has become generalized and has intensified in West European countries, independently of the political colour of governments, somewhat like the situation prevailing in the United States (after thirty years of what J. Simon (2007) calls the 'Crime Deal').

If it is true that officially racial profiling has not been institutionalized in Europe (an institutionalization described in Harcourt's chapter on the USA), we still follow the custom of 'facies offences' or 'facies checks' or 'ethnic profiling' (Sayad, 1999; Palidda, 1999). On top of this the police are under pressure to increase their crime-solving rates (Mucchielli, 2008a), or fulfil their arrest quotas, i.e. to tot up the numbers (Slama, 2008), which is what public opinion wants from *a government based on fear* (Palidda, 2000; Simon, 2007; Jobard, 2006). In this way we can see how administrative offences are converted into penal offences, asylum seekers are transformed into alleged terrorists and deviants, and why administrative custody has been invented and introduced in Europe in recent years (see Valluy's chapter).

In addition, many young people from countries seriously hit by processes of disintegration labour under the illusion of making a fast buck, while young people living in the suburbs of Europe refuse to accept job insecurity or low-wage work. There has thus been a process of change whereby the native deviant or criminal has been replaced by the young foreigner, mostly from countries situated at the periphery of Western Europe. Furthermore, the majority of foreigners arrested and imprisoned (especially in South European countries) are of Maghrebian or Balkan descent.

Despite the differences, there is a certain similarity between the actions of the French and British governments that, as described by Bosworth and Guild and Mucchielli and Nevanen, seem to experiment with the criminalization of (young) urbanites of foreign extraction. Indeed, the British and French cases seem to

---

3   On shadow economies see Schneider (2004).

suggest that the criminalization of aliens again has a 'mirror function', in the sense that it prefigures or exaggerates the tendencies that apply to a section of nationals. We can see this from the tougher measures applied to minors and youth in general (in this regard, see the contribution of Yasha Maccanico). Similarly to the United States, where it is the young blacks and Latinos who are the specific targets of repressive and penal actions, in Europe it is the young aliens who have to bear the brunt, especially if they are *sans papiers*, but also lower-class native youths, who apparently represent an 'inappropriate posterity'.[4]

The Spanish case (as well as the Greek) is quite similar to the Italian case. In particular, Spain does not seem to be done with Francoism (in the normative sense). After the end of the dictatorship, it directly embarked on the development phase that took place between 1980and 2006, fuelled by the informal economy (see Brandariz Garcia and Fernandez Bessa). Having said that, it is in Italy that the judicial guarantees of foreigners have been undermined the most. For more than twenty years, the increase in the irregularity of immigrants/aliens has been a formidable trump card for the country's economy, going hand in hand with their criminalization, which ensures an unfailing consensus between local and national governments, and rising sales for the security business.

Change and Continuity

Similarities and changes between the past and the present with regard to the criminalization of immigrants and aliens are also examined in this book. Indeed, the phenomenon of the criminalization of aliens was well known in the past. As highlighted by several contributions to the book and in other researches,[5] neo-immigrants always run the risk of occupying the lowest rungs of the social ladder and figuring as the 'dangerous classes' alongside the native dropouts from society or in partial substitution of the latter, especially in adverse conditions where peaceful and stable integration becomes difficult. In other words, the latest arrivals on the social scene are very likely to find themselves banded with the dropouts and deviants and potential criminals, becoming an easy target for police repression (think of the fringe elements migrating from the countryside to Paris in 1848, described by Buret (Chevalier, 1984; Foucault, 1975, 2004a), immigrants

---

4   The term 'inappropriate posterity' is in reference to Sayad (1999) who talks of immigration as a total social phenomenon essential for prosperity and posterity in the development of the industrial society; now, one of the most important consequences of neoliberal development (which is contrary to the liberal-democratic development as envisaged by Schumpeter, Keynes, and others) is that only *hic et nunc* prosperity is favoured, while posterity is discounted, thereby neglecting the future and especially the youth (from the perspective of stable and properly paid employment, higher education, social problems etc.). See Muchielli (2002, 2008); Castel (2007); Palidda (2008a, 2009a).

5   Among others see Castles and Miller (2009); Palidda (2008a, 2009a).

and blacks in the late 1800s/ early 1900s United States (Franzina & Stella, 2002), internal migrants moving to Northern Italy in the post-1945 period (Alasia & Montaldi, 1961; Fofi, 1964), and numerous other examples found in the works of historians and social scientists).

It is also interesting to recall that the discourse that accompanied the criminalization of immigrants/aliens in these different periods and contexts, was often superimposed on a discourse that upheld the criminalization of the 'mob', or of the subaltern classes when they veered towards revolt. At other times it was superimposed on the discourse in support of colonization with racist justifications (Le Cour Grandmaison, 2005; Palidda, 2008a).

As we can see through the history of migrations that took place during the nineteenth and twentieth centuries until the present time, there have been periods of mass migration (internal and external) which did not raise any alarm with respect to 'law and order', and this independently of any short-term increase in criminality. Conversely, periods of lesser migration have been accompanied by the fierce criminalization of migrants – i.e. greater repression – sometimes even without an increase in the number of offences.[6] It is moreover important to remember that present-day migrations toward richer countries are less sizable than the domestic and international migrations of the past. In particular, the migrations occurred during the Thirty Glorious Years (from 1945 to 1975 in developed countries, members of the OECD) did not give rise to feelings of fear or insecurity, even though deviance and criminality among immigrants existed, as attested by the increase in their number among recent inmates over this period. Thus, we are forced to conclude that the criminality and criminalization of immigrants was not of great interest to the political and social sciences in the post-World War II period: it was the preoccupation of the occasional criminologist.

It was especially during the 1990s that the criminality attributed to immigrants increasingly caught the attention of scholars from the social sciences in Europe and in the United States, as well as in other countries of immigration. And it is since the terrorist attacks in the United States, London and Madrid that the emphasis on the enemy and the rhetoric centred upon the conflict of civilizations has led many to talk about the 'impossibility of the integration of immigrants', and thus contributed to the growing criminalization of immigrants (see Petti, 2010).

---

6   In other words, the evolution of delinquency was not connected with immigration trends, but with economic and political, conditions and especially with something that since the nineteenth century has been the periodic criminalization of the social question; see Baratta (1982); Franzina and Stella (2002); Palidda (2008a).

Chapter 3

Do Conflicts between Cultures Really Exist?
A Historical and Methodological Reflection[1]

Alessandro Dal Lago

E digghe a chi me ciamma rénegôu
che a tutte ë ricchesse a l'argentu e l'öu
Sinàn g'ha lasciòu de luxî au sü
giastemmandu Mumä au postu du Segnü

(Fabrizio de André, *Sinàn Capudàn Pascià*)[2]

Questions of Civilization

Samuel P. Huntington's famous essay on the 'clash of civilizations' (Huntington 1996) is inevitably called into question when it comes to discussing the thorny issue of the 'conflict of cultures'. It might well be argued that 'civilization' and 'culture' are not equivalent terms, given that the former is used predominantly in historical and philosophical discussions, while the latter is more typical of sociological and anthropological research.[3] This said, the matter in question is pretty clear:

---

1   A first version of this chapter appeared in Galli (2006). I would like to thank Salvatore Palidda for his critical comments.

2   And tell all those who call me a renegade/ that for all the riches, silver and gold/ Sinàn has conceded to sparkle in the sun,/ cursing Mehmed instead of the Lord (De André 1999, 221).

3   Today the terms 'civilization' and 'culture' are used as synonyms, even though they refer to very different linguistic and lexical traditions. There is clearly an impossibility of translation or in any case only a partial overlapping between the notion of civilization used for example by Elias (1969) or Braudel (1979) and the idea of culture in a sociological or anthropological sense. In the case of the former, 'civilization' is the overall form that a society reaches during a particular historical period (such as the 'civilization of good manners' for Elias or the broad idea of 'capitalism' for Braudel). In the case of the latter (exemplified in sociology by Parsons [1937], in anthropology by Kroeber and Kluckhohn [1952] and in general by Kroeber and Parsons [1958]), 'culture' is the structured symbolic dimension of society. Braudel also speaks of culture, but this is marginal and coincides more or less with the rituals and ceremonies of power (Braudel 1979, II). In a sense, historians of civilization owe much more to the German tradition – where *Kultur* implies a 'spiritual' achievement, while *Zivilization* denotes the 'material civilization' – than does the principal,

the clash of civilizations or cultures is used to imply a conflict between *symbolic formations that are binding for those social actors who identify themselves within them*, and this first and foremost means religion. Today we immediately think of 'Islam versus Christianity', just as a century ago in Germany the talk would have been about *Kulturkampf* between Catholicism and Protestantism. Each historical era selects some sort of symbolic conflict, and the predominant conflict in scientific and popular debates over the last fifteen years has been that between religions as expressions of civilizations or cultures. In order to appreciate the global impact of this recent trend, there is no need to scour the internet or produce an extensive literature review: one can do no better that browse the pamphlets of Oriana Fallaci, where the late famous Italian journalist announces to her millions of readers around the world the advent of the war between the civilization (or culture) of Islam and the civilization (or culture) of the Christian West (which Fallaci modestly proclaimed to be its standard-bearer).

Although Fallaci is not in the habit of quoting her sources, it is clear to readers that her spiritual guiding light is Huntington. It is therefore useful to briefly discuss a text, the cultural importance of which plainly transcends its scientific significance. Indeed, *The Clash of Civilizations and the Remaking of World Order* sums up much of current scientific and popular opinion regarding the decisive conflicts that arise out of the 'opposition' of symbolic worlds. I want to say straightaway that Huntington's book is much more interesting for its lacunae than for its thesis. As the 'self-appointed' synthesis of various intellectual traditions, the book takes for granted (i.e. it ignores) a range of epistemological problems that have traditionally been discussed by cultural specialists. First of all, the notion of civilization, around which Huntington constructs his doctrine of a clash between the West and the rest of the world, is vague and lacks a rigorous definition. Despite the different ways in which the term is used, 'civilization' for Huntington is the *general* form that large political-cultural formations adopt in a given historic period. These incorporate cultures (in their narrow definition) and religions, as well as economies and different types of societies. Therefore, as well as a civilization construed in classic, almost metaphysical terms such as the West (Europe, North America, Australia and New Zealand), we find in Huntington's typology civilizations defined in geographic-continental terms (South America, considered as a poor relation of the West, and Africa), while others are delineated according to island nation (Japanese), political-linguistic (Chinese), religious (Orthodox Christian and Islamic) or religious-cultural (Buddhist) perspectives. The variety, and therefore the scientific arbitrariness, of this typology does not actually hide its geopolitical character. It is as if, at a given moment (the beginning of the 1990s), Huntington had taken a global snapshot of what the world was like (or what it appeared to him) and had frozen its configuration. In contrast to

---

especially American, current in contemporary social sciences. Huntington fuses the two meanings together, so that 'civilization' becomes the significant symbolic, political and material formation of a certain era at the same time as being integrated and homogenous.

a West that has developed as a result of its capacity to free itself from conditions (a capacity perceptible in religious secularization, scientific rationalism, political democracy etc.), there are the different peripheries of the world, identified almost exclusively by religion, political authoritarianism, economic backwardness and strategic marginality.

On close analysis, this is an extreme reformulation at a global scale of the time-worn opposition between the principal forms of *Gesellschaft* and *Gemeinschaft*, which Huntington seeks to legitimate in the first couple of dozen pages where the entire history of humanity is summarized through references to the work of Toynbee, Braudel and other minor writers (Huntington 1996, 43–68).[4] The opposition between the West and other worlds is in essence the opposition between, on the one hand, a universalistic modernity and, on the other, various community versions largely blocked and therefore influenced by various kinds of backwardness. And so the 'clash of civilizations' is the clash *between a civilization and non-civilizations*. This historical mould would appear to be far removed from Fukuyama's formula (1992) about the end of history in the wake of the triumph of the liberal West, but in actual fact it is only separate in terms of diagnosis. While for Fukuyama, history came to its conclusion during the 1990s, for Huntington the path towards the triumph of a universalistic West was still encumbered with obstacles.[5] This was a 'realistic vision', attentive to the political dimension of global conflicts, and although it was formulated by a scholar close to the Democratic establishment of the United States, it would directly or indirectly inspire the aggressive political strategies of neoconservatives on both sides of the Atlantic. While the original emphasis upon the conflicts between the West and the 'Orthodox' world and Japan reflects the period in which the book was written (the early 1990s just when the conflicts in the Balkans were exploding and the Japanese economy seemed to undermine U.S. supremacy over the markets), the Islamic threat has since become the fixed obsession of the rich global North, while China now looms as the most threatening competitor for Western political and economic culture.

---

4   Huntington's 'sources' include classic theorists of sociology of culture (Durkheim, Alfred Weber and Max Weber) anthropology (Kroeber and Kluckhohn), late-nineteenth century apocalyptic philosophies (Spengler), long-term historical syntheses (Braudel, Toynbee), recent theories of globalization (Wallerstein) etc. Due to the lack of any preliminary clarification of the terminology of such different scientific and cultural traditions, Huntington's treatise is little more than an assemblage of necessary references to legitimate at an academic level a discourse which wavers between common sense and a report for political decision makers. A non-specialist reader can ignore the fact, for instance, that Weber would have rejected such a generic historical synthesis or that the terminology employed by Wallerstein is primarily historic and economic.

5   As an influential member of the Project for the New American Century, Fukuyama appears to have changed idea. Recently (since the terrorist attacks of 11 September 2001), the West is faced with a new task: to help the rest of the world to build 'nations'. In other terms, history has not finished and can set off again under the benevolent watch of Western democracies (Fukuyama 2004).

Huntington's implicit premise is that, in contrast to the West, all other civilizations are inevitably conditioned by a specific cultural stigma, whether this be Orthodox traditionalism, Chinese authoritarianism, Islamic fanaticism, African tribalism, South American parasitism or Japanese arrogance. As Edward Said has noted (2000, 569–90), this represents the projection of timeworn and essentially colonial clichés about how the inhabitants of other worlds do not evolve because they are eternally conditioned by their culture. In actual fact, it would not take much to demonstrate that the real object of these general theories is not the backwardness of the other civilizations, but, on the contrary, the capacity of a number of emergent countries to integrate themselves with extreme ease into global (i.e. Western) economic and political systems, maintaining at the same time their own political systems and goals that differ from those of North America and Europe. It is the classic spectres of Japanese rearmament, Russian and Chinese nationalism, the political autonomy of oil-producing (and predominantly 'Arab' and 'Islamic') countries, that motivate Huntington's seemingly sophisticated and realistic analysis. At heart, the 'clash of civilizations' is nothing more than the representation of a global political clash for hegemony disguised as the conflict between civilizations or cultures.[6]

Much more so than the Democrat Clinton, it was the visionary Republican Bush who, after 11 September 2001, would draw the practical consequences of a geopolitical doctrine that would become, over a period of a few years and under false pretences, common sense. If the doctrine had such overwhelming success, this was, however, not just the result of its hegemonic implications. It reflects a common Western sentiment that also prevails among scholars of the Islamic world, observers of international politics and opinion makers.[7] Huntington, in short, gave synthetic form (despite the size of his books) to a widespread system of thought that was waiting only for a prophet. It would then be up to the big-name journalists, such as Oriana Fallaci, to translate the scholar's vision into sensational formulas: Islamic 'barbarity', Western 'cowardice', 'timid' democracy, the 'invasion' of Islamic immigrants and so on.[8] The Huntington–Fallaci style of thought offers

---

6 On this point, see Dal Lago (2003, 2005c).

7 Here I am referring to experts on the Near East and Islam such as Fouad Ajami and Bernard Lewis. Ajami (1992, 2003) is an influential supporter of global democratic interventionism and of the forced modernization of Islam. Lewis is the author of numerous texts on the 'relations' between Europe and Islam, in which, under the appearance of a neutral analysis and versed in the Islamic view of Europe, Islamic 'culture' is stigmatized in general as having always been hostile to the West (Lewis 1982). Said (2000) has discussed Lewis's contribution to the theory of the clash of civilizations.

8 A degree of intellectual snobbery has probably prevented for the time being an attentive analysis of these pamphlets (Fallaci 2004). They need to be considered expressions of a discourse accessible to a mass audience which is also expressed by a substantial part of the 'scientific community'. Giovanni Sartori (2000), an acclaimed political scientist in Italy, says more or less the same things. Similarly, it does not seem at all to be a coincidence that Huntington's reflections over the last ten years of his life began with the invocation

a highly simplified, if not caricatured, rereading of history on the basis of a few simple oppositions, all of which reflect the purely linguistic transformation of hegemonic and geopolitical problems in cultural questions. In the following pages, I will first seek to demonstrate how such oppositions – starting from the basic opposition between a civilized 'us' and a barbaric 'them' – actually have little resonance over the course of history, and I will then proceed to discuss the problematic relations between the concepts of culture and conflict.

The Imaginary Genealogy of the 'Clash of Civilizations'

Everyone remembers from their history lessons at school the distinction between Greeks and barbarians. The first lot represents 'us', political animals who speak Greek, whereas the second group represents 'them', people who express themselves in a strange if not incomprehensible language. The opposition is both political and cultural. The Greeks are free, in so far as they live in self-governing *poleis*, while the barbarians are subject to despotic powers. The Greek political-cultural space is like an island surrounded by Barbarian kingdoms and sub-kingdoms: Italic tribes and Carthaginians to the west and south-west, Illyrians, Gauls and Thracians to the north, Persians to the east and Egyptians to the south. The best-known example of the difference between Greeks and barbarians can be traced to the Persian wars. The small Greek *poleis*, forever in conflict over border issues and questions of hegemony and perennially troubled by *stasis* (civil war), for once put their arguments to one side and united firstly against Darius and later against Xerxes, defeating them at Marathon and in the great naval battle of Salamis. With the Greek victory in Plataea, the Persian efforts to conquer Greece came to an end. The cohesion and the rationality of the Greeks triumphed over the undisciplined hordes of Orientals, while the accounts of Herodotus and Thucydides bequeathed us with the first conflict of civilizations according to Western tradition.[9]

---

of the threat that other civilizations present to the West and ended in alarm at the danger that migrants (particularly Latin Americans) represent for the identity of the American civilization (Huntington 2004). If the 'other civilizations' are an external danger for the West, the migrants are the internal Fifth Column. In both cases, there is a caricatured description of who 'we' are, and it is 'them' who create the idea of an irremediable hostility between cultures. In the case of Huntington, the caricature is not exempt from paranoid tones. He tries to make the reader believe not only that liberal (i.e. Anglo-Saxon) culture is threatened by Latin American migrants, but also that these represent the fifth column of the governments of their countries of origin, and as such are able to influence American politics.

9   This representation is highly popular among historians today. See, for instance Hanson (1989). The clash between Greeks and Persians essentially provides the underlying framework for any political-military opposition between 'us' and 'them', in other words between Westerners and barbarians of any era (see also Hanson 1999, 2001).

In reality, things went somewhat differently. The Greek cities in Ionia but also in the motherland such as Thebes served on the side of Persians. Moreover, despotism was not at all unheard of among the Greeks. Both the colonies and the peripheral zones of Hellas (Sicily, Ionia, Macedonia and Thessaly), as well as the important centres of the motherland were usually dominated by kings or tyrants. Even the principal *poleis* experienced tyranny, as demonstrated by the events of the Athenian Peisistratos and his sons, one of whom fought with the Persians against his fellow citizens (Herodotus, VI, 107–8).[10] The opposition between Greeks and barbarians was also much more blurred than is conveyed by the rhetoric about Greece's cultural superiority. Egypt was acknowledged as a trove of wisdom and religiosity that predated the Dorians and Ionians.[11] As for the strategists who defeated the Persians in Salamis and Plataea, Themistocles the Athenian and Pausania the Spartan were both suspected of 'medism', in other words sympathies for their age-old adversaries: Themistocles died in exile, while Pausanias was walled up alive on the orders of the ephors because of his alleged inclination towards despotism. The penchant for Persians – whether motivated by political opportunism or cultural attraction – is a constant throughout Greek history. Alcibiades found refuge among the Persians when hunted by the Athenians, while during the decline of the *poleis* the King of Kings was often summoned as guarantor of the *koiné eirène*, the general peace among Greeks, that was always invoked but never achieved (Xenophon, *Hellenica*, V).[12]

After Herodotus, himself born in Ionia (an area of Persian influence) and who therefore knew and respected oriental cultures, it was Xenophon who provided us with the first major, if imaginary, example of cultural hybridization. The central theme of his *Cyropaedia*, the originator of the European *Bildungsroman*, is the education of Cyrus the Great, founder of the Achaemenid dynasty. Even if the cultivation of the ideal monarch in actual fact suggests the model of the Spartan *paideia* (similar to Plato's philo-Laconism in the *Republic*), it is worth noting that his hero is a Persian. Translated into the present day, this would be like if the main character of a North American or European educational novel were, let us say, Colonel Gheddafi. With Xenophon, an Athenian and pro-Spartan with oligarchical tendencies, the model of Greek democracy founded upon *isonomia* (the equality of citizens before the law) disappears forever to be replaced by the myth of an 'enlightened' and multicultural despot. But he confirms, as do numerous other

---

10   Following convention, here references to classic texts indicate the specific book and paragraph.

11   According to Herodotus (II, 4 and ff..) the Ionians recognized that they had learnt the fundamentals of science from the Egyptians. See also Diodorus Siculus, I, 96–8.

12   Finally, it should not be forgotten that Alexander aimed to create at a sort of Euroasian empire, from Macedonia to India in which Greek and Persian elements would have merged together (as recounted in Arrian's *Anabasis Alexandri*). Oliver Stone's recent cinematic reconstruction of Alexander's conquests completely ignores this fundamental aspect of Macedonian ecumenical imperialism.

Greek thinkers, travellers, geographers and historians, that the opposition between Greece and barbarians (at least with regards the Orientals) was far less salient and intrinsic than the conventional image passed down to us over the centuries. Indeed, contemporary historiography, mindful of the contribution of anthropology, has recognized that the ancient Mediterranean was a common area of exchanges and influences between West and East where Greek culture did not reign supreme but evolved among other cultures (Prontera 1996).[13]

It is clear that during the fifth century BC there was a clash between two political mentalities. The Persians could not accept that on the edges of their empire (which, should it not be forgotten, spanned from present-day Afghanistan and Pakistan to the Aegean Sea) there were small quarrelsome urban communities (the cities of Ionia) which shunned an ecumenical and, in its own way, well-organized system. Neither did they understand how the *poleis* of the Greek motherland, which were each able to deploy armies of a few thousand men, were so arrogant as to challenge an immense military power. The Greeks, for their part, scorned Persian absolutism, the magic character of their practices (as in the case of Xerxes who had Hellespont whipped) and the heterogeneous dimension of their formidable war machine, which for the most part remained primitive and unable to withstand the onslaught of the phalanxes. But the extent to which all this amounts to a true conflict, ignoring for one moment the contemporary production of patriotic rhetoric, needs to be reassessed.[14] It would not be another 150 years before the Greeks, under Alexander, permanently established a foothold in Asia Minor. More importantly, this geopolitical altercation did not coincide with any real cultural hostility. Aeschylus, who fought at Salamis, offers us in his *Persians* a stirring representation of the disaster that befell the court of Xerxes following defeat (imagine today a play on Broadway about the last days of Saddam in Baghdad that takes an interest in the Iraqi dictator's feelings). Certainly, the tragedy was supposed to arouse Athenian patriotism, but this was *political* not *cultural* patriotism. The Athenian audience was supposed to learn from a fate that could well have also been theirs. The primacy of the political over the cultural in the relations with other worlds is also a constant aspect during the Hellenistic kingdoms. With the exception of Alexander, who thought about constituting a mixed Greek and Persian political-military elite, his successors did not attempt to totally Hellenize the kingdoms they conquered. What for a long time appeared to be a cultural confrontation (Greeks *against* barbarians) was thus an interaction, closer to a problematic osmosis than a conflict.

---

13   For an excellent analysis of this aspect, see Musti (2004).

14   The state of war was endemic during Ancient Greece: around sixty conflicts of varying intensities took place between 480 and 330 BC, which means about one every two years (Garlan 1972; Pritchett 1971–85). It is into the context that we must position the clash between Persians and the political communities where military service was a condition of citizenship, and was expressed outside the city through the practice of war. See Cartledge (1996).

The radical opposition between West and East is, for the most part, a historiographic invention constructed around the idea of the Graeco-Roman tradition as the foundation of the West. But this is an ex-post construction. The Romans, who at the time of their first contacts with the Greek world were considered by the latter as themselves *barbarians*, were, on their part, more interested in political than cultural hegemony.[15] The extraordinary unifying power of the imperialist Republic and later the Empire can be largely explained by the shrewd extension of citizenship to peoples as and when they were conquered (which culminated in the third century AD, under Caracalla, with the attribution of Roman citizenship to all free inhabitants of the Empire) and, at the same time, by a notable syncretism (or tolerance) in cultural and religious matters. The divinities of the Phoenicians, Egyptians and Syrians were all assimilated into the Roman pantheon (Turcan 1989). The oriental cults readily found citizenship in Rome and were privately observed by the emperors. Provinces and cities often maintained their local rules, cults and own languages alongside the official language of the Empire, which was Latin in the West, but Greek in the East. If one glances through *Historia Augusta* one will note how, from the Flavian dynasty onwards, the emperors came from all four corners of the Empire (Spain, Africa, the Balkans and also Italy). Above all else, it was the army, the backbone of the Empire, that best represented Roman 'multiculturalism'. Inscriptions found in many different places tell of legionaries who kept their original names alongside their Roman *praenomen* and *nomen*. For example, Britons who found themselves defending the Roman outposts in Libya or Egypt, after having served along Hadrian's Wall or the fortifications in Dacia, ended life as small landowners in Memphis.[16] Long before the proclamation of the end of the Western Empire, the Roman army had ceased fighting the 'Roman way' and the legions, which remained so in name alone, were mainly comprised of *foederati*, heavy cavalry troops, archers and others recruited from the border tribes.[17]

---

15   As Nero's famous journey to Greece demonstrates, the politics of some emperors, in contrast to senatorial conservatism, was in favour of Hellenization. Obviously the Romans did not possess a distinction similar to ours between political and cultural sphere; also in the sense that religion and institutional structure were closely connected. It is indisputable however that in the phase of maximum expansion, the Empire managed to assimilate religions, customs, lifestyles – that which would be called 'culture' – alien to those originally Latin.

16   On the Roman army as an element of mobility and social integration, see Wells (1984) and Le Bohec (1989). Naturally this was an integration that did not conceal in anyway the intensely classist structure within and militaristic structure on the outside of the Empire. The classic studies of Veyne (1975) and Hopkins (1983) relate funeral rites, festivities and gladiatorial rituals with this fundamental aspect of imperial society. In particular, Hopkins discusses how the gladiator games (which used slaves, war prisoners, condemned etc.) had the aim of reminding everyone the fate in store for whoever opposed the internal and external order of the Empire.

17   Rostovtzeef's classic study (1926) shows how the Imperial army, at least from the time of the Flavians, had been largely de-Romanized.

The hybrid form through which Roman citizenship was expressed, above all during the Imperial era, can not be explained without a substantial cultural and religious heterogeneity. Certainly, there were important exceptions. Palestine and Egypt were provinces periodically convulsed by nationalist risings and real religious conflicts (between Greeks and natives and between Greeks and Jews). The most famous case was the insurrection of Judea, which ended with the expulsion of Jews from Palestine, and represented perhaps the only example of wholesale political-cultural genocide during the Roman era. The most important exception is, of course, the intermittent persecution of Christians. But, even here, the reality needs to be separated from the mainly hagiographic perspective that would later become prevalent. When Constantine signed the Edict of Milan proclaiming religious toleration, Christians probably did not number more than 10 per cent of the Empire's population. The late persecutions (under for instance Valerian and Diocletian) did not target so much Christianity itself, as the Christian communities' claim to exclusivity; in other words their refusal to see themselves as *one* of the many religions of the Empire. The absorption of Christianity by Rome – which marks the beginning of the end of Roman history in the true sense of the term – ultimately testifies to the absence of a unity between political structure and cultural and religious structure. Without exaggerating the universalistic significance of the Empire, one needs to recognize that Rome's integrating capacity has few parallels in history. The two basic ideas in Gibbon's *The History of the Decline and Fall of Roman Empire* – the central concept of decline and the anti-Christian polemic – have both been refuted by successive historiography. But Gibbon's evident sympathies for paganism (still echoed today, for instance in Gore Vidal's fictionalized reconstruction of the life of Julian the Apostate) is based on an accurate assessment of Roman ecumenism (Gibbon 1973).[18] Julian wanted to revive paganism and was disgusted by the fanaticism of Christians, but his face-to-face disputes (in the sense that he would actually engage directly with bishops and Christian theologians), coupled with the fact that he was not responsible for large-scale persecutions, demonstrate how the Empire at the beginning of the fourth century AD could still see itself as a politically unified structure but culturally and religiously diverse.[19]

Despite the Christianization of the Empire, something of Roman ecumenism managed to survive even in Byzantium, which ruled over a vast variety of peoples. First of all, the Eastern Roman Empire was the result of an extraordinary historical, cultural and linguistic synthesis. Christian by faith, heir to Rome in its institutions, law and self-representation (the Byzantines continued for a long time to call themselves *romaioi*, Romans), Greek in language, but imbued in the East in

---

18   For a balanced reappraisal of Gibbon which in some ways corrects the curse that modern historiography had cast upon the great English historian, see Brown (1982).

19   A curious testimony of Julian's geniality is the *Misopogon*, the essay written in defence of his beard (and with it pagan philosophy), that Julian had posted on the doors of the churches of Antioch.

its customs, the Empire managed to survive for a millennium thanks to its capacity for political and social assimiliation.[20] Texts from the ninth and tenth centuries describe Costantinople as a melting-pot where as well as Greek, other languages such as Latin, Alani, Russian, Turkish and Iranian dialects and Arabic were all commonly spoken (Bréhier 1970b). Cultural malleability went hand-in-hand with diplomatic flexibility. Goths, Alans, Pechenegs, Slavs, Bulgars, Turks, Rus' and Arabs may all have been at some time the mortal enemies of Constantinople, but they were also its possible allies.[21] Byzantine diplomacy was ready at any moment to make compromises, to pay tributes and to transform enemies into friends. Perhaps the only irremediable conflict of Byzantine history was with the Western Christians, especially during the crusades, and it is this last group who should be considered the real culprits for the irreversible decline of Constantinople. But even here we need to avoid generalizations. The magnificent portrait of the Norman crusader Bohemond penned by Anna Komnene is not immune from fascination, while it is well known that the last of the great emperors of the Komnenos dynasty, Manuel, was drawn to the feudal and chivalric culture that the crusaders had sought to install in the Near East.[22] If anything, there existed a radical cultural opposition (once again, more with the West and the Church of Rome than with pagans and Muslims) in the ways in which historians, chroniclers and court literati portrayed their own world as an island of civilization surrounded by barbarians. But this ultimately indicates how the representation of cultural conflicts offered by scribes is only a partial (and not entirely valid) image that a society uses to depict its adversaries and external enemies.[23]

---

20   Ronchey (2002) sees the Empire's capacity to assimilate foreigners, beginning with the political elite, as precisely its strong point and condition of survival. Goths, Armenians, Slavs, Franks and others entered into the upper echelons of imperial bureaucracy (and sometimes into the reigning families).

21   Arabs also served as soldiers. From the time of Justinian, mercenaries and auxiliaries recruited in borderland provinces formed the predominant part of the Byzantine armies (Bréhier 1970a). The *Wars of Justinian* by Procopius of Caesarea are a vivid illustration of conflicts in which barbarians serving for imperial armies could find themselves facing their own kind fighting on the side of the Goths.

22   Anna Comnena (1969, XIII).

23   Apparently, the Byzantine historiographical tradition (as in Michael Psellos or in Niketas Choniates) insists on the contradiction between 'our civilization' and the barbarism of those peoples that Empire continually fought against. Yet, shortly before the definitive fall of Byzantium, while the Turks relentlessly surrounded Constantinople, at the beginning of the fifteenth century, emperor Manuel II Palaiologos found time to write a dialogue – not dissimilar in spirit to Gotthold Ephraim Lessing's 1779 drama *Nathan the Wise* (Lessing 1986) – where he calmly confronts an Ottoman (Manuel II Paléologue 1966). As Brown notes (1982, 64) old-school Byzantinists consider such a text as proof of the 'mysterious' Byzantine spirit; something that appears less mysterious if one abandons the traditional assumption of a conflict between West and East since the time of Greece and Rome.

This also holds true for Islam, which a reflourishing tradition today has indicated as the absolute other in the self-representation of the West. It would be pointless here to insist on the role that various Islamic societies have played in completing and enriching the transmission of ancient cultural and scientific heritage. A few examples would be sufficient, however, to demonstrate how the idea of cultural confrontation between Islam and Christianity has long been an ideological stereotype as well as a historical simplification.[24] The first obvious example is provided by the relative coexistence between the Christian dominions in the Holy Land and the so-called Islamic 'world' at the time of the first crusades. Pegged back on the Palestinian coast, the crusader seignories of Outremer had to contend, through a continual succession of wars, truces and alliances, with an Islamic universe split between Sunnis and Shiites (and seven Muslim Minorites), Turks, Kurds, Arabs, Mamelukes and a host of potentates incapable of uniting politically. As a result and shortly after the conquest of Jerusalem, political realism and a degree of religious tolerance replaced the initial crusading spirit.

During the period of the greatest number of Christian dominions in Palestine and Syria, new arrivals were often disgusted by the Arabization of those who had arrived and settled before them. These veteran crusaders latter were less fanatical and pragmatic in their relations with the small and large powers that surrounded them. They had, to some measure, become orientalized in their daily habits, they made and undid alliances with Muslim rulers so as to share the enemy front, they were inevitably tolerant towards Islam and the other Christian confessions, even when they represented the majority in their region, in exactly the same way as the Muslim sovereigns behaved with their Christian subjects.[25] So, while the political boundaries between the two worlds were clear-cut, the social and cultural borders were not. This was certainly the case with the Norman kingdom of Sicily which, more than anywhere else, stood at the interface between Europe and the Muslim world. Just like their natural successor, Federick II of Swabia, who was renown for his indifference towards religious distinctions,[26] the Norman kings did not care for the idea of crusades for contingent political reasons (hostility towards the Papacy) but perhaps also because of their familiarity with Arabs (which in some cases went as far as admiration) due to the continuous interactions and exchanges

---

24   Norman Daniel has demonstrates, in contrast to the readings à la Bernard Lewis that prevail today, that there existed a common courtly culture, even during the era of the crusades across the Mediterranean space, which was reflected for example in literary production and lifestyles (Daniel 1975). The influence of Arab poetry on its medieval courtly literature (especially in Occitan) is amply illustrated in Various Authors (1981).

25   On this point, see the classic work of Runciman (1951), and the more recent studies by Partner (1998) and Flori (2001).

26   Besides Runciman (1951), two biographies of Federick II, the eulogistic Kantorowicz (1927) and the more disenchanted Abulafia (1988), both agree on this point. This was naturally a case of theological and not political indifference. When necessary, Federick could be ruthless towards the Arabs of Sicily or heretics, when through their resistance, they undermined imperial authority.

that they had with the Muslim worlds and all the peoples of the Mediterranean. Indeed, the churches of Palermo with their Arab domes, Byzantine mosaics and Romanesque cloisters remind us that the Normans, once famed as warriors and adventurers, had created in Sicily one of the most syncretic political and cultural experiences of the whole of the Middle Ages.

Rather than a conflict between faiths, the tradition of remorseless hatred between Christians and Muslims has its origins in the indiscriminate massacres carried out in the Holy Land firstly by the crusaders and later also by their adversaries. During the conquest of Jerusalem, the entire civil population of every confession was exterminated. As for Richard the Lionheart, the untainted king, it should be recalled that he had three thousand Muslim prisoners executed in Acre because Saladin was late in paying an instalment of their ransom (Flori 1999).[27] This is not to deny that, especially from the expulsion of westerners from Palestine onwards, faith did not constitute a powerful stimulus for the recapture of territory and later the Muslim expansion under the Turks.[28] But in all these cases, the idea of a 'conflict between Islam and Christianity' does not bear exclusive explanatory weight. It is essentially a retrospective label through which conflicts of a political, social, economic as well as religious and cultural nature are synthesized for the purpose, at best, of simplification and, at worst, of ideological falsification. An analogy would be if some time in the future a historian decided to explain the war in Iraq on the basis of the opposition between the evangelical fundamentalism of George W. Bush and the alleged Islamism of Saddam Hussein.

A period would arise when Christian Europe would feel threatened by the Turks and this threat would assume a religious tone. This more or less coincides with the fall of Constantinople in 1453 to the beginning of the decline of the Ottoman Empire during the second half of the seventeenth century and the subsequent end of Turkish expansion in the West. But even here it would take a somewhat outlandish historiography to view this period – the advent of modernity – as an era of exclusive conflict between civilizations or religions. In fact, 1453 marks a fundamental date because it is from this year that the destruction of the remnants of the Byzantine Empire – by a military power capable of uniting the Turkish, Arab and Berber dominions in the Mediterranean and the Near East – begins to be interpreted as a *religious threat against the whole of Christianity*. However, while this cultural showdown would become the object of a vast literaray output and has ultimately survived through to the present day in the form of the 'Turkish

27   Napoleon behaved in exactly the same way 700 years later when he exterminated Mameluke prisoners at Acre.

28   The collections of Arab chronicles of the crusades edited by Gabrieli (1987) and Maoluf (1999) document how the reaction of the Arabs to the Western invasion was for a long time without an organic conception, both in a religious and a political sense. Even Saladin's short-lived unification of Islam did not necessarily lead to the persecution of the Christian, Orthodox and heretical communities.

Terror',[29] it did not coincide with a defined political alignment nor with a common Western consciousness.

On the whole, the European kingdoms avoided helping Constantinople, while the Italian Maritime Republics were more interested in the survival of their commercial bases in the Aegean than in defending Christianity.[30] France, for one, maintained for centuries a non-committal alliance with the Sublime Porte. Neither does it seem that the Turks, despite the inflammatory sermons that the Imams delivered to the Janissaries prior to battle, really played the part of defenders of the whole of Islam for, over and above their ecumenical claims, they only represented its Western frontier.[31] On the absence of a clear-cut division, the examples abound. It is suffice to note that the self-representation of the West as a culture united by a common faith and opposed to the duly common faith of the other side finds no confirmation in history besides the papal bulls and appeals of humanists and rhetoricians; although while these were certainly part of an official culture, they were unable to orient politics. During the era of the supposed war to the death between West and East (the epicentre of which was the Mediterranean), the wind of history was blowing strongly elsewhere: in the Atlantic and, from the perspective of other worlds, in the Pacific. The crusades had ended centuries before, the Genovese and Venetians were festering in the salt lake that extended from Gibraltar to Constantinople, while the history of the relations with Muslims would now weave between piracy and legends about seraglios. A final anecdote can show how arbitrary and distorted it is to speak of a millennial conflict between religions and cultures, in particular between the West and Islam. When Napoleon returned home after his expedition to Egypt, there were few traces of his endeavours in Muslim accounts of events. Someone merely went as far as to recall that the pilgrimage to Mecca that year had faced delays.[32]

What do these various references to the West's presumed bimillenary conflict with barbarians (firstly Persians, later Arabs and Turks and finally Muslims) actually tell us? They indicate that the historical accumulation of separate and heterogeneous facts (at both a logical and empirical level) easily and inevitably

---

29   On this point, see Ricci (2002). As already observed, Bernard Lewis's take on the relations between Europe and Arabs is not immune from an underlying anti-Islamic bias (Lewis 1982, 1995, 2003), see also Said (1985). A more balanced view is provided by Wheatcroft (2004).

30   The fundamental documents for understanding the indifference of Western kingdoms regarding the fate of the Byzantines and the simultaneous rise of an anti-Turkish obsession as a reaction to the fall of Constantinople are collected in Pertusi (1976).

31   On the ultimately marginal role of the Mediterranean with regards the Muslim dominions at the time of the Turkish expansion, see the collection of studies in Various Authors (1970).

32   The episode is cited in Chandler (1966, I, 329). Bernard Lewis, on this regard, speaks of the favourable impression that the 'tolerance and justice' of the French in Egypt had upon some Turkish observers (quoting just one source).

overlaps with the unified readings that every present makes of its past.[33] One does not need to have read Nietzsche's *Untimely Meditations* or Gadamer's *Truth and Method* to realize that historical narrative (*Historie*) is a means by which every contemporary stage projects *its* problems onto events in the past (*Geschichte*). Huntington's narrative – which is of interest to us here as an example of the Western discourse[34] about the conflict of religions, cultures or civilizations – postulates a clash that is as old as history itself and in doing so remodels the past, so as to then historically justify the existence of a present-day clash, in a sort of 'loop' that is characteristic of every rudimentary philosophy of history. Thus, a literary construction – the conflict between cultures – ends up becoming the cause of the complex historical situation that it is supposed to explain. As such, the protagonists of history are no longer social actors in *their* societies, religions and cultures, but entire civilizations or cultures understood as symbolic macro-actors that are endowed with long-term aims and respective strategies.[35]

Epistemological Digression

The reader will recognize in the irremediable discrepancy between the empirical dimension and the historiographical and social science reconstructions a classic concern of Max Weber's methodology; a concern that remains instructive to our discussion here about the 'clash of civilizations' or 'conflict between cultures'. While a Durkheimian lineage lies at the basis of the conceptual formulation of much of contemporary sociology and anthropology, Weber's epistemological approach instead continues to harry us, if nothing else because the problems he poses are more open and, one might add, more ambiguous. Weber was famously tormented, also at a personal level, by the conflict between, on the one hand, 'value orientations' (cultural demons) and, on the other, the rational and material orientations (interests and every other kind of motive that we define as social). Moving through his labyrinthine oeuvre, one discovers that he always oscillates between both. Or put another way, thanks to his well-known dualistic tendency, he recognizes both of them, attributing pre-eminence to either one or the other. This is demonstrated by the following sequence of examples: modern economic

---

33   That a socio-historical event is discontinuous (or 'occasional') simply means that it should be studied through its interactions with other events, without presupposing the existence of some metahistoric or metasocial structure that unites them. See Veyne (1998).

34   By discourse here I mean, following Michel Foucault (1970), the sets of texts that are predominant in a society and which, without necessarily being theorized in an explicit way, orientate the thought of an era. With regard to the themes discussed here, a fundamental reference is Foucault (1997). For a overview of Foucault's contribution to the explanation of contemporary conflicts, see Dal Lago (2005a).

35   My methodological considerations here owe much to the fundamental work of Paul Veyne (1978 and 1998).

rationalism is ultimately favoured by religious factors; religious, political or any other sort of charisma is the most irrational of social ties, but inevitably ends by becoming rationalized in some form of institution; the field of political action is the sphere in which rationalities prevail, but daring is the political actor who forsakes, in the name of opportunity, the force of their ultimate convictions (an excess of rationalism compromises political action). As a contributor to public scientific debates towards the end of his life and following the end of the European catastrophe of the First World War, Weber appears to argue that as the result of the rejection of cultural monotheism the world has become a terrain where the multiplicity of 'gods' (i.e. values or 'cultures') clash and where everyone is forced to *choose* between them (but does not the act of 'choosing' mean that rationalism reappears exactly where it was supposed to have been ousted?).[36]

This is not the place to explore Weber's metaphors and rhetoric. Given their poignancy, these will never cease to fascinate scholars and elicit different interpretations. What is worth underlining is that Weber's typical style of argumentation seems to be obsessed, as was fashionable during his day, by the *relationship between words and things*. The same meticulous desire to classify, define and list was shared by the likes of Karl Kraus and Ludwig Wittgenstein. Each of Weber's conceptual definitions that draws on some aspect of empirical reality contains the caveat that in other circumstances things might work out differently. The exceptions are so numerous that in the end they negate the definition itself, which is supposed to apply in a majority of cases. Here I present an example that leads us straight to the heart of the problem of cultural conflicts: the *nation*. If one reads the section of Weber's *Economy and Society* dedicated to the nation, it is difficult to figure out what is going on. In a few pages Weber explains to us what the nation *is not*: it is not identified with a 'people', a 'language' or, least of all, an 'ethnic community'. In the end, Weber writes that the nation does indeed have something to do with the act of 'community', but perhaps more with political 'prestige'. On reading and rereading the text and confronting it with similar passages, we might well be forgiven in considering Weber's idea of 'nation' as just the name we give to the empirically varied, broadly subjective and arbitrary set of claims with which a group declares to believe in 'something', for the purpose of political prestige or power, and which keeps them together and justifies their existence before other groups (Weber 1922, 23–7).[37]

Weber's method of reasoning is undoubtedly contorted, but it has, in my opinion, an extraordinary virtue of preventing a word from being mistaken as the cause of actions or forms of behaviour.[38] Take note: at no point does Weber say that

---

36   Weber's political work rather than his methodological writings is the most important source for an understanding of Weber the philosopher (Weber 1958).

37   The paragraph in question is incomplete. However, it all makes us think that in final analysis the driving impetus for the assertion of 'nations' was, for Weber, power.

38   This is nothing more than Whitehead's famous warning against the *fallacy of misplaced concreteness*. In an essay from the 1930s, Gregory Bateson (1973) noted how

the nation does not exist (after all, a whole host of different words have played key roles in history). He says that it is a claim – a set of assertions and performative expressions – with which different groups establish or justify their existence. It is at the same time a myth, a symbolic configuration, a legitimating narrative, a *process* (and not something fixed and solid) which, like all processes, has a beginning and an end, and therefore produces memories, interpretations, legends and ideologies. In each case, we need to study how such processes influence the actions of a group, how they convey or obscure interests and so on. The nation, as in the case of 'values' and culture, is not a word that explains, but rather a word that needs to be explained: this is Weber's epistemological message, entirely consistent with his theory of method in historical and social sciences.

I have mentioned these old discussions not because they contain in themselves useful clues for understanding contemporary conflicts, but because they indicate the gap between analytical readings of the past (and present) and what Max Weber himself would have defined as the rhetoric of literati. According to Weber, the literati – as opposed to researchers who work *sine ira ac studio* (without anger or bias) – tend to explain historical political problems by generalizing their *own* ideological categories. Think, for example, of the German scholars during the second half of the nineteenth century who interpreted ancient history on the basis of their own nationalist romanticism,[39] Clearly, the literati's style was not limited to Germany. Indeed, during the same period, philosophers and historians with fervent imaginations such as Renan, Carlyle and Gobineau began to reconstruct European history as a conflict between civilizations, cultures or, worse still, races. On this note, it is difficult not to bring Nietzsche into discussion. But although Nietzsche was responsible, at least indirectly, for a number of tasteless stereotypes (such as the 'blond beasts'), he was clearly averse to the mythopoeic historiography of the day. Indeed his hostility towards anti-Semitism, cultural Prussianism or Wagnerism was bound to a sort of *methodological individualism*, while the force of his philosophical hammer was aimed at what he saw as an improper use of collective concepts. For Nietzsche, exactly as for Weber, it was one thing to recognize the existence of historical-cultural formations such as socialism, statalism, nationalism, Christian morals, anti-Semitism and so on; it was completely another thing to adopt the narrow-minded conceptual frameworks devised by such formations to study historical processes.

This is exactly what we are faced with when it comes to pseudo-problems such as the 'clash of civilizations' or the 'conflict between cultures'. It is indisputable that today there exists a formidable literary output that legitimates or takes for granted the existence of such conflicts – from essays with scientific pretensions to press reports – and that this has given rise to a particular ideology. But must we then assume that such an opaque conceptual system is the cause of this historical

this is a risk to be avoided, especially when studying cultural conflicts.
    39   On this point (which is of great importance for our theme), see Momigliano (1984).

(the immigrants are 'hordes', while citizens are engaged in a 'revolt', 'crusade' or 'truce') that are filtered through this state thought (the 'outpost', 'base', 'citadel', 'safe house' are all 'stormed'). Immigrants are an alien body, entrenched and removed from the rule of the state that has to reimpose its control. Again, we are presented with the language of invasion: this 'army' has 'conquered' a territory pertaining to the state and must be 'liberated'. Their presence is an intrusion that disrupts the integrity of an ethnically pure national order.[38]

What unites the 'bellicization' of international, external and internal fronts, despite their differences, is the police–military mechanisms of constraint that govern migration. The continuum between these wars and real wars as well as the police–military hybridization of security activities (Palidda 2007, 2010a, 2010b) is the outcome of the asymmetry that governs relations between rich nations (free to delocalize, control resources and govern at a distance) and poor countries, whose citizens are denied by military means the freedom of movement. Access to rich countries is only granted at the price of a citizenship that is perpetually in question, held back and liable to be withdrawn through the instruments of police and military control.

In summary, this brief review of the media's treatment of immigration demonstrates how exclusionary and control practices on the three main fronts are objectivized into discourse, and in categories, images and narratives that frame aspects of reality into unitary, stereotypical and tautological representations that guarantee the legitimation of these same practices. The media's role in mediating but also self-constructing these representations has been extremely instrumental to the criminalization of immigration, while the politics of fear, on the one hand, and the search for visibility and consensus by the entrepreneurs of commonsense, on the other, have together provided the raw material that has fuelled the 'immigration emergency'. However, behind the discourse on immigration, lie above all the practices of Fortress Europe which are particularly radical in the Italian case. The closure of borders, the withdrawal of policies of reception and assistance and the obsession with control leave their mark, for it is in the acts of expelling, arresting, evicting, searching and identifying that the discourse on immigration is originally spelled out.

---

38 As already noted, the national coordinates of state thought correspond to those of mobilized citizens. For example, during the frequent protests against 'nomad camps', it is often argued that 'they must go home', phrases that are continuously repeated even after it has been noted that the camp is only occupied by Roma with Italian citizenship. Clearly, as Roma, they appear to disrupt the purity of national identity. For an eloquent example, see the RAI current affairs programme 'Presa Diretta' (2009) available at http://www.presadiretta. rai.it/category/0,1067207,1067208-1083740,00.html; on the business of persecution of Roma see http://www.unmondoacolori.rai.it/sito/scheda_puntata.asp?progid=906

Chapter 6
The Detention Machine

Federico Rahola

Questioning Borders

Political modernity can be represented as a relentless struggle on maps. Indeed, against any naturalistic claim, the relation between a map and 'its' territory – that is the very political notion of space – is far from being a simply descriptive matter. 'The map is not the territory' is a kind of mantra that from Korzybski up to Gregory Bateson has been continuously repeated. It means, above all, that instead of simply reflecting or being defined by a territory, a map effectively produces it, defining the way we make experience of the space. In other words, once we have fixed a map, we have at the same time decided how to organize the space, how to circumscribe it, to think about and to govern it. Yet, if political modernity has signified, above all, the ultimate subsumption of the territory under the rationality of several (and often conflicting) maps, such an over-determining relation seems now to have come to an end. Indeed, current geography(ies) appears to exceed and transcend any possible map, any kind of cartographic rationality.[1] For this reason a renewed geographical imagination has to be developed, in order to give an account of the whole array of processes that, at different levels, are definitely overpassing any singular and discrete (or national) scale. Saskia Sassen deals with this kind of predicament when she suggests conceiving the new geography of globalization in terms of an intricate/imbricated and multi-scalar dimension, encompassing territories, authorities and networks, where working out the distinction between an inside and outside becomes increasingly arduous, and where the global interpenetrates the national generating new solid concretions of borders.[2] As a matter of fact, borders are the places where global tensions and geographical pretensions end up precipitating and becoming particularly visible. In other terms, the overall reshaping of current geography starts from the borders, from the very notion of border. But what are we talking about when we talk about borders?

Even in this case, we have firstly to detect a radical change according to which borders tend to transform themselves from linear manifestations into points of intensity. There is a persistent, commonsensical notion of border, at least in the geographical and political literature, according to which a border is first and

---

1   On the crisis of the 'cartographic rationality', see Farinelli (2003).
2   Sassen (2007) insists on the multiscalar character of globalization, where the national and the global intersect, generating new kinds of borders.

foremost a line separating two political entities differently defined in terms of sovereignty. It is precisely this linear dimension that, about a century ago, the German geographer Fredrick Ratzel defined as a 'geometrical abstraction' (Ratzel, 1923). To the abstract idea of a *Grenzlinie*, Ratzel opposed the more complex and realistic notion of a *Grenzsaum*, that is, a bi- or three-dimensional border-zone, making the case of the *terrains vagues* and the no-mans-land occupying the space in between two national states: places whose sovereignty is uncertain, that, according to Ratzel, are nonetheless filled with 'scattered manifestations of border'. Ratzel, by the way, gives us a further and more enlightening example of *Grenzsaum*, making the case of the desert, as a place nomadic groups move through while carrying the border with them. We are thus confronted with borders that are first and foremost dynamic, mobile, at least individualized and deterritorialized: borders on the move, following people on the move.

It is worth insisting on this specific dimension of border and space, insofar as it directly concerns a crucial point of distinction and transition. While a *Grenzlinie*, the border as a line, is basically oriented to distinguish between an inside and outside, the *Grenzsaum*, as a zone, is characterized by a proliferation of borders that, rather than being linear, assume a specific 'point' form. The movement is therefore from lines to points, whose function, rather than separating an inside from an outside, is basically devoted to the production of distinctions among the individuals within an open-ended dimension of space – as it was for the nomads moving in the desert. Indeed, Ratzel suggests that a *Grenzilinie* is the direct border manifestation of a closed and mono-scalar form of territoriality (namely, the nation-state one), while the scattered and punctiform manifestations of borders of the *Grenzsaum* belong to an open territoriality. It is precisely this latter dimension of both borders and territoriality that appears to be more responsive to the imbricate and multi-scalar geography of what we typically refer to as globalization. For this reason, as suggested by Paolo Cuttitta, the geography of the present could be conceived as a global *Grenzsaum*, that is, a surface characterized by an open dimension of territoriality, yet crisscrossed by scattered and dispersed manifestations of border (Cuttitta, 2007).

There is a thaumaturgic and multipurpose term that is continuously evoked in order to describe the transformations investing global geography, and it is 'deterritorialization'. In a way, we can say that while shifting from lines to points borders deterritorialize both themselves and their functioning. More precisely, borders seem to describe a double deterritorializing movement, according to which, while leaving aside their linear dimension, they either project themselves far away from the line they are supposed to preside over, and they reflect inward, within the territory they are supposed to delimit. It is a process that becomes particularly evident in the case of the control of human mobility (I prefer this generic term to the more connotative way the specific literature talks about migrations, distinguishing between 'forced' and 'economic' ones). In the first case, indeed, a border can act 'at distance', in a preventive way, by selecting people potentially on the move (no matter whether as migrants or asylum seekers) in their own country, as in the case of a consulate or an embassy acting as a punctiform manifestation of a linear border in a foreign territory. It is what Didier Bigo and Elspeth Guild refer to as 'police at distance' (Bigo and Guild, 2003), by this alluding to the preventive action of selecting people *in loco*, before their very movement. In the second case, at stake there is a more complex movement of reflection inward, within the national territory, to the extent that the weight, or the ghost, of a linear border retrospectively follows those who have crossed it, hanging over them and defining their status in terms of temporariness or clandestinity – and, in so doing, producing differences of status among a population within the same territory. It is worth noting, in this case, the almost literal hypostasizing of the very idea evoked by Ratzel, of a nomadic and almost individualized border that accompanies people on the move.[3]

Yet, the very notion of deterritorialization reveals itself to be but a partial truth, just one half of the story. It is worth reminding here the way Gilles Deleuze and Felix Guattari describe the interplay between deterritorialization and reterritorialization as an ongoing, open-ended process: any form of deterritorialization exerts retorritorializing effects; any deterritorializing pressure is already a kind of reterritorialization (Deleuze and Guattari, 2004). This is true, first, for human mobility. Broadly speaking, contemporary migrations reveal themselves to be increasingly 'autonomous' and beyond the national scale. As opposed to the past, they seem to increasingly exceed any regulatory capacity of government by individual states, while they can hardly be reduced to mere 'objective' economic factors (such as 'push and pull').[4] Accordingly, in order to capture this exceeding and deterritorialized dimension, a new conceptual tool-box and new terms have been adopted. This is the case for transmigrations and diasporas,[5] both of which suggest a dimension that transcends the discrete, national scale while redefining the very experience of proximity and distance.

This is not the place for an in-depth analysis of the transformations in current migrations. The point here is that even in the case of diasporic and transnational

---

3   Ratzel's notion of *Grenzsaum*, as an open surface filled with scattered manifestations of borders, also suggests that, in the case of the government of migrations, rather than simply blocking the movement, borders act as device that introduce lines of discontinuity within the very condition of movement (by selecting, 'bridling', clandestinizing and blackmailing it).

4   A growing literature recognizes the increasing and specific 'autonomy' of current migrations. See, among the others, the study by Castles and Miller (2009, 4th edn), and Mezzadra (2004).

5   The notions of diaspora and transmigration seem to better grasp the complex and multi-situated geography enacted by contemporary migrants experience – though, by privileging the organizing capacity from below of informal and familiar networks, the latter often runs the risk of erasing any notion of public space. For an in-depth analysis of the transnational approach in migration studies see Portes and DeWind (2008); for an enlightening attempt to rearticulate and extend the notion of diaspora to the forms of contemporary displacement, see Clifford (1997).

migrations, we are always confronted with forms and projects of mobility that, while expressing a deterritorializing force, end up somehow reterritorializing themselves, insofar as they precipitate into new forms of territory and organization (such as a transnational family or an extended and ideal notion of 'home'). More importantly (at least here), this complex and ongoing relation is also true for borders, though at a more abstract level. Indeed, to affirm that borders deterritorialize themselves by transforming their manifestations from lines to points, also means that they reterritorialize themselves (as punctiform places, as in the case of a consulate, or, more roughly, in terms of walls and fences surrounded by barbed wire, like the ones between the U.S. and Mexico or around Cisjordania), and even re-naturalize themselves, by encompassing entire deserts (as the Sahara, the Teneré, or the Sonoran desert) and seas (the Mediterranean, the ocean surrounding Australia etc.). This means, above all, that borders, while deterritorializing themselves, forcibly reterritorialize the forms of human mobility, by imposing new forms of confinement and producing radical differences of status.

It is possible to translate this movement – that is, the interplay between deterritorialization and reterritorialization and thus between movement and borders – into a kind of relational sequence. As a matter of fact, the border is always an inert device whose existence is first and foremost a reaction to movement: it does not exist and act until it is crossed, violated, profaned by something or someone's movement. Movement is therefore the condition of possibility for the existence of borders. And borders act to transform the smooth surface assumed by the very experience of movement into a striated one. Starting from this premise, Deleuze and Guattari develop a complex and abstract model referred to a specific historical instance. This is the case of the relation between what they define as the 'nomadic machine', alluding by this to the way the Barbarians moved over and used the space in their assaults on the territories of the Roman empire, and the 'apparatus of capture', that is, the military answer that the Empire opposed to the Barbarian machine, transforming the smooth surface assumed by the latter into a striated space (Deleuze and Guattari, 2004: 387–552). The fact is that, in so doing, the detention apparatus itself has to become nomadic too, in order to master and reterritorialize the deterritorializing movement of the nomadic machine. At stake, therefore, there is a kind of isomorphic or mimetic relation – that is, a relation that is far from being dialectical, to the extent that it does not assume any possible synthesis; on the contrary it develops itself into a relentless becoming. In other terms, and in a very Deleuzian way, we can say that movement 'comes first': by conceiving space as a smooth surface to be continuously crossed and violated, it opens up territories and places, deterritorializes them and produces 'global' relations and connections. And borders only come after, by taking on the new deterritorialized surface defined by movement and trying to reterritorialize it while deterritorializing and turning themselves into nomadic machines. This complex, isomorphic relation is synthesized by a specific device that, in the case of human mobility, can be considered as one of the main material manifestations of border of the present: the detention camp.

A New Apparatus of Capture

There is a map produced by a collective group of researchers and activists (www. migreurop.com) that directly illustrates this complex, de- and reterritorializing movement. It represents the impressive proliferation of transit, identification and detention camps for persons variously 'out of place' which is investing the EU space as well as the territory surrounding its external borders. It is a map that, at the same time, directly enacts the geographical predicament mentioned above, insofar as to any point indicated on the map corresponds a material and punctiform manifestation of the EU border. In other words, the real borders of the European Union will coincide with the overall picture realized by those scattered points rather than with lines. Two different directions intersect in these places: the first implies an attempt to enter, while the second a forced exit. And both the directions are 'governed' through recourse to this particular border device, whose aim is basically to control, select and slow down the movement of persons in transit. Indeed, it is through this specific 'apparatus of capture' that the European Union is trying to govern and reterritorialize the mobility (essentially of migrants and asylum seekers) either within the member states' territory or outside of it. As the map shows, the proliferation of camps does not only limit itself to the EU territory, but on the contrary stretches well beyond it: it penetrates into the Maghreb, goes up to Libya, touches the Atlantic coast of Mauritania and extends east, from Turkey up to the Ukraine, in order to control the EU frontiers from the outside.

The hypothesis advanced here is that we are dealing with a new apparatus of capture, which deterritorializes itself in order to reterritorialize the 'nomadic machine' of human mobility, and, in so doing, ends up re-territorializing the deterritorialized borders of the EU, by precipitating their weight into an archipelago of scattered points, each of them being a manifestation of border. The whole effect of the stains affecting (as if it were an exanthematic disease) the European map is therefore that of an overall system, the EU detention apparatus, whose certain (though not at all systemic) coherence and integration as well as the specific 'productiveness' I would like to stress here.

It is better to start with 'coherence', that is, with the relation allowing us to keep together the different (and apparently opposed) current manifestations of the camps. Consider, as an example, the case of an extremely unlucky yet possible life-story – whose implications, that I summarily synthesize here, should need a more detailed account. It is the case of someone, let us call her Halima, who is persecuted (for reasons of religion, gender, or political and ethnic belonging) in her own country. Suppose the country is Sudan, a place where international organizations (either UNHCR or different NGOs) directly operate in terms of minority protection. Halima should therefore be lodged within a temporary shelter centre for the internally displaced (whose official definition could be 'Emergency Temporary location' – ETL). Consider, then, that Halima is able to leave her own country, crossing the national border: in the specific case of Sudan, it means that she would reach Libyan territory, passing through a series of informal camps spread around Chad or Niger.[6] Once she arrives, a further constellation of camps (informal and/or of detention, that is, directly managed by Libyan police[7]) is waiting for her, before her probable forced repatriation or the abandonment on the Libyan borders, near the desert. But there is also the frequent possibility for Halima to succeed in getting a passage to the north, by sea, and reaching, for instance, the Italian coast. In this case, Lampedusa Island represents a kind of forced arrival – being the only southern island of Italy to be equipped with an airport and a 'shelter' centre for migrants and asylum seekers. Indeed, once here, Halima will be confined for a while (from two up to ten weeks) in the local first-asylum and identification centre (the Italian acronym being CPSA). From there, despite a thousand obstacles, it is possible that she will be allowed to apply for asylum. After the first undefined period of detention in the local centre, she will therefore be transferred to a further facility, a shelter and identification centre for asylum seekers (the new Italian acronym is CARA), staying there for the time required to assess her application. We have thus to consider both possibilities: the far more likely situation of a denial (to the extent that a form of protection, a humanitarian centre/ETL, already exists in her own country, thus avoiding the acceptance of her application abroad), and the possibility implying the start-up of asymptotic procedures for the release of a generic and temporary humanitarian status (a form of temporary protection that substantially differs from the right to asylum as it has been defined by the 1951 Geneva Convention, insofar as it does not imply any kind of permanent recognition of civil and social rights –UNHCR, 2006). However, in the first case Halima will be considered as an 'irregular' migrant and thus virtually destined to a detention centre (an 'identification and expulsion centre'– CIE). In the second and rarer case, for the overall in-between time before the ultimate release of a new humanitarian status, Halima will most likely be lodged in a protection facility. In any case, the right to asylum is today conceived as a temporary instrument which presupposes the normalization of the situation in one's land of origin. And once the asylum expires, it is assumed that Halima will spontaneously return to her own country; otherwise, she will be threatened with a deportation order that in most cases will remain unexecuted, but which will nevertheless subsume her prior existence as an internally displaced 'asylum seeker' and 'temporary refugee' under a situation of precariousness and blackmail that hastens her advance toward a definition of 'illegality'. Another facility, an identification and expulsion centre (CIE), will therefore hang over her, from where to organize her possible repatriation (that is, deportation) to the third 'safe' country she passed through before touching

---

6   For an account of the various and often extreme conditions of migrants' movements and displacement in the south of the Sahara, see Liberti (2008).

7   An Italian documentary (*Come un uomo sulla terra*) directly describes the harsh conditions of detention within the Libyan camps where migrants are blackmailed and often kidnapped by the local military police. Some documentaries and photos are available at the websites http://fortresseurope.blogspot.com/ and http://dailymotion.virgilio.it/video/x6hqwb_migration-europe-sans-frontiere_news

her final destination, namely Libya. Once the 'repatriation' has been organized, according to the specific bilateral agreements Italy and Libya have stipulated, Halima will be confined to one of the several transit centres (TPC) that have been set up by the Libyan government with European funds and the supervision of inter-governmental organizations such as the IOM[8]. Here she will be detained for a time and in conditions that nobody can verify – insofar as Libya does not allow any kind of intrusion and control, nor has it ratified the Geneva Convention for refugees – before being accompanied to the frontier with Sudan or abandoned in the Teneré desert.

Of course, this is an extreme instance, to the extent that it is not at all necessary to pass through all the places and centres mentioned above, each one corresponding nonetheless to a different formal definition and a specific juridical status (from internally displaced, to asylum seeker, to temporary refugee, up to irregular migrant). Yet, such an extreme example quite eloquently shows us the specific link between different devices of detention. At every step, for each border that has been crossed and for any status that has been acquired or denied, there is always a camp that, at least potentially, hangs over the person on the move. It is from this constancy – the permanent transit through temporary places – that the hypothesis of a 'detention machine', based upon what I have elsewhere defined as the 'definitely temporary zones' of present time (Rahola, 2003), takes shape. In this perspective, camps represent first and foremost the only 'possible' territory for persons that exceed any form of univocal belonging. As suggested by Hannah Arendt, in a complex chapter of *The Origins of Totalitarianism* dedicated to the impressive proliferation of camps in Europe in between the two world wars, the 'internment camp' reveals itself to be 'the only practical substitute for a nonexistent homeland' (Arendt, 1958: 284), the place where to confine individuals exceeding that nationalistic landscape and its claustrophobic declination of political belonging. The relevant differences between the two historical moments notwithstanding, that exceeding political dimension seems to be reproduced today and to define one of the main traits of contemporary migrations.

There exists a substantial literature which describes camps in terms of exception. Through a rereading of modern sovereignty around the dialectical pairing of biopower and bare life (Agamben, 1998), Giorgio Agamben (1998, 2005), for example, sees the camp as a paradigmatic place where sovereign power and life confront each other, leading to a suspension of any mediation and right. Agamben attempts to reflect upon that which is produced as an 'outside' in relation to a given legal system, and which can be captured and 'taken outside' (or, to use the Latin term, *excipere* – Agamben, 1998: 92), by suspending ordinary legal instruments and appealing to a transcendent idea of sovereignty, as the instance that decides the state of exception. In a perspective closer to the Foucaultian idea of

---

8   A series of specific studies demonstrate the pivotal role the International Organisation for Migration (IOM) is playing in Europe's expanding deportation machine. See Hamood (2006) and Andrijasevic (2006a).

governmentality, I believe that it is necessary to focus above all on the meaning of places and practices that define and govern subjects, without necessarily referring to the transcendence of a sovereign decision, which on the contrary comes true on an immanent level, in the gestures and in the immediate effects produced by such places and practices (Foucault, 2007). Put in other terms, this means assuming the dispositive of the 'camp' for its specific 'positive' and therefore productive capacity. We are thus confronted with a productive form of power, to the extent that it defines and ratifies differences of status among a population within the same political territory. But what kind of difference is produced by a camp, and according to what logics?

Colonial Genealogies

In order to answer this question we have to outline another path, to be added to the horizontal and synchronic one which allows us to gather together all the different manifestations and forms (protection, identification, detention) of present-day camps. It is a vertical and diachronic line. Indeed, a genealogy of the first facilities for the administrative detention of civilians amounts to the colonies: Cuba in 1894 (as an answer to the insurrection of the colonized people against the Spaniards), and then South Africa in 1900 (when the British colonial troops interned thousands of Boer civilians in special 'relocational centres'), and then again Namibia in 1910 (when the whole Herero population was concentrated and exterminated by the Germans, through recourse to special camps that anticipated *à la lettre* the Nazi KZ), Kenya (during the Mau Mau insurrection), Libya (together with the first experiments with chemical weapons made by the Italian general Augusto Graziani), Algeria, by the French colonial power, and so on. Colonial history is filled with internment camps for civilians, whose presence has been explored by a sizeable literature: from that drafted by Arendt, to the 'angry' study by Andrzej Kaminski (1982), up to the more recent and contentious work by Kotek and Rigoulot (2000). Actually, these origins could be dated back even further to the time of the first reserves where Native North Americans were interned – though, if the idea of colonialism is conceived along Gramscian lines (that is, in terms of an internal colonization), the colonial matrix of camps seems to be confirmed in all these cases. A lacuna however exists, only partially attributable to Arendt, who in fact forcefully denounced the 'administrative massacres' of colonialism, but one which is more serious in successive work, and that is the capacity to interrogate the sense of this origin, without simply acknowledging it as a historic fact.

Indeed, the colonial origin of the camps and of the detention machine compels us to cope with a specific political subject, the colonized subject, whose existence directly reflected the peremptory action of the radical border – or Meta-Border, as Etienne Balibar (2005) conceives It – that used to spatially separate and politically distinguish two worlds and the two respective figures inhabiting them as citizens or subjects. Incidentally, it is worth noting here that in the colonial realm, instead of a suspension of the law, there existed a particular separation of the legal system – that is, the coexistence of a national law and a juridical system for the metropolitan spaces, citizens and settlers, together with a specific colonial law for the colonized subjects. The colonies, in other words, represented an excess space, which evaded and questioned dialectical images of national boundaries and an inside–outside logic, and for this reason was governed by a colonial law that 'exceeded' (rather than being an exception to) the legal system of each colonial power.[9] Accordingly, the colonial origin of internment camps and administrative detention, instead of referring to a particular 'state of exception', seems rather to suggest the idea of a juridical system that was differentially enforced along the line of the Colonial Divide. However, our point here is that the colonial origin of camps materially defined the colonized subject as the first 'internable', confinable and deportable subject. It is therefore along the Colonial Divide that the existence of subjects liable to be interned and deported has been defined. These are subjects whose presence is nonetheless recognized, in a way included, though according to a strictly differential status and within a dichotomized yet integrated geography.

The problem therefore consists in how to consider and eventually update this origin, wondering whether a Colonial (B)order and a colonial subject still exist. In this sense, drawing on the area of studies known as postcolonialism, it is useful to recover the sense of a transition which has been taking place but has by no means been resolved, a sense which inevitably problematizes the very prefix 'post' (Hall, 1996; Mezzadra and Rahola, 2006). In short, this entails detecting the continuing traces of a past of domination and exploitation in the present, but without being able to situate them within a polarized geography and an absolute Border. If today the geography, overdetermined by the Colonial Divide, has been 'technically overcome' (by the disruptions which, from the struggles for independence onwards, have redrawn an entire geography and forced capital to establish itself at another, necessarily global level), the two figures that used to inhabit it, the metropolitan citizens and the colonial subjects, end up living, so to say, side by side. And the delocalized and deterritorialized borders of the present eventually act upon this specific dimension of proximity. They are devices that substitute the action of that peremptory Border, thus governing the movement of persons by producing and ratifying differences of status and by dislocating everywhere in the global *Granzsaum*, in the former colonies as in the former metropolitan spaces.

For this reason, according to its colonial matrix, the detention machine acts above all as a separator of status, as the material and reterritorialized signal of deterritorialized borders, and its own productivity consists in this specific action. Michel Foucault outlined the particular productivity of the apparatuses of power (*dispositifs*), their specific domain of 'positivity'. More precisely, he suggested that it was the prison and the hospital that produced and diffused a social notion of normality and deviance, of health and illness. Besides, he also suggested the

---

9   The double standard between colonial law and national legal system is theorized, for example, by the Italian jurist Romano (1918: 14–123).

central and material role these apparatuses played in producing 'docile bodies', in defining the subject to be interned and in disciplining their behaviours (Foucault, 1975). The question is therefore rather immediate: what do the present-day camps produce and ratify?

The Sign of the Camps

The hypothesis advanced here is that the specific 'productiveness' of the camps consists in the very act of decreeing the existence of individuals liable to internment, over and above individual responsibility and biographical factors. In the absolute temporary dimension they condemn, and in the transitoriness they ratify, camps are not simply the only territory for displaced individuals, but, as a looming possibility, differentially define human beings who exceed borders and forms of belonging as 'detainable' and 'deportable' (De Genova, 2002). This appears to me to be the governmental character of camps: places where power is produced; *dispositives* through which a 'difference' is established. Accordingly, the detention machine directly produces and ratifies a difference of status among the population of a given territory, and, in so doing, differentially decomposes the forms of political membership, the recognition of rights, ultimately the very notion of citizenship (Rahola, 2007). In this regard, Etienne Balibar has recently denounced EU migration politics, defining them as a revisited version of the South African apartheid regime, and particularly emphasizing the central role played by the detention centres in the material constitution of a European citizenship, by prismatically decomposing it. Balibar's (2005) denunciation appears totally uncontroversial, though it needs a clarification: an apartheid regime such as the one in South Africa, formally ceased in 1991, implied a substantially static model of segregation, whereas the way the EU detention machine governs migrants mobility turns out to be much more dynamic and stratified, and, above all, seems to be more virtual/potential than real.

It is worth insisting on this point. Instead of defining an ultimate condition, the recourse to camps materially subsumes the lives of migrants and 'displaced' persons as potentially internable and deportable. In other terms, it is not the specific act of detention and of expulsion that matters - insofar as (luckily, we have to add) the huge majority of 'economic', 'forced' and whatsoever migrants do not pass through a camp, and the majority of those who are detained in a centre are thereafter released (as irregular, 'clandestine') instead of being expelled. On the contrary, it is the constant, virtual possibility of being interned and deported that matters, and that literally makes the difference. In this very possibility, or threat, we can thus detect the specific productiveness of the overall 'detention machine' which has been set up within and around the EU borders. We are confronted here with a productiveness that corresponds to logics of flexibility rather than of closure, and that ratifies the presence of *definitely temporary subjects with a definitely flexible status*. By borrowing an expression of Pierre Bourdieu, these apparatuses of capture materially produce a '*precarization*' of the conditions of life and of permanence within a given territory. They are tools that, instead of simply excluding, define the presence of subjects that in different ways are 'out of place' in terms of an absolute, political as well as economic, precariousness (Bourdieu, 1993). If this is true, rather than ratifying a form of exclusion, the EU detention machine seems to continuously produce forms of differential inclusion (incidentally, a dimension that replicates the one of the colonial subject, though beyond the Colonial Divide). Hence, the camps, as border devices, directly suggest and enact the new role borders play within the global *Grenzsaum*: rather than ratifying a distinction between an inside and outside, they seem to operate in decomposing the forms of membership and recognition within an all-encompassing yet highly selective geography, and they directly produce differences in a context defined by proximity.

There exists a further and more immediate productive dimension to be ascribed to the current detention machine. It concerns the criminalization of migrants and of migrant mobility. In a way, the overall detention system set up within and around the EU borders (the same being for the U.S.–Mexico border as well as for the archipelago of islands-camps surrounding Australia) can be considered as a punitive measure to objectify a specific 'crime'. In particular, the detention centres become a sort of prison through which it is possible to punish a person responsible for the 'crime' of having crossed a border (spatial or temporal, in terms of an expired visa), thus exceeding the forms of political belonging. The specific productiveness of this apparatus thus consists in ratifying and hypostatizing as a crime the act of crossing a border without a visa or of being in possession of an expired one. In this regard, it is worth noting here that, in juridical terms, these two acts have been both, until yesterday, considered as violations to be administratively sanctioned (i.e. via an injunction or a decree of expulsion) – that is, not criminally punished with detention. For this reason, the recourse to detention has always been defined as an administrative act. The ploy consisted therefore in 'magically' transforming an administrative sanction into a form of administrative detention. The evident unconstitutionality of the recourse to administrative detention has provoked a rather violent protest, particularly focused on the double standard it directly introduced within a legal system, according to which certain individuals could be detained on the basis of an administrative act. To these voices must be added those of the thousands of persons who, as European and/or migrant citizens, have demonstrated and struggled for the abolition of the detention centres.

While totally sharing the meaning of this struggle, I would like to suggest here a further level of productiveness to be ascribed to the detention machine. It is a sociological effect, that directly concerns the inverted relationship between punishment and crime as well as the social construction and perception of the crime this reversal determines. If, following Foucault, the prison (either as a material apparatus and as a broader social discourse) produces the detainee, and if the punishment over-determines the crime (by socially fixing a notion of guilt), then the detention centres produce both the specific crime of 'clandestinity' and the specific criminal figure of the clandestine. From this point of view, the crime of clandestinity, whose introduction is violently distorting Italian and European juridical and constitutional structures, seems to obtain a sort of preventive or *ex ante* legitimization by the very existence of the detention machine that has been set up within and outside the EU borders. The punishment, in other terms, ends up pre- and over-determining the crime, and this in turn should be considered as a further symptom of the productiveness of the detention machine and of the camps. The introduction of the crime of 'clandestine migration' seems to suggest a relevant change of course in European migration politics, by increasing repressive policies and leading to a formal assimilation between detention centres and prisons, thus reducing the 'extraterritorial' dimension of the former. However, in this tragic game, it has yet to be determined which one of the two apparently opposite logics (that is, the differentialist and expulsive one, and the securitarian and repressive one) is going to prevail. In the meanwhile, European territory and its borders are literally filling with camps, to the point that the map mentioned above appears to be constantly outdated. On the one hand, the growing presence of camps outside EU borders seems to testify to a violent increase in repressive policies. On the other hand, their exponential proliferation within the EU territory confirms how European borders remain porous and permeable: how, while letting in, they hang over those who have crossed them, thus bridling their presence and marking their biography. Either materially (by intercepting 'irregular' subjects and releasing them as clandestine) and in terms of social perception (by hypostatizing the definition of a person as 'expellable') camps are, above all, 'factories of clandestinity'. To define women and men as internable and deportable subjects, to discipline them as precarious and flexible bodies, to criminalize them as clandestine subjects: it is in all these multiple effects that the specific productivity of the current detention machine resides.

Chapter 7

The Metamorphosis of Asylum in Europe: From the Origins of 'Fake Refugees' to their Internment[1]

Jérôme Valluy

In the modern history of the idea of the right to asylum, the most significant statement dates back to 10 December 1948 and is contained in articles 13 and 14 of the Universal Declaration of Human Rights of the United Nations:

> Art. 13: 1. Everyone has the right to freedom of movement and residence within the borders of each state; 2. Everyone has the right to leave any country, including his own, and to return to his country.

> Art.14: 1. Everyone has the right to seek and to enjoy in other countries asylum from persecution; 2. This right may not be invoked in the case of prosecutions

---

1 [*Editor's note*: According to UNHCR data, there are around 67 million refugees in the world, of whom 11.4 million fall under the UNHCR's mandate, 4.6 under the UNRWA mandate, 26 million are displaced as a result of conflicts and 25 million due to natural disasters. From 1998 to date, there has hardly been a variation as regards traditional refugees, whereas there has been a large increase in the people displaced as a result of wars, which have passed from little over 5 million to more than 14 million. Europe only hosts 14 per cent of the total of UNHCR refugees; Germany hosts 578,879 of them, the United Kingdom 299,718, France 151,789, Holland 86,587, Sweden 75,078, Italy, 38,068, Austria 30,773, Denmark 26,788 and Belgium 17,575. (Germany, the United Kingdom, France and Italy have populations of around or over 60 million; Italy only hosts 2.4 per cent of the refugees in Europe). In Italy, the number of asylum seekers has supposedly increased threefold since 2005. In 2008 (January–November), there were 26,898 new asylum applications. In 2007, refugee status was granted to only 1,408 people, whereas it was denied to 6,318 people who received humanitarian protection, and it was denied to other 4,908 people, without forms of assistance being provided. 875 cannot be found or have given up, 894 are undergoing appeals and 544 are awaiting the outcome. It is well known that Italy has never passed a veritable law regulating humanitarian and political asylum. CIR (*Consiglio Italiano per i Rifugiati*, a non-profit entity) defines itself as 'an independent humanitarian organization' that was established in 1990 under the patronage of UNHCR (whose spokeswoman in Italy is Laura Boldrini).]

genuinely arising from non-political crimes or from acts contrary to the purposes
and principles of the United Nations.

Following this statement, in 1949 the High Commissioner for Refugees was created
within the UN Secretary General's office and negotiations began that would result
into the 1951 Geneva Convention on Refugees. The Convention was born out
of a clash between two ideologies: the rather extensive protection for exiles vs.
the primacy of national sovereignty. In the negotiations between diplomats, who
essentially represented the interests of states, the second rationale easily prevailed.
According to the former, the right to asylum cannot be separated from the freedom
of movement. It is what may be termed an 'axiological right to asylum': it derives
from a value system that calls for a policy of open borders, and thus offers a basis
for the protection sought by refugees and entails providing symbolic and material
support to people who are recognized as refugees, as well as to the cause for which
they are persecuted.

Conversely, according to the second rationale, because the sovereignty of states
is the philosophical principle that oversees the legal and material status of borders,
the right to asylum is here conceived as an exception: a small door left open
on the margins of the vast, closed barrier of national frontiers. Thus, associated
to the closure of borders, this 'derogative right of asylum' only exceptionally
offers authorization for entry and residence in the country of refuge to escape
persecution.

While the 1948 Declaration did not choose between the two options, between
the wide open door of axiological asylum and the half-closed small door of
derogative asylum, the 1951 Geneva Convention made the political choice to put
an end to a matter which, retrospectively, appears to be more philosophical than
diplomatic:

> Art. 1.A.2: For the purposes of the present Convention, the term 'refugee' shall
> apply to any person who ... owing to well-founded fear of being persecuted for
> reasons of race, religion, nationality, membership of a particular social group or
> political opinion, is outside the country of his nationality and is unable or, owing
> to such fear, is unwilling to avail himself of the protection of that country.

By restricting the right to asylum to a definition of refugees, the Convention
essentially stated some criteria for selecting individuals and entrusted the
power of selection to states, leaving them free to define the modalities for its
implementation. This Convention thus established the ideology of derogative
asylum that has been developed over half a century by the High Commissioner
for Refugees (UNHCR) which was created to draft the Convention and which is
responsible for its implementation, alongside the totality of actors from individual
governments (administrations, jurisdictions ...) and non-governmental actors
(NGOs, associations, social workers ...) that come into play.

Following such start, the right to asylum became a matter for experts, particularly international or national officials, who had large room for discretion in their decisions, due to the vacuity and the weak binding power of the Convention. Direct observation of the evaluation of asylum applications (Valluy 2005) shows that, far from being the final assessment of an in-depth process of legal reasoning strictly based on international law, unspoken political assumptions quite simply guide the decision-making process over asylum. A simple combination of subjective and intuitive opinion replaces the search for information and the legal syllogism that should supposedly guide judicial rulings. Thus, the lack a reasoned basis for the decision is often concealed, as is the relatively discretional character of technocratic power-wielders that are subject to political and ideological bias.[2]

The Genesis of 'Fake Refugees' (1960s and 1970s)

Technocratic power concerning refugees was initially constructed through the creation of UNHCR (1949) and of national organizations such as the French OFPRA (1952, *Office français de protection des réfugiés et apatrides*) and CRR (*Commission des Recours des Réfugiés*). But it was only more recently, in the 1970s and 1980s, that, in France and other rich countries, professionalization occurred for what has become the public, institutionalized management of the right to asylum, enabled by the thrust provided by the increase in the funding and human resources going into these government agencies, which also applied to their academic and civil society counterparts. This community of experts on the right to asylum has been growing quickly, precisely while the right to asylum has been steadily decreasing. The professional references of this world were constructed in direct relationship with the large-scale reversal of the policy on the right to asylum at the expense of exiles and refugees.

During the first phase of the modern right to asylum, approximately from 1948 to 1968, this part of international policy basically depended upon the willingness of states to let exiles into their border, or, within the NATO camp, to welcome dissidents fleeing the Soviet bloc in order to show the moral and political failure of the rival. The individual, restrictive and selective definition of refugees, in accordance with article 1A2 of the Geneva Convention, perfectly satisfied this dual political function. In France, a few thousand people requested asylum every year and a sizeable majority – between 80 per cent and 100 per cent – obtained it. However, during this period Western borders were 'open', a fact which allowed whoever sought refuge to obtain social asylum without passing through the procedure set forth by the Geneva Convention.

Starting with the early 1970s, the policy on the right to asylum, which had previously reflected the Cold War struggle between the 'communist' and the

---

2   [Editor's note: This discretionality is entirely analogous to the one guiding the actions of the police and judiciary alike.]

'capitalist' blocs, became entwined with a different story: decolonization. In effect, the 1951 Geneva Convention on Refugees was not international, but European. Many European states were still colonial empires, whose colonized citizens could not obtain anything in terms of asylum, other than deciding to submit to a different colonial power by moving to the European continent. This made the asylum phenomenon unlikely and demographically marginal.

Nonetheless, after the decolonizations of the 1960s, decolonized people became subjects of international law (that is, citizens of a state) in their relation with the colonialist state. France only agreed to ratify the 1967 New York Protocol that extended the Geneva Convention to the international arena after several years of internal negotiations. This only happened after a lengthy power struggle between technocrats from the interior ministry, who feared that this extension would open a route for the immigration of decolonized peoples, and from the foreign affairs ministry, who were more concerned about preserving French influence, both on the African Continent and within the United Nations General Assembly, in which the new decolonized states played a significant role. Diplomats managed to have their views prevail in 1971 ... but the interior administration was able to express its refusal in other ways: from 1972 onward, non-European asylum applications were massively dismissed, with rates approaching 100 per cent, whereas refusal rates remained around 15 per cent for European asylum-seekers (in flight from the USSR).

From 1972 to 1973, the number of asylum applications rose quickly due to influxes from Indochina and South America.[3] From that moment on, the rejection rate of asylum applications by OPFRA began its steady growth. However, the overall trend was slowed down by the good reception reserved to the Indochinese

---

3   [Editor's note: In that period, 'boat people' were very visible on international media. It was the end of the Vietnam War and of the geopolitical catastrophe that had stricken Indochina. The West tried to restore its moral image by showing the atrocities committed by Pol Pot's Khmer Rouge, and by mobilizing for the reception of refugees expelled by the Vietcong from Indochina. France (defeated by Giap in Diem Bien Phu in 1956 and hence driven out of Vietnam) was the European country that received the largest contingent. In most cases, boat people were descendants of the Chinese diaspora that had spread across Indochina; among them, there were many shopkeepers and small entrepreneurs, as well as a few collaborators, first of the French and later of American colonialist regimes, as well as of regional regimes that were corrupt and traffickers of weapons and drugs. In France, small Chinese and Vietnamese communities had existed since the start of the twentieth century. In the 1980s, people whose origins lay in Indochina became particularly numerous among shopkeepers and in small-scale manufacturing, first in some Paris neighbourhoods and later in other cities. A substantial majority of them was obviously anti-communist and linked to Chinese-Americans, as well as to Taiwan and Hong Kong. Following the new mantra of 'business is business', in the 1990s the Asian community in France has established ties with the Popular Republic of China which, in the meantime, has developed a policy to penetrate European markets which effectively controls the new wave of Chinese emigration around the world.]

(and the Chileans). The 'boat people' benefited from favourable public opinion and political interest. This was reflected by a very low rejection rate for applications: lower than 10 per cent until the mid-1980s. During the following two decades, the Indochinese became the leading immigrant nationality and they accounted for a majority of the asylum applications that were granted. The privileged reception of Indochinese people enabled France to certify the moral and political failure of its victors in the war of decolonization, within the context of the conflict between the communist and capitalist camps in which it had lost political influence on its former Asian colonies.

Nonetheless, this privileged reception concealed a more important phenomenon: rejection rates rising dramatically for all other nationalities. Asylum applications filed by Africans were rejected wholesale: 95 per cent of refusals in 1973. The overall refusal rate rose immediately afterwards: to 30 per cent in 1973, 35 per cent in 1974, 45 per cent in 1975, and 80 per cent in 1976. After three years of respite between 1977 and 1979, the trend towards refusal reaffirmed itself in 1981 (70 per cent) climbing steadily until refusal rates of 70 per cent and 100 per cent were reached in the mid-1980s (85 per cent in 1985, then 90 per cent in the three subsequent years).[4]

It can hence be seen that the policy on the right to asylum for non-Europeans was strictly linked to decolonization, both as regards the reception of Indochinese people and the rejection of other nationalities, especially Africans. OPFRA operates under the oversight of the foreign affairs ministry, but it is also under the authority of the interior ministry (naturalization, controls on entry, initial recording of asylum applications in police headquarters ...) and of the social affairs ministry (reception and taking charge of asylum seekers in specialized centres for recognized refugees ...). These three ministries and their respective bureaucracies were strongly involved in the decolonization process during the 1960s.

During the Algerian war of liberation, the interior ministry played its part in the French home country. The signing of the Evian agreements in 1962 (which decreed Algeria's independence) did not suddenly cancel the mentality of officials who were trained during the eight years of war against the Algerians. In effect, the Algerian war of independence certainly constituted a training laboratory for the police in dealing with non-European foreigners. This approach was extended to the totality of African nationalities, as is shown by the distribution by nationality of the people expelled from France from 1963 to 1973: 73.1 per cent were Algerians at the start of this period, in comparison with 45.4 per cent at the end (Spire 2005: 218), amounting to a number of annual expulsions that was almost constant; the difference is even larger for other nationalities of the Maghreb and Africa.

As Bernardot's (2008) research shows, on the social front the will to control decolonized people/ immigrants better was manifest in the creation of Sonacotral (National company for the construction of lodgings for Algerian workers) in 1956, re-named Sonacotra in 1962, when it lost its Algerian focus to extend its

---

4   Legoux (1995: 148). The statistical data are drawn from this work.

competencies to the totality of Africans. At the end of the decade, 90 per cent of the directors of Sonacotra comprised former military personnel involved in the colonial wars. The genesis and evolution of the DPM (Directorate for Population and Migrations), created in 1966 within the social affairs ministry, also illustrates this approach as regards the policy vis-à-vis immigration. As Laurens shows,[5] the majority of high-level officials in the new directorate and, most importantly, the highest ranking ones in every service came from the former colonial administration and brought attitudes and references from their previous professional experiences into the new service.

Hence, in the 1960s there was an authentic political process that led to the decisions of the early 1970s and lent them a meaning that was unrelated to economic crisis and deindustrialization in the following decade, even though they would serve as retrospective justification for the policies to refuse asylum that has resulted from a different historical dynamic: the closing of borders (1974), restrictions on family reunions (1976), punishment of irregular residence (1980), identity checks based on physical features (1981).

After the 1980s, a reinterpretation of the story would assert itself, based on ex-post knowledge of the crisis that nobody had ten years earlier: the oil shock was presented as the main determinant to tell the story of the reversal of the policy on the right to asylum. It would thus appear that it was basically an outcome of entrenched xenophobia which was mainly technocratic in nature, and would only become politicized in the mid-1980s with the electoral rise of Le Pen's far right. However, at the time when this new political force emerged, the bases of the great reversal of the right to asylum against exiles had already been enacted, especially for non-European nationalities with the exception of the Indochinese. Hence, it can reasonably be argued that the far right's success was a consequence of the previous narrative on decolonization and asylum: the hypothesis of a reversed relationship would be absurd. Once the *Front National* appeared on the country's political scene, an acceleration of the processes occurred amid the so-called 'lepenisation of spirits' (Tévanian and Tessot, 2002), often deemed to be the driving factor in this historical development … whereas it was merely a symptom of the deeper and more ancient phenomenon of the institutionalization of xenophobia.[6]

After several decades of technocratic preparation by civil servants repatriated from the colonies, by high-level officials from the foreign affairs, interior and social affairs ministries, but also by experts and intellectuals who were close to these circles …, asylum and immigration issues were blended together and became part of the electoral agenda. Other elements intervened and favoured this

---

5   S. Laurens, Hauts fonctionnaires et immigration en France (1962–1981) – Socio-histoire d'une domination à distance, Paris: Ecole des Hautes Etudes en Sciences Sociales, PhD in sociology, 8 December 2006.

6   Le Cour Grandmaison (2005). [Editor's note: Here, the author alludes to the long history that Le Cour Grandmaison traces back, in particular, to Tocqueville's proposals against Algerians who resisted French colonialism –'civilization'.]

process: when it reached power, the left had to deal with ministerial technocracies and was forced to strike bargains with them for the conduct of public action. The political shift from right to left in 1981 only led to a brief interlude, mixing spectacular measures for the benefit of *sans papiers* with the first signs (1982) of the socialists' conversion in the fight against immigration: measures against irregular migrants, thereby stoking a conflict between old and new immigrants. The electoral victory of the National Front in March 1983 marked a change in the left's mentality, but it was limited in scope and nothing indicated that it would last. Nonetheless, in the following year the socialist prime minister Fabius uttered his famous phrase ('The far right is a false answer to a real problem') that reflected the new arrangement between socialist elites and technocrats from the ministries and high-level bureaucracies.

The National-Securitarian Shift (1980–90)

The evolution of the policy on the right to asylum was favoured by wider and deeper developments. The 'asylum/immigration' or 'left/right' distinctions are not very useful to describe this transformation in the ideological power relations between the three ideologies that imbued local, national and European administrations (Valluy, 2006, 2009): utilitarian, 'national-securitarian' and 'humanist/asylum supporting' (Tsoukala, 2000: 251).

These three value and belief systems correspond to three coalitions that are transnational, but have greater or lesser strength depending on what country one is looking at. Each of them brings together a collection of experts on migrations (officials, experts, journalists, leading NGOs, academics, lawyers etc.) who share the same analysis of migrations, of the problems that they pose and of the possible solutions. The customary mode of action of the actors from any of these coalitions consists in spreading their ideas to all the segments of public actors at different governmental levels in each country.

To summarize, the European history of migration policy since the middle of the twentieth century has been characterized by the continuous decline of the 'humanist/asylum supporting' faction and the corresponding strengthening of national-securitarian ideological forces. In the meantime the utilitarian vision that had been progressively marginalized in the middle of the period in question has resurfaced, particularly at the European level, but appeared to be a long way away from acting as a counterweight to political forces that supported closure and refusal of entry. The policy on the right to asylum was an element of this ideological competition and, like any other public policy in this realm, it was not the expression of a single coalition, but of their power relations, of the tectonics that they jointly produced.

This swing resulted primarily from the endogenous growth of national-securitarian forces (the precocious conversion of the high-level civil servants to the idea of migration as a 'problem', starting with the 1960s; the administrative closing of borders and intensification of policies against migration from which the reversal of asylum stems, in the 1970s; the emergence of a nationalist far right in the political arena during the 1980s). Nonetheless, the shift was also an effect of less visible aspects which tended towards the weakening of humanist-asylum supporting forces, a weakening whose origins must be sought in the transformation of associative, academic and political forces that had explicitly embraced the values of humanitarian and social action.

During the 1980s, when far right parties emerged in Europe and took over the issue of the arrival of foreigners as a reason to criticize government policies … governments had been discrediting exiles for ten years already, relentlessly raising asylum application rejection rates and producing justifications for such restrictions in the public sphere: the stigmatization of exiles as 'economic refugees' attracted by our wealth who took advantage the Geneva Convention on Refugees. Its electoral use by political forces and government actors alike, merely amplified this public stigmatization and increased the political significance of rejection rates.

From this perspective, the internment of immigrants became a crucial element of policies to counter immigration, with two important collateral effects: it strengthened the social perception of the supposed dangerousness of immigrants, while simultaneously trumpeting the authorities' mobilization against this threat. Massive research about the strong increase in the imprisonment of foreigners in Europe has led to converging conclusions: since the 1980s, the figures on foreign detainees have grown as a result of breaches of immigration legislation (irregular residence, refusal to comply with expulsion …),[7] offences that are directly linked to being force to live underground (forgery and use of false documents, contravening employment laws …) and preventive imprisonment, which was even more frequent because foreigners do not offer the guarantees (stability and lawfulness of residence, a home address, family situation, employment, schooling, etc.) that are required to benefit from alternative measures to preventive imprisonment. Beyond these aspects, the over-representation of foreigners is not linked to their national origins, but rather, to their statistical distribution on the basis of other variables: age, gender and socioeconomic condition. Hence, the basic story is told by the correlation between imprisonment rates for foreigners and factors linked to irregular residence, as shown by the research carried out in 1998 by James Lynch and Rita Simon (1999) on seven countries (U.S., Canada, Australia, United Kingdom, France, Germany and Japan). This fundamental correlation is compounded by 'incidental' factors, particularly discrimination by the police and the judiciary. The collection of these analyses shows that the foreigners' imprisonment rate is a sociologically relevant indicator of the degree of criminalization of exiles in our societies [*editor's note*: insofar as the critical analysis of this process of criminalization of foreigners is concerned, see the other contributions in this volume].

---

7   The phenomenon is particularly clear-cut as regards four countries in southern Europe, see Calavita (1998), Palidda (2008a).

The attacks of 11 September 2001 have engendered a considerable acceleration in the process of criminalization of exiles. But one must not overlook the historical depth of the phenomenon to understand its breadth correctly. The trends described above predate 2001 by decades.

Europeanization and Externalization of Asylum (2000)

The European harmonization of asylum policies effectively began in 1999, on the occasion of the Tampere Summit. The first five-year plan ended in May 2004 and is worthy of some consideration.

a. The capability of associations to mobilize, already weak at the national level, became almost non-existent at the European level. Except for associations that could hire multilingual experts from the old European legal tradition, small militant organizations campaigning for the right to asylum and the foreigners' right to stay could no longer have an influence over political decision-making: thus, the humanitarian-asylum supporting coalition was effectively eliminated.

b. UNHCR played a crucial political role at this level of governance because – being very European in terms of its history and funding – it had played an essential part in the coordination of European policies before the European Commission managed to assert itself. UNHCR's political drift, its conversion to utilitarian themes and its concessions to securitarian projects of 'camps for exiles' weighed upon the evolution of the nascent European policy.

c. The Europeanization of such policies occurred firstly within the European bureaucratic camp, for the benefit of the DG-JFS (General Directorate for Justice, Freedom and Security), that is, by adopting police-minded and securitarian view of the problem that has dominated the European Commission until today. Nonetheless, the securitarians at the DG-JFS are more receptive than their national counterparts to economic priorities, since they are part of the bureaucracy of the European Commission, a body which has historically devoted itself to economic management.

Finally, the policy calling for 'externalization of asylum' was established by the Hague Programme: obviously, the DG-JFS programme could not be implemented in territories bordering the EU without the help of European diplomacy, that is, of the EC's Rel Ex Directorate (Foreign Relations). Now, Rel Ex is an essentially economic diplomatic service and the EU's consular offices often resemble chambers of commerce rather than actual embassies. Rel Ex officials called upon to take charge of this neighbourhood policy have spontaneously approached it in accordance with mental categories that are more economy-minded than police-minded.

'The externalization of asylum' is a commonly used expression in the network of experts on asylum and migrations to indicate a political idea that is rather simple, as are the public policies implementing it: 'We agree to grant refugees asylum, but preferably far away from us: in places, detention camps or geographic areas of concentration from where they will have a hard time to reach Europe.' The idea is not new; it became explicit in a project drafted by the Austrian government in 1999 and was then theorized in 2002 by the UN High Commissioner for Refugees, Ruud Lubbers, formerly Holland's prime minister, and by the British prime minister Tony Blair. It has been more recently institutionalized as the central European policy with the support of the EU's most xenophobic national governments – those of the Netherlands, Denmark, Austria and Italy – and with the explicit or implicit backing of all others.

The externalization of asylum is not a radical innovation, but rather, the radicalization of previous trends. It constitutes an epitomic figure of the great reversal of asylum policy at the expense of exiles and refugees: it serves the purpose, without formally disowning the principle of the right to asylum, not just of blocking borders and forbidding refugees' access to the territories of refuge of their choice, but even more so to hold them in camps referred to as 'processing centres' or in so-called 'special protection' zones. It has also introduced a new dimension in the reversal of asylum: its spread beyond European frontiers and, more precisely, to the bordering countries that appear to be simultaneously attracted by entry into the EU, but also destined to remain outside of it that is, to become the 'buffering regions of empire'. These are sensitive zones for any empire, since its internal and external tensions find expression there at the same time; such sensitivity is heightened by the fact that such boundaries can be fuzzy and uncertain, still subject to fluctuations.

The process of the 'Europeanization of public policies', that is, the European convergence in national policies and the strong emergence of actors and fields of action that are specifically European, is not neutral in terms of political choices made about asylum. Europeanization alters the balance of power between the ideological coalitions over immigration and asylum: it definitively erodes the humanitarian-asylum supporting coalition by ensuring the promotion of securitarian ideas while balancing them with utilitarian preoccupations; it progressively strengthens the utilitarianist coalition at the expense of strictly police-minded approaches. This phenomenon affects the various actors' possibilities of enacting strategic actions: human rights defenders, for example, do not just have to struggle against rival approaches, but also against the Europeanization process because it strengthens rival coalitions on asylum and immigration.

Conclusions

The metamorphosis of the right to asylum against exiles appears to reflect a phenomenon of governmental xenophobia understood as a combination of discourses and acts made by public authorities that tend to designate foreigners as a problem, risk or threat. Xenophobia is not just the psychological phenomenon of hostility towards foreigners, but also the social phenomenon of stigmatization of foreigners. In the case analysed here, the policy of the right to asylum in France and in Europe, this social phenomenon appears to be the product of a struggle between ideological forces that is evolving towards the rise of national-securitarian ideas that are increasingly less opposed by countervailing ideas and forces. Hence, governmental xenophobia is basically an ideological imbalance produced by the interplay between the strengthening and the weakening of rival ideologies on immigration. It is also a historical process of institutionalization of perceptions of foreigners as a 'problem', 'risk' or 'threat' in the current references produced by the different types of authorities (ministerial, administrative, judicial, media, scientific, intellectual, school, economic, party-based, associative …). The development of this historical phenomenon is driven by the activity of technocrats, administrative staff, experts and politicians who have occupied the key posts in the transformations of public action in this field over the last fifty years.

Without odious gestures and vulgarity, and well before the resurgence of the 'critical xenophobia' of the small far-right groups, governmental xenophobia expressed itself with the cold detachment that befits ruling elites in designating a threat, and in the technocratic development of the means to counter it.

The origins of the great return of xenophobic nationalism in the European political sphere at levels unseen since the 1930s must be sought in the elites' objective interest to focus attention and energies on the fight between 'ethnic groups' rather than on the struggle between 'classes', on immigration rather than recession. Europeans are capable of identifying this rather universal mechanism of power, that of the holy alliance against foreigners, when it is a matter of analysing situations in Africa or in Asia, but they find it very difficult to recognize it when it operates closer to home.

Chapter 8

The (re)Criminalization of Roma Communities in a Neoliberal Europe

Nando Sigona and Nidhi Trehan

Introduction

The history of Romani communities in Europe is dramatically marked by episodes of mass persecution, violence and discrimination perpetuated by both institutional and non-institutional agents.[1] The *Baro Mudaripe* (the 'large murder') or the mass killing of hundreds of thousands of Roma systematically carried out by the Nazi regime before and during World War II was the tragic culmination of a series of events, rather than an isolated episode.[2] The construction of the Romani communities as a 'race of criminals' genetically inclined to crime, was a central component of the ideological apparatus that provided a 'justification' for the genocide of European Roma. However, the racial criminalization of Romani communities started far earlier, with the Enlightenment, and found in positivism and social Darwinism a great expansion. In particular, the work of the Italian doctor criminal anthropologist Cesare Lombroso contributed to the creation of a strong link between features generally associated to social deviance and racial belonging (Gibson, 2002). For Lombroso and his scientific contemporaries, Gypsies were by nature predisposed to crime, as suggested in this extract from Lombroso's book, *L'uomo delinquente*:

> [Gypsies] epitomise a thoroughly criminal race, with all its passions and vices. [They] have a horror of anything that requires the slightest effort. They prefer to suffer hunger and misery rather than to subject themselves to any sort of continuous work, and they want only the minimum they need for survival. They are deceitful with one another, ungrateful, cruel, and, at the same time, cowardly … Gypsies have the same lack of foresight as savages and criminals. Lovers of orgies and noise, in the market they make a great hubbub. Ferocious, they

---

1   Vaux Defouletier (1990 [1970]); Fraser (1992); Hancock (1987). For a critical interpretation of the role of the Holocaust in the construction of modernity in Europe, see Bauman (1989).

2   See Friedlander (1995); Bernadac (1996 [1989]). The Holocaust of Roma is also known as 'Porrajmos', 'Pharraijmos' or 'Samudaripen' by some authors. See also Barsony and Daroczi (2008) and Hancock (1995).

kill for money without remorse. Years ago, they were suspected of cannibalism. (Lombroso, 2006 [1879]: 119)

Moreover, idleness and vagrancy were for centuries two defining features of the 'Gypsy lifestyle' and continuous sources of concern for public order and safety[3]. In 1852, the Italian Minister of Home Affairs in his introduction to a bill on public security stated:

> The idle and vagrant can be considered in permanent infraction of law, depriving society of what is due to it by each and every citizen ... And if we do not extend police surveillance, at a time when crime is so frequent, to people legitimately deemed suspects [the Gypsies], to whom should we extend it?[4]

This chapter addresses the contemporary spread of anti-Gypsyism in a neoliberal Europe and explores the link between the racial criminalization of the Roma and discriminatory policy and practice. Anti-Gypsyism is not a new phenomenon, we will argue; nonetheless, in its current configuration, it is strongly intertwined to the transformations that followed the break-up of the Soviet Union, the consolidation of liberal democracies and neoliberal economic principles in the European Union, and linked to the process of pauperization that many Romani communities are undergoing. This chapter is divided into three parts. In the first part, we discuss the impact of neoliberal policies on the socio-economic situation of Roma in Europe, the growing impoverishment of Romani communities and the virulent rise and spread of anti-Gypsyism in the context of the collapse of the Soviet Union and its satellite states, along with the concomitant crisis of European socialism. The second part outlines the institutional responses to these phenomena and their rationale – in particular the fear of Romani westward migration – and the emergence and salience of minority and human rights frameworks, as well as their limitations. In the final section, we look at the spaces of political participation for Romani communities in the context of the critique of the racialization of political spaces and the (re)criminalization of Roma presently occurring in Europe.

---

3   The institution of slavery of Roma in present-day Romania, particularly in the principalities of Moldavia and Wallachia from the early fifteenth century to the time of emancipation in the mid-1800s was also connected to the 'migrancy' of Roma within Europe. Thousands upon thousands of freed Romani slaves sought to build new lives in other European lands after their emancipation in the late 1850s in Romania; for further details of this key episode of Romani history in Europe, see Achim (2004: 120–7).

4   Galvagno, cited in Mereu (1974).

Poverty and anti-Gypsyism

> Roma have been among the biggest losers in the transition from communism
> since 1989. They were often the first to lose their jobs in the early 1990s, and
> have been persistently blocked from re-entering the labour force due to their
> often inadequate skills and pervasive discrimination.[5]

This statement by the former president of the World Bank, James Wolfensohn,
and the financier and philanthropist George Soros accompanied the launch of an
important report 'Roma in an Expanding Europe' by the World Bank and predated
by two years the 'Decade of Roma Inclusion', an initiative promoted by the World
Bank, the Open Society Institute, the Council of Europe and the United Nations
Development Programme, together with others, 'to accelerate progress toward
improving the welfare of Roma and to review such progress in a transparent and
quantifiable way' (www.romadecade.org).

Importantly, it recognized that in countries undergoing profound economic
restructuring, a significant number of Roma people – for various reasons – have
not found any adequate and socially acceptable position in the new order, and have
been pushed to the margins of society. The post-socialist pauperization of Europe's
Roma – particularly those who are citizens of 'transition' countries – became
increasingly visible in the 1990s, during the climax of the neoliberal triumph.[6]
Precisely then, while some citizens benefited from the new prosperity, the income
of the majority of Romani families plummeted alongside the closure of state-run
factories and the drastic reduction of employment by public administrations. The
case of Hungary, one of the most economically advanced countries in the former
Socialist bloc, is emblematic: in 1985, the employment rate of men belonging to the
Romani communities was almost equal to that of the rest of the male population;
today, in sharp contrast, it is estimated that at least 70 per cent of the men are
officially unemployed.[7]

The poverty rate of Roma people in the countries of central-eastern Europe
is often as many as ten times higher than that of other citizens. In 2000, almost
80 per cent of Roma people in Bulgaria and Romania lived on less than 4 euro
per day, compared with 37 per cent of the rest of the population in Bulgaria and

---

5   Wolfensohn and Soros (2003).

6   In a comprehensive piece on neoliberal practices and Romani minority governance
issues, Van Baar (2009) argues that 'social policies that European institutions and
international organizations, such as the European Union, the World Bank and the United
Nations have recently developed and supported rely heavily on a neoliberal trend to govern
… through processes of decentralization, the "outsourcing" of public services to private
stakeholders, the support of "public–private" partnerships, and the correlated mobilization
of civil societal agencies'.

7   Kertesi (2005). For an analysis of the impact of neoliberal policies on the Roma in
Hungary, see Forrai (2006).

30 per cent in Romania. In Hungary, instead, 'only' 40 per cent of the Roma lived below the 4 euro threshold, a figure that, however, must be compared with the 7 per cent of the rest of the population. These figures, combined with a high birth rate, make it possible to foresee a further growth of poverty and a reproduction of chronic poverty in Hungary.[8]

Apart from structural tensions resulting from the quick economic transformation, the transition towards capitalism in formerly Socialist countries has also been characterized by a search for foundational myths to re-define the relationship between state and nation after the fall of Communist ideology.[9] In such a context, nationalist movements have acquired strength and, alongside them, so have numerous far-right racist and xenophobic groups that have managed to etch out increasingly large spaces in the political life of most European countries. This overall slide to the right, exacerbated by the existing confusion in the social-democratic camp, has turned the Roma, a minority without significant political representation, into a preferred target for racist campaigns that at times culminate in overt displays of violence. In fact, a recent US State Department report on human rights in Hungary stated that:

> In the wake of the economic downturn, there have been a number of killings and incidents of violence against Roma, including in Italy, Hungary, Romania, Slovakia, and the Czech Republic … Roma are the largest and most vulnerable minority in Europe; they suffer racial profiling, violence, and discrimination.[10]

Hence, in contemporary Europe, racism against Roma does not only concern some extremist fringe elements.[11] Indeed, Eurobarometer surveys from 2007 and 2008 underline just how widespread prejudice and stereotypes about this minority are. 77 per cent of European citizens deem it a disadvantage to belong to the Roma minority and 24 per cent would consider it inconvenient to have a Roma as a neighbour. This figure rises to 47 per cent in Italy and the Czech Republic, where only one person in ten states that they would have no problem living close to a Roma person.[12] Data on Italy from the Institute for the Study of Public Opinion (ISPO) research (2008) offers a picture that is even more worrying,[13] confirming the

---

8   Ringhold, Orenstein, Wilkens (2003); UNDP (2002).
9   Brubaker (1996). This research mainly, but not exclusively, concerned countries in central-eastern Europe. Countries such as Italy, for example, have undergone two decades of transformations, births and refoundations that have deeply redrawn the country's political-ideological map.
10   US State Department (2009) reported in Politcs.hu (accessed January 2010): http://www.politics.hu/20100312/us-human-rights-report-on-hungary-highlights-violence-against-roma
11   For the Italian case, see Sigona (2006); Simoni (2008); Colacicchi (2008).
12   Eurobarometer (2007, 2008). Interestingly, similar results are also obtained in countries like Denmark and Malta, where there is a minimal presence of Roma people.
13   ISPO (2008). See also Arrigoni and Vitale (2008).

scepticism expressed by some Romani activists and experts about the reliability of the Eurobarometer data. As the ISPO findings suggest, Italians have an extremely negative view of Roma: 47 per cent of the interviewed people see them primarily as thieves, delinquents and layabouts, while 35 per cent link their image to that of nomad camps, to degradation and dirtiness. This latter view is certainly linked to long-term policies of the Italian local authorities, which since the late 1980s have built *campi nomadi* to house Romani migrant families from the Balkans and eastern Europe, and which the media covers in a sensationalistic manner on a regular basis (Piasere, 1991; Brunello, 1996; Sigona, 2005).

Despite this spread of intolerance towards Roma in Europe, terms such as anti-Gypsyism and Romaphobia have only recently entered Europe's political language. The first official document in which the matter of forms of discrimination against the Roma is dealt with in depth, is the European Parliament's resolution adopted on 28 April 2005 (P6_TA(2005)0151), in which the European Commission was invited to intervene to combat Anti-Gypsyism/Romaphobia across Europe:

> underlining the importance of urgently eliminating continuing and violent trends of racism and racial discrimination against Roma, and conscious that any form of impunity for racist attacks, hate speech, physical attacks by extremist groups, unlawful evictions and police harassment motivated by Anti-Gypsyism and Romaphobia plays a role in weakening the rule of law and democracy, tends to encourage the recurrence of such crimes and requires resolute action for its eradication.[14]

As Nicolae (2008: 1) suggests, Roma are faced with a specific form of racism:

> An ideology of racial superiority, a form of dehumanisation and of institutional racism … fuelled by historical discrimination. A complex social phenomenon that expresses itself publicly through episodes of violence, expressions of hatred, exploitation and discrimination, but also through the discourses and portrayals produced by politicians and academics, spatial and housing segregation, widespread stigmatisation and socio-economic exclusion.[15]

The failure to recognize the Roma as holders of rights has also resurfaced in research on the discrimination of Roma in Italy (ERRC, 2000; Sigona and Monasta, 2006). Sigona and Monasta's report (2006) on racial discrimination against Roma and Sinti in Italy reveals a two-fold phenomenon: a) the widespread discriminatory policy and practice by institutional agents at national and local level and b) the public denial (and lack of acknowledgement) of the discriminatory nature of such measures which led the authors of the report to define the position of the Roma in Italian polity as an 'imperfect citizenship', wherein the boundaries of

---

14   European Commission (2008); European Parliament (2008).
15   Nicolae (2008: 1). See also Sigona and Monasta (2006).

citizenship, as well as the entitlements, rights and duties attached to it are always fluid and subject to negotiation, producing amongst 'imperfect citizens' a sense of uncertainty of their rights and entitlements and, importantly, affecting also their perception of what discrimination is.[16].

In sum, the deteriorating living conditions of Roma people in central-eastern Europe over the last twenty years and the episodes of anti-Roma racism are two separate phenomena which are simultaneously related. The primary cause of the impoverishment of Roma after the end of the USSR was not racism, which certainly played its part and still has a central role in defining experiences and life opportunities for people belonging to the Roma minority, but rather, the *structural transformations* that have radically redefined the economy and social contract on which the former Socialist countries were founded.

From Migrants to Minority

Even more so than in previous years, after the expansion of the European Union and the suppression of visa requirements, abandoned by all governments and at the mercy of the sudden transformations imposed by an embrace of neoliberal policies, the Roma of central-eastern Europe (along with many citizens of post-socialist states) sought a chance to better their lives through emigration, giving rise to alarm in Western governments.

Until the 1990s, the main countries from which the Roma emigrated had been Macedonia, Bosnia-Herzegovina, Yugoslavia (Serbia, Montenegro and Kosovo) and Romania,[17] while subsequently they were Romania, Bulgaria and Slovakia. Among the countries of arrival, Germany, France and Italy were historically the main destinations for Romani migration, but over the years, a significant flow has also affected the UK, Austria and Spain.[18]

The perceived threat represented by the mass arrival ('tidal wave' as portrayed popularly in the press) of Roma people was, from the 1990s onwards, the main reason for the European Union and other leading European organizations, i.e. the Council of Europe and OSCE, to become interested in this population (Guy, 2001; Guglielmo and Waters, 2005).

---

16   See also B. Sigona, Ethnography of the 'Gypsy problem' in Italy, unpublished PhD thesis, Oxford Brookes University, 2009.

17   During certain phases, particularly at the start of the 1990s, substantial groups of Roma people also emigrated from Croatia and Bulgaria and, as of 1995, from Poland, the Czech Republic and Slovakia (Matras, 2000).

18   The introduction of new measures to manage flows like, for example, bilateral repatriation agreements and lists of safe third countries during the 1990s, have given rise to secondary migrations and changes in mobility patterns; see Sobotka (2003).

As is well known, the so-called 'invasion' of the West never happened[19] and, quantitatively, the migration of Roma people corresponds with that of the rest of the population in their respective countries of origin. In spite of this, the fear of such an 'invasion', manipulated through the distorted use of data, stories and images, has influenced the policy choices of several governments and has pushed them to adopt draconian measures to stop 'the gypsies'.[20]

The process of EU expansion has led to a gradual transformation of this approach for two types of reasons, one demographic, and the other more strictly political. With the expansions of 2004 and 2007, in fact, around two million Roma people became European citizens and therefore putatively, members of the largest European ethnic minority. As a result, 'social, rights, and security issues surrounding Roma became *internal* issues' (Guglielmo and Waters, 2005: 776–7). Moreover, with accession, it has become more or less impossible to stop the mobility of Roma people within the territory of EU countries – in spite of recent efforts undertaken by countries like France, Italy, the UK and Belgium – safeguarded as it is by one of the key EU pillars: freedom of movement. Conversely, third-country Roma are increasingly encountering greater obstacles in entering the EU through legal channels, both as a result of the selectiveness of EU migration policies towards TCNs (third-country nationals) as well as the general restriction of the right to political asylum, which is even more evident for citizens of countries that currently aspire to join the EU, like Macedonia, Kosovo, Croatia, Serbia, Turkey, Albania and Montenegro.

Measures of a purely repressive, restrictive and deterrent nature that have mainly characterized the pre-enlargement phase, such as bilateral agreements for the immediate repatriation of migrants, intelligence exchanges and training of police forces of neighbour countries, the discriminatory application of norms on visas and the increasing reduction of the effectiveness of the right to asylum, have produced a segmentation of the concept of citizenship and of the rights associated to it.[21] As time passed, such measures were accompanied by others of a different nature, aimed at encouraging the Roma to stay in their countries of origin, the enforcement of human and minority rights framework and development-like initiatives are part of this strategy. The political reason for this change in approach has been summarized by Guglielmo and Waters (2005: 764):

> Although the EU and other European institutions were initially concerned with externally oriented migration control, the fact that the case for enlargement

---

19   The literature on Roma migrations is rather limited and often within the bounds of a restricted milieu of experts within Romani studies (Guy, 2001; Matras, 2000; Liegeois and Gheorghe, 1995; Reyniers, 1999), with some rare attempts to frame the issue within a wider debate on migrations (Sobotka, 2003; Sigona, 2003; Piasere, 2006).

20   See CDMG (1998); Clark and Campbell (2000); Guy (2009); Sigona and Trehan (2009).

21   Rigo (2007); Balibar and Wallerstein (1991). See also Huysmans (2006).

was articulated in terms of 'common values' compelled EU Member States to elaborate a more internally oriented, rights-based approach to minority protection and towards Roma.

Hence, as enlargement approached, it became necessary for the EU to tackle issues concerning Roma people within a different framework, one whose hinge was no longer 'if' the Roma should be integrated into the EU, but 'how'. It has certainly not been a process whose outcome was a foregone conclusion, and the issue of the migration of Roma people seemingly threatened to derail the enlargement process of countries such as Hungary and Slovakia, which were accused of being unable to protect the Roma's fundamental rights and of not being ready for freedom of movement.

In spite of these obstacles, and with a series of restrictions on freedom of movement that were more or less temporary, in 2004 and 2007 the enlargement of the European Union changed the situation significantly. Thus, while in certain countries the tensions were appeased, in others, like Italy, the issue of freedom of movement for Roma people acquired a growing urgency, as did the exasperation of the public debate and the spreading of Romaphobic sentiment in the public sphere.[22]

The Europeanization of the Roma Issue

In spite of the announcements and declarations of principle, the priority concern for European Union policies towards Roma people since the 1990s has been to control and limit their westward migration.

While it must be acknowledged that the protection of minorities, one of the requirements set for aspiring EU member States at the 1993 Copenhagen Council, represents an important advance towards the recognition of the protection of minorities among the foundational norms of democracy, it must also be stressed that the relationship between 'democracy' and 'respect and protection for minorities' was wilfully left vague and ambiguous in the Copenhagen document.[23] Moreover, as Guglielmo and Waters (2005) point out, the protection of minorities as formulated in the Copenhagen criteria are only valid for countries seeking to enter the EU and not for current member States.

---

22   See Sigona (2008). To make the situation even more complex, a number of European countries –including countries like the Czech Republic, Poland, Slovenia and Hungary– after being long-term source countries for migration of Romani people, have themselves become countries of destination.

23   About this matter, Sasse points out that the linguistic formula employed by the EU carefully avoids the notion of 'minority rights'. Moreover, it does not refer to 'national minority' and does not specify what types of minority are covered, see Sasse (2006: 4).

Furthermore, even without an explicit reference to rights, the criterion raises legitimate conceptual and empirical objections about the type of democracy that the EU sought to promote in the candidate countries. In fact, there is an evident risk of fostering the fragmentation of society along ethnic lines and heightening social and political conflict, as the recent displays of intolerance and racism that have burst out in Hungary and Czech Republic have, to an extent, confirmed.

The reception of the principle of the protection of minorities by the candidate countries has been effectively described by Tesser, who has underlined the instrumental and top-down character of this process, as the 'geopolitics of tolerance' (Tesser, 2003). The referral to OSCE as to the definition of the reference framework for the protection of minorities provides further evidence of the fact that at the start of the 1990s, the European Union did not wish to commit to defining its own normative framework on minorities.

This attitude gradually changed when, following enlargement, the concrete reality was altered and it was no longer possible to envisage managing the Roma issue only in terms of the control of mobility. In fact, even if the Roma do not move, the conditions of marginality in which many of them live are, on their own, insofar as they are EU country nationals, a sufficient reason to justify interest from the EU: rather than being the Roma who migrate, rights have migrated towards them, at least in theory. Nonetheless, there is a substantial gap between theory and practice in this regard. In the UK for example, often unskilled Romanian Roma migrants face great difficulties in obtaining jobs and NI (National Insurance) numbers. They are caught in a 'Catch 22' trap as on the one hand, employers want an NI number before hiring them, while on the other hand, NI numbers are only granted if either proof of an offer of employment is provided (or alternatively, documentation showing that jobs were applied for with three employers, and the applicant was not successful). Many migrants are unable to obtain this documentation, and thus, permission to work, and therefore become vulnerable to unscrupulous 'agents' who may exploit these administrative barriers.

In Italy, the 'nomad emergency' decrees issued by both left-of-centre Prodi (Presidential Decree no. 181/2007) and right-of-centre Berlusconi governments (Prime Ministerial Decree no. 122/2008), the pogrom in Ponticelli (Naples) in May 2008 and the mass collection of biometric data in nomad camps, caused the outrage of progressive European public opinion and diplomatic tensions between two EU member States (Romania and Italy). As a response to the crisis, the process of 'Europeanization of the Roma issue' speeded up. According to Guy (2009): 'The consequences of both EU enlargement and Roma exclusion combined to threaten not only the relationship between two Member States but also the fundamental right to freedom of movement within the EU.

The episodes of anti-Gypsyism that emerged in Italy also revealed that systemic and institutional discrimination against the Roma and violent expressions of racism do not only take place in countries of the former Soviet bloc, but also in Western Europe (something that was wilfully underestimated by the European Commission in previous years). Moreover, the events in Italy served to remind the

Commission that, in spite of a decade of EU involvement in the 'matter' and the numerous assistance projects that were funded through the PHARE programme, the problems of a large majority of Roma people in the new member States – whose causes are structural – remain unresolved, pushing many Roma to migrate westwards in search of a better life.

In December 2007, for the first time, the European Council, the EU's highest political body, tackled the issue 'of the very specific situation in which many Roma find themselves in the Union' and invited member States to 'adopt any means to improve their inclusion'.[24] In January 2008, an urgent invitation came from the European Parliament to draw up a European framework strategy for the 'inclusion of the Roma' (EP, 2008, par. 6); a similar invitation also arrived in the following months from the countries involved in the 'Decade of Roma inclusion' (Hungary, the Czech Republic, Slovenia, Romania, Albania and Macedonia) and from the European Roma Policy Coalition, a network formed by key international NGOs that promote rights of Roma in Europe (ERPC 2008).

For the time being, the pressure on the European Commission to draw up a new approach to the Roma issue has not had the expected results. In a report published in July 2008, the Commission acknowledged that:

> Although the European institutions, Member States and candidate countries as well as civil society have addressed these problems since the beginning of the 1990s, there is a widely shared assumption that the living and working conditions of Roma have not much improved over the last two decades. (European Commission 2008a: 4)

The Commission's view is misleading and self-exculpating: the material and working conditions of the Roma in central-eastern Europe have never been priorities of the interventions backed and funded by the EU, especially in the 1990s. Moreover, to state that the situation 'has not improved much' is insulting to Roma, considering that numerous indicators confirm that their socio-economic situation has deteriorated quite significantly since the fall of the Socialist regimes.

In September 2008, the European Commission organized the first EU Roma Summit in Brussels, with the participation of hundreds of activists, politicians and administrators from all over Europe. The presence of the president and several commissioners from the European Commission sent out a clear sign of how the matter of the social inclusion of the Roma has become an important theme in the EU's political agenda, even though President Barroso's approach shows continuity with policies enacted in previous years, rather than a willingness to acknowledge the failure of this path and to suggest new forms of intervention.

---

24 European Council (2008, par. 50).

Roma Politics in Europe: Potential and Limits

Starting from the second half of the 1990s, in response to the dramatic living conditions of a majority of Roma people and to increasing anti-Gypsyism, two discourses have acquired growing relevance in the EU context: the human rights and anti-discrimination discourse, and the minority rights one (Vermeersch, 2006). Within these discourses and their related apparatuses and practices, the presence of a 'Roma civil society' that seeks to dialogue with European and national institutions at various levels, has progressively taken shape. Nonetheless, these (neo)liberal human rights discourses often overlook the socio-economic roots of the problems that Romani communities face.[25]

Two recent initiatives are emblematic of the process that is underway and of the change in scale with regards to the direct involvement of Roma people in decision-making processes at a European level. They also underline the two main directions that are forming: on the one hand, the European Roma and Travellers Forum (ERTF), established in 2004; on the other, the European Roma Policy Coalition (ERPC), established in 2008.[26] The first organization, born within the Council of Europe under the patronage of the president of Finland, Tarja Halonen, has attempted to structure itself on a representative basis. It involves the presence, on a basis that is more or less proportional to the number of Roma in each country, of representatives from over twenty different groups belonging to the Roma communities, NGOs, Roma political parties and representatives of faith organizations. The stated goal of the ERTF is that of facilitating the integration of the Roma population in European societies and their participation in public life and decision-making processes (ERTF statute, article 2). In contrast, ERPC is a coalition of key NGOs which was created in response to increasing episodes of violence and racism that have taken place in various EU countries, and has as its main objective that of exerting pressure on the European Commission for it to draw up a framework strategy for the social inclusion of Romani people. Among the coalition members and the founders – who define it as an 'informal group' (ERPC, 2008) – there are not just European and national Roma associations, like the European Roma Grassroots Organization (ERGO), the European Roma Information Office (ERIO) or the Fundacion Secretariado Gitano (FSG), but also NGOs that have specialized in promoting respect for human rights, minorities and

---

25   N. Trehan, Human Rights Entrepreneurship in Post-Socialist Hungary: from 'Gypsy Problem' to 'Roma Rights', London School of Economics and Political Science, unpublished thesis, 2009.

26   J. Nirenberg, Romani Political Mobilization from the first International Romani Union Congress to the European Roma, Sinti and Travellers Forum, in Sigona and Trehan (2009); Vermeersch (2010); see also A. McGarry, Ethnicity-Blind and Differentiated Treatment: Fine-Tuning the EU Policy on Roma, unpublished paper given at the international conference on 'Romani Mobilities in Europe: Multidisciplinary Perspectives', Oxford, 14–15 January 2010.

the fight against racism: the Open Society Institute (OSI), the Spolu International Foundation (SF), the European Roma Rights Centre (ERRC), Amnesty International (AI), the European Network Against Racism (ENAR) and Minority Rights Group International (MRGI).

Identification with the ethnonym 'Roma' has become the main channel for political action and access to EU resources for people belonging to the varied and diverse Romani communities of Europe, priming important transformations within the latter and promoting the consolidation of the idea of a pan-European Roma minority and the birth of a trans-European, mainly English-speaking, Roma élite.[27] If identifying all the Roma as a single political community may appear to be a rational and effective choice to enhance their visibility in the mainstream political sphere, at the same time it is a choice that consciously subsumes the historical, linguistic and cultural specificities that exist amongst the diverse communities; nonetheless, this act of constructing a political community often overlooks the concrete opposition – both political and legitimate – that some of the communities express as regards their assimilation into the ethnonym 'Roma'.[28]

Brubaker et al. have compellingly argued that 'ethnicity is not a thing, an attribute, or a distinct sphere of life, it is a way of understanding and interpreting experience, a way of talking and acting, a way of formulating interests and identities' (Brubaker, Feischmidt, Fox, Grancea, 2006: 358). Political organizing around a Romani identity has been almost universally perceived as a positive development lacking any ambiguity, representing the long-awaited entrance into the political arena of a people and a community that have been excluded from decision-making processes and from participation in public life for a long time. Nonetheless, as Kovats (2003) highlights, one must not look at Roma politics in isolation, nor at the Roma issue in general as being outside of the political, social and economic context in which it arose, and without taking into account the growing inequality and phenomena of widespread racism that are becoming consolidated in contemporary, neoliberal Europe.

The construction of an ethnicized political agenda and of the bodies to support it, not only conceals the interests that Roma have in common with fellow citizens, but it also places them in competition with one another. Kovats (2003: 3) writes:

> Money spent on Roma is quite simply, money not spent on 'non-Roma'. This
> occurs within the context not only of intensive competition for scarce public
> resources, but also the historic political culture of Central and Eastern Europe,

---

27   The training of the Roma élite has been brought forth through workshops, specialization courses, scholarships, and internships, particularly by the Open Society Institute, the European Roma Rights Center, and by the Project on Ethnic Relations (PER). Among the initiatives, there has also been a training course in diplomacy for Roma.

28   Marushiakova and Popov (2001); Kovats (2003); see also www.opendemocracy. org

characterised … by the often problematic relationship between ethnic/national identity and political power.

Research on the forms and modes of political participation of the Roma who currently reside in Kosovo confirms the concerns expressed by Kovats, highlighting how the policies for ethnic minorities imposed by international and European institutions end up exacerbating tensions between communities that live in Kosovo by placing them in competition with one another on an ethnic basis, rather than transversely responding to the real needs and concrete situations that exist on the ground. Moreover, some Kosovo Roma activists have noted how the allocation of resources and the imposition of the human rights and minority rights vocabularies sometimes places them in conflict with members of their own communities and forces them to continuously carry out a role as translators (not merely linguistic) between the humanitarian language and that of the people with whom they interact.[29] On the matter of talking or not talking the same language, Brubaker (2004: 167) recalls that 'the beliefs, desires, hopes and interests of ordinary people cannot be uncritically inferred from the ethnopolitical entrepreneurs who claim to speak in their name'.

Conclusions

Poverty, social exclusion and racism are three phenomena that dominate the daily life of European Roma today, determining their expectations and opportunities for the future. Poverty and anti-Gypsyism are different phenomena, but they are strictly interrelated. In fact, the roots of the process of pauperization of the Roma minority in central-eastern Europe cannot be reduced to being a product of racist policies, but rather, they must be traced back to systemic factors such as the transformation in a neoliberal direction of the economies of countries from the former Socialist bloc and of the welfare state. Kovats (2003: 5) caustically argues:

> The fashion for attributing objective disadvantages — unemployment, low life expectancy, slum housing — to racism, ensures not only that conditions continue to deteriorate, but enables elites to deny political responsibility by blaming the popular prejudices for their failure to act.

Moreover, van Baar (2009: 28–9), in his examination of European neoliberal states' response to Romani socio-economic marginalization, suggests neoliberal activation schemes and welfare reforms instituted to tackle the problem of large-scale unemployment of Roma (and hence enhance their social inclusion) 'actually

---

29   An interview with two Kosovo Roma activists carried out in June 2008 (see Sigona and Trehan, 2009).

function as a form of ethnicity-based governmentality that has naturalized the ethnic differences between Romani and other parts of the population'.

It was only as EU enlargement approached that there was an evolution in the policies of European institutions, with a gradual shift from a rhetoric that centred on concern over the destabilizing power of migration by Roma people to placing a greater emphasis on the concept of discrimination and the protection of minority rights. This transformation may be attributed to the objective fact that, with the entry of new EU member States, at least two million Roma people became EU citizens from one day to the next, and the political consideration that, once EU citizens, previous legal tools for governing their mobility in the EU space Would become ineffective and a new policy vocabulary was needed. Nonetheless (unfortunately), the Roma élite has been unable to etch out an adequate political role for itself; in fact, political participation has been structured and is strongly conditioned by the priorities imposed by neoliberal and racializing discourses, while communities on the ground continue to experience the damaging effects of poverty, social exclusion, and in some cases, (re)criminalization.

Chapter 9
The U.S. Penal Experiment

Alessandro De Giorgi

Punitive Democracy

The graph reproduced below (see Figure 9.1) offers a disturbing picture of the process of mass-imprisonment that has been taking place in the last three decades in the greatest of Western democracies. At the outset of the twenty-first century, the U.S. prison population has reached the historically unprecedented number of 2.3 million individuals, confined inside a carceral archipelago of almost five thousand penal institutions. With an incarceration rate of 756/100,000, the 'productivity' of the American penal system is unmatched by any other country (democratic or not) in the world.[1]

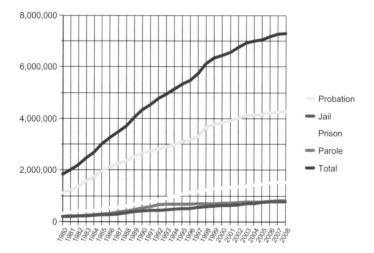

Source: Bureau of Justice Statistics: http://www.ojp.usdoj.gov/bjs/glance/corr2.htm

Figure 9.1   Correctional population in the U.S. (1980–2008)

---

1   The U.S. incarceration rate of 756/100,000 can be compared to 413/10,000 in post-*apartheid* South Africa, and 523/100,000 in post-Soviet Russia. Overall, between 1972 and 2004 the American prison population has increased by 600 per cent (Mauer, 2006: 20).

However, not all Americans have shared the weight of mass-imprisonment equally. Among the convicted population African Americans are dramatically overrepresented, with rates of conviction six to eight times higher than those of whites, whereas for Hispanics (again, compared to whites) the rate of over-representation narrows down to a factor of three to one. Overall, 66 per cent of the convicted population belongs to the vast group of 'non-whites', and these racial disproportions are reproduced across gender lines. Indeed, although African American women are in absolute terms less numerous in prison than white women, they are currently convicted three times more often, whereas among Hispanic women rates of conviction are two times higher than those of their white counterparts (see Tables 9.2 and 9.3).

Table 9.1   Prison convictions by gender and race in the U.S. (2000–2007)

Year		2000	2007
Convicted males		1,331,300	1,532,800
White		435,500	521,900
	% of total	33 %	34 %
Black		564,600	586.200
	% of total	42 %	38 %
Hispanic		255,700	318,800
	% of total	19 %	21 %
Convicted Females		84,300	105,500
White		33,600	50,500
	% of total	40 %	48 %
Black		32,200	29,300
	% of total	38 %	28 %
Hispanic		13,100	17,600
	% of total	16 %	17 %

Source: elaboration by S. Palidda and A. De Giorgi on Mauer and King (2007).

Table 9.2   Conviction rates (x 100,000) and gender/race ratios in the U.S. (2000–2007)

Year	2000	2007
White males	410	481
Black males	3,188	3,138
Black/White ratio	8	7
Hispanic males	1,419	1,259
Hispanic/White ratio	3	3
White females	33	50
Black females	175	150
Black/White ratio	5	3
Hispanic females	78	79
Hispanic/White ratio	2	2

Source: elaboration by S. Palidda and A. De Giorgi on Mauer and King (2007).

It is also worth remembering here that the carceral archipelago constitutes only one side of the great penal experiment undertaken in the U.S. In fact, outside the walls of the prison, a true and proper 'nation within the nation' has come into existence in the last decades as a consequence of the vertical increase of semi-custodial or non-custodial punishments collateral to incarceration. Today, the total population living under some form of correctional supervision (including probation, parole, electronic surveillance, house arrests etc.), has reached the astonishing number of 7.2 million. This means that in the 'land of the free', 2.3 per cent of the citizenry live under conditions of limited freedom (cf. Glaze and Bonczar, 2007).

The construction of what 15 years ago abolitionist criminologist Nils Christie (1993) described as an emerging '*gulag* Western-style', constitutes one of the main features of the neo-liberal and neo-conservative revolution started during the last quarter of the twentieth century by Ronald Reagan and then continued by the following administrations (Democratic and Republican) along the coordinates of a twofold by-partisan commitment: to the 'invisible hand' of economic deregulation and welfare retrenchment on the side of socio-economic policies, and to the 'iron fist' of mass-incarceration on the side of penal politics (Wacquant, 2009a). Not surprisingly, the American prison crisis represents one of the greatest emergencies the Obama administration must face today (although not the only one, as shown by the recent economic recession and by other social emergencies generated by the neoliberal ideology of deregulation and risk-individualization in such areas as housing, health care and education. We live in the aftermath of three long decades of neoliberal socioeconomic policies constructed in a symbiotic relationship with an exclusionary paradigm of governance based on the punitive regulation of social marginality. As Loic Wacquant argues in his latest book:

> America has launched into a social and political experiment without precedent or equivalent in the societies of the postwar West: the gradual replacement of a (semi-)welfare state by a police and penal state for which the criminalization of marginality and the punitive containment of dispossessed categories serve as social policy at the lower end of the class and ethnic order. (Wacquant, 2009a: 41)

The foundations for the punitive overturn of the welfarist model of social regulation that had prevailed in advanced capitalist democracies (including, though to a lesser degree, the U.S.) in the aftermath of World War II, were laid down in the second half of the 1970s. Consolidating its governmental rationality in an era dominated in much of the Western world by a restructuring of the economy in the direction of a post-Fordist model based on deregulation, labor flexibility, and the 'abolition of welfare as we know it', the American punitive turn expressed its exclusionary logic in the form of vertically increasing incarceration rates and an increasing use of non-custodial forms of penal control (see Beckett, 1997; Parenti, 2000; Tonry, 2004; Simon, 2007). As the twenty-first century unfolds, the result of this ongoing trajectory of punitive governance is that the U.S. is the world leader in punishment and it spends more on prisons than on higher education.

Despite the sort of collective amnesia surrounding public debates on the penal question, whose effect is to 'naturalize' and de-historicize current penal policies, this has not always been the case. In fact, until the early 1970s – that is, at the height of the reformist era defined by David Garland (2001b) as 'penal modernism' – U.S. incarceration rates were comparable to (and in some states even lower than) those of other advanced Western democracies: so much so that some authors ventured to announce an era of 'decarceration' in American society (Scull, 1977). Just 30 years later, those rates are between five and eleven times higher than those found in European countries: the U.S. has become the world's first 'punitive democracy', and this has been the intended consequence of a specific politico-economic plan undertaken by U.S. power elites over the last few decades.

However, it is not simply from the statistical picture of this second 'great confinement', to borrow from Michel Foucault (1975), that we can get an exhaustive image of the construction of a punitive democracy in America. In fact, besides the advent of what sociologists of punishment have come to define as 'mass-imprisonment' (Garland 2001a), it is important to note that the wars against crime and drugs – which since the late 1970s have replaced (both in the political agenda and in public debates) the 'war on poverty' launched by president Lyndon B. Johnson in 1964 – have witnessed also the return of some 'non-conventional' penal weapons, such as the death penalty, chain gangs, solitary confinement, 'supermax' prisons, chemical castration and other kinds of 'de-civilized' punishments (Pratt, 1998): pre-modern penal practices which the progressive ethos of earlier decades (to which the Supreme Court had significantly contributed with path-breaking decisions not only in the field of punishment) seemed to have once and for all consigned to the arsenal of history. Just to give one example, 1,099 death row inmates have been executed in the U.S. between 1977 and 2006, at an average of three executions each month (Bureau of Justice Statistics, 2007).

At the same time, at other latitudes of the U.S. penal archipelago, there has been a silent proliferation of 'invisible punishments' (Mauer and Chesney-Lynd, 2002) aimed at consolidating a model of punitive regulation of the poor and the socially vulnerable which takes place at the intersection between penal and social policies. As Loic Wacquant (2009a) suggests, the result of these developments has been the creation of a 'carceral-assistantial' *continuum* whose foundations were laid down by president Clinton's 1996 'welfare reform'. Among a vast array of stigmatizing measures targeting the 'underclass', the *Personal Responsbility and Work Opportunity Reconciliation Act* has excluded convicted drug offenders from access to food stamps, educational grants, and unemployment benefits – thus projecting the socially destructive consequences of imprisonment well beyond the walls of the prison, and onto the families of prisoners (and ex-prisoners). Another case in point are the draconian 'One Strike and You're Out' provisions adopted in several urban areas during the late 1990s, which allow public housing authorities to evict entire families from subsidized houses if *just one member* of the household is convicted of a drug-related felony, and in some cases even if the crime took place outside the building.

It has been also as a consequence of these neo-authoritarian and revanchist policies, which intentionally targeted a population largely composed of poor African Americans and Latinos confined in the most derelict areas of the American inner cities, that race, welfare and crime have come to be associated in public discourse to the point of becoming almost synonymous. As Glenn Loury has recently argued:

> Before 1965, public attitudes on the welfare state and on race, as measured by the annually administered General Social Survey, varied from year to year independent of one another: you could not predict much about a person's attitudes on welfare politics by knowing his or her attitudes about race. After 1965, the attitudes moved in tandem, as welfare came to be seen as a race issue …. The association in the American mind of race with welfare, and of race with crime, was achieved at a common historical moment. (Loury, 2008: 14–15)

Meanwhile, particularly between the end of the 1980s and the early 1990s, in the wake of cyclical moral panics prompted by some highly mass-mediated criminal cases (e.g., Polly Klaas and Megan Kanka), highly symbolic and revanchist penal strategies gained new legitimacy: the death penalty also for the mentally ill (it is worth remembering here that in 1992 presidential candidate Bill Clinton interrupted his campaign to preside over the execution of Ricky Ray Rector, who suffered from self-inflicted cerebral damages as a consequence of an attempted suicide; Rector was so mentally impaired that at the time of having his last meal before execution he asked the prison personnel to put aside the dessert for him, so that he could eat it after the execution); life imprisonment also for juveniles, ever more often tried as adults in cases of serious crime (currently 44 states have enacted legislation permitting juveniles to be tried as adults in cases of violent crime, with Vermont and Kansas extending this provision to children aged 10); 'Three Strikes and You're Out' laws mandating life in prison for any third felony (in some cases even if the previous two offences were only attempted crimes[2]); the reintroduction of forced labor and chain gangs in some Southern states; sex-offender laws mandating the public registration (and, in many cases, public notification) of former sex offenders.

An analysis of these practices of social and political neutralization collateral to mass-imprisonment unveils an even clearer image of the racial connotation of the American great confinement. As we have already seen, penal statistics show that African Americans constitute the majority of the U.S. prison population, although they represent only 12 per cent of the general population. Within the African American population this means that one every three males aged 20 to 29 is today under some form of correctional supervision; at current rates, a black male born in 2001 has 32 per cent of chances of ending up in prison during his lifetime – a probability which for Hispanic males of the same age group is 17 per cent, whereas for the whites is as low as 6 per cent (Western, 2006; Mauer, 2006).

However, the process of social excommunication of the 'truly disadvantaged' (cf. Wilson, 1987) prompted by the American punitive turn has not been limited to civil and social rights: in fact, it has extended to the realm of political rights as well. Today, 14 states impose a temporary ban from electoral participation on individuals convicted of a felony, even after the sentence has been fully served, while eight states impose a *lifetime ban on voting rights*. Just 40 years after the civil rights revolution (and less than 60 years after the beginning of de-segregation), 13 per cent of African American males are politically disenfranchised as a consequence of the

---

2   In November 1995, U.S. Army veteran Leandro Andrade was arrested in a K-Mart while attempting to steal nine videotapes he needed as Christmas gifts for his nieces, for a total value of $153. In March 2000, Gary Albert Ewing was caught in a golf shop near Los Angeles while trying to hide some golf clubs for a total value of $1,197. Both have been convicted under the Three Strikes laws, since both were considered 'third strikers' as a consequence of previous convictions for minor crimes. Andrade will be able to apply for parole in 2045, while Ewing will be eligible in 2025. In March 2003, the U.S. Supreme Court upheld California's Three Strikes laws, establishing (in *Lockyer* v *Andrade* and *Ewing* v *California*) that none of the two sentences was grossly disproportionate, and that California's Three Strikes laws did not violate the Eighth Amendment's prohibition of 'cruel and unusual punishments'.

voting bans mentioned above (Mauer, 2002: 50–58). During the 2000 presidential elections, which saw George W. Bush famously defeat former vice-president Al Gore by a handful of (contested) votes, almost 4.7 million U.S. citizens could not vote as a consequence of earlier criminal convictions. Reliable estimates suggest that – given the current electoral trends within the African American population – if only those black voters who were banned from the 2000 and 2004 elections despite having served their sentences *in full* had been allowed to vote, George W. Bush would have never been elected to the White House (cf. Davis, 2003; Manza and Uggen, 2008).

The Myth of Crime and Punishment

The commonsense perspective on crime and punishment, according to which the obvious catalyst for any change in punitive 'reactions' must be a concomitant change in criminal 'actions', has been popularized by mainstream criminologists, embraced by politicians in search of populist consent and amplified by the mass media.[3] However, a growing body of critical literature in the sociology of punishment has shown that crime is not a plausible explanation for the advent of mass-imprisonment in the U.S. (see Donziger, 1996; Western, 2006; Mauer, 2006). As has recently been suggested, any attempt to explain the American penal hypertrophy of the last few decades, and the condition of 'internal exile' to which the construction of a 'penal state' has consigned the most economically and racially marginalized fractions of the population, must guard itself against the 'crime and punishment poke, which continues to straightjacket scholarly and policy debates on incarceration, even as the divorce of this familiar couple grows ever more barefaced' (Wacquant, 2009a: 287).

Indeed, after a significant rise between the end of 1960s and the early 1970s, street crime constantly declined over the next three decades, with particular intensity during the 1990s and the early 2000s (see Figure 9.2). The American crime decline has been so sharp and constant that criminologists from very different theoretical perspectives are still in search of possible explanations (*cf.* Zimring, 2008; Blumstein and Wallman, 2000).

---

3 Already in 1984, Stuart Scheingold warned that the widespread 'myth of crime and punishment' would legitimate among the American public opinion the war on crime and drugs just launched by the country's power elites: 'The core of the myth of crime and punishment is a simple morality play that dramatizes the conflict between good and evil: because of bad people, this is a dangerous and violent world … . This frightening image triggers off a second and more reassuring feature of the myth of crime and punishment: the idea that the appropriate response to crime is punishment. Punishment is both morally justified and practically effective' (Scheingold 1984: 60).

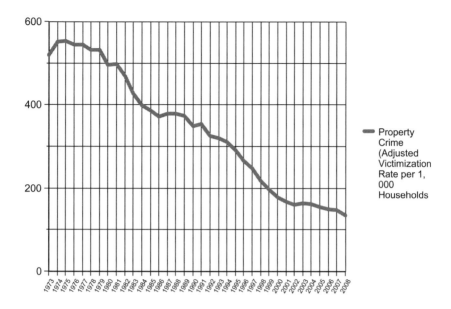

Source: National Crime Victimization Survey, http://www.ojp.usdoj.gov/bjs/glance/house2. htm

Figure 9.2   Property crime trends in the U.S. (1973–2008)

A partial exception to this downward trend has been represented by gun-related violent crime, which increased sharply during the 1980s (see Figure 9.3), mostly as a consequence two related factors. On the one hand, the sudden spread of crack cocaine across the streets of U.S. inner cities lured a generation of underprivileged young African American males into a burgeoning drug economy which for many represented the only path to economic inclusion in the age of capitalist restructuring (Bourgois, 2003). On the other hand, the war on drugs waged by the Reagan and Bush administrations prompted a militaristic approach to the drug issue by the police, which in turn contributed to escalate drug-related violence on the streets. In any case, since the early 1990s rates of violent crime have also been declining steeply, although this has not prevented incarceration rates from continuing their vertical increase.

The conclusion we can draw from these data is that the U.S. penal experiment has been launched while rates of criminal activity were *already declining*. In this respect, it would be as incorrect to argue (like mainstream criminologists tend to do) that increasing crime rates are the main cause of the vertical rise of incarceration, as it would be to suggest (as politicians and the mass-media tend to do) that mass-imprisonment is the main cause of the steep decline in criminal activity across the U.S. Quite simply, there appears to be no relationship at all between the two.

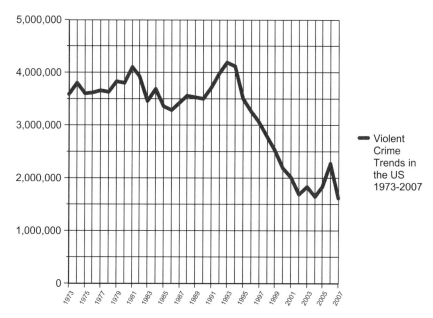

Source: National Crime Victimization Survey, http://www.ojp.usdoj.gov/bjs/glance/viort.htm

Figure 9.3   Violent crime trends in the U.S. (1973–2007)

In the U.S., and to a lesser extent also in Europe,[4] we have witnessed an increasing disconnection between trends in crime and rates of imprisonment. Even as crime rates declined, the number of people arrested, convicted and incarcerated has been constantly increasing. Thus, while the rhetoric of penal severity was able to consolidate itself successfully even in the absence of any connection to the actual size of the criminal problem, public discourses and political debates about social issues traditionally framed in the language of civil and social rights, and of a more equitable distribution of resources in a chronically unequal society, were easily reshaped according to the logic of punishment and its exclusionary practices:

> Since the about-turn of the mid-1970s the carceral system of the United States serves not only to repress crime: it also has for mission to bolster the social, racial, and economic order via the punitive regulation of the behaviors of the categories prone to visible and offensive deviance because they are relegated

---

4   With particular reference to the criminalization of immigrants (see other contributions to this volume), whose chronic overrepresentation across European prisons is in some cases even higher than the overrepresentation of African Americans in the American prison system (cf. also Palidda, 1996; Tonry, 1997; De Giorgi, forthcoming).

at the bottom of a polarizing class and caste structure. The prison has been called upon to contain the disorders generated by the rising tide of dispossessed families, street derelicts, unemployed and alienated youths, and the desperation and violence that have accumulated and intensified in the segregated urban core of the metropolis as the 'safety net' of the U.S. semi-welfare state was torn, and desocialized wage labor in the low wage service was made the normal horizon of work for the deskilled fractions of the working class. (Wacquant, 2005: 15)[5]

As Jonathan Simon argues in his recent book (Simon, 2007), the diffusion of practices of securization at all levels of American society – but particularly among those middle classes whose social mobility has been jeopardized by a new economy that has 'corroded' their character (Sennett, 2000) and crippled their faith in the American dream – and the consolidation of policies of mass-criminalization against the most vulnerable fractions of American society, have both converged to define a new paradigm of 'governing through crime'. By fomenting and then 'governing' widespread social anxieties, from street crime to illegal immigration, from paedophilia to Islamic terrorism, this governmental paradigm, whose strategies of privatization of risk and individualization of security are entirely consistent with the neoliberal ideology of 'possessive individualism' (MacPherson, 1962) and economic deregulation, generates a constant source of political legitimacy built on fear:

> If the experience of mass economic insecurity associated with the Great Depression formed a major impetus for the New Deal model, it must be agreed that the experience … of mass insecurity about violent crime since the late 1960s has provided the impetus for the Crime Deal. Liberty, security, and community have been renegotiated by governing actors and agents of all kinds on the basis of this crime priority. In place of spreading risk across broad social and economic groups, the Crime Deal has promoted disaggregation of risk that reaches its most potent form in the assignment of a historically unprecedented portion of our population to incarceration, as well as in patterns of consumption, such as the ubiquity of the gated community form of residential subdivision, the high security office park form of business development, and the militarized SUV with names like Expedition, Armada, and Suburban, which advertise their militant commitment to security and liberty without community. (Simon 2008: 54)

While Simon's analysis refers specifically to the U.S., and might somehow reflect the 'exceptionalism' of the American experience, it would be difficult to deny that

---

5   Several authors have also illustrated the 'globalizing' character of punitive discourses and practices (such as the myth of New York's *zero tolerance*) which have been imported into Europe from the U.S. throughout the 1990s (see Bigo 1998a, 2004, 2005; Palidda, 2000).

some elements of his diagnosis point to tendencies that are emerging within the European context as well.

Across the European Union we witness the consolidation of a governmental logic which on the one hand nourishes public fears and insecurities about 'public enemies' (e.g. illegal immigrants) against whom periodic wars must be waged, and on the other hand abandons the welfarist model of socio-economic regulation in favor of punitive approaches to social problems (e.g. drugs). Through an opportunistic escalation of what Italian sociologist Alessandro Dal Lago has defined as 'tautology of fear' (Dal Lago, 1999b), in the U.S. as well as in Europe, this paradigm of governance has been able to consolidate the hegemony of a populist-punitive approach to the penal question, which in turn has contributed to neutralize (if only temporarily, as the current global crisis has shown) the catastrophic social consequences of neoliberalism (cf. Harvey, 2005).

Moreover, beyond its propensity to accumulate political capital around the vocabularies of personal insecurity, criminal dangerousness, zero tolerance and the war on crime, this new paradigm of punitive governance has revealed also a strong capacity to generate capital *tout court*, functioning as a catalyst for the booming profits of insurance companies, private security, and the so called 'prison-industrial complex' (cf. Sudbury, 2005).[6] Not surprisingly, the development of this 'penal capitalism' has been particularly visible in a highly neoliberal socio-economic system like the U.S.:

> The prison industrial complex is fueled by privatization patterns that, it will be recalled, have also drastically transformed health care, education, and other areas of our lives. Moreover, the prison privatization trends – both the increasing presence of corporations in the prison economy and the establishment of private prisons – are reminiscent of the historical efforts to create a profitable punishment industry based on the new supply of 'free' black male laborers in the aftermath of the Civil War. (Davis, 2003: 93–4)

Finally, at a broader level it is possible to trace the development of an intense circularity of interactions between national and transnational actors involved in the construction of punitive discourses, as well as in their economic and political productivity: a punitive whirl which from the U.S. has made its way throughout the Western world, reaching a status of a global cultural hegemony (Wacquant, 2009b). Particularly between the late 1980s and the early 2000s, in many neoliberal societies the result of this process has been the consolidation of vocabularies (and practices) of war – against drugs, crime, terrorism, illegal immigration – as the main tools to frame social issues and shape public policies.

---

6 According to Glenn Loury (2008: 5), the U.S. correctional system 'employs more Americans than the combined work forces of General Motors, Ford, and Wal-Mart, the three largest corporate employers in the country'.

The powerful rationality of governing the contradictions of neoliberalism through fear, which revolves around the symbolic and material criminalization of whole categories of subjects stigmatized as dangerous, undesirable, or simply incompatible with a more and more militarized concept of security as personal safety, has thus recruited to the ongoing war against our ubiquitous 'suitable enemies' (Christie, 1986) a vast array of social and institutional actors: an army composed by frightened citizens in search of protection, police forces invested with the mandate to defend 'communities of fear' from criminal (or immigrant) invasions, city mayors acting as warriors against urban disorder, embedded criminologists eager to give scientific validation to the latest moral panic, and moral entrepreneurs raising public fears only to capitalize later on the political and economic profit they generate.

In the midst of a global recession which in the U.S. is bringing back the spectre of the Great Depression, the 2008 presidential election seems to have at least made possible a public debate about the exclusionary effects produced by three decades of uninterrupted symbiosis between economic deregulation and penal severity. In the 1930s, Americans built their way out of the great depression and its devastating consequences through the New Deal, whose inclusionary ethos paved the way for several decades of prosperity and expansive social citizenship. Time will tell whether the new-New Deal envisioned by Barack Obama will be able to awake American society from the prolonged punitive torpor in which it fell almost 30 years ago, and above all whether this awakening will extend beyond the boundaries of the U.S.

PART II
National Case Studies

Chapter 10

Delinquency, Victimization, Criminalization and Penal Treatment of Foreigners in France

Laurent Mucchielli and Sophie Nevanen

Introduction: The Strength of Suspicion

In France, like in other European countries, for around the last thirty years the issue of immigration and that of security have become impossible to separate in the political–media debate. As has been shown for some time by certain authors,[1] the history of foreigners or immigrants in France is structurally linked to the construction of the nation-state and industrialization. In the French case, however, one must also add the impact of de-colonization and, in particular, that of an Algerian War that was traumatic in various senses and not acknowledged as such for a long time, even when, in the 1960s and 1970s, Algerian workers and then their families became the most numerous group among immigrants.[2] The consequence has been a powerful anti-Arabic racism (Gastaut, 2000). Finally, over the last few years, the new research approaches point to a third dimension

---

1   See, for example, Noiriel (1988), Viet (2004).

2   See Stora (1991, 1992). Since then, Algerian immigration (and later Moroccan immigration) has become more important than Italian or Portuguese immigration. In the last census (2004–2005), there were around 700,000 Algerian immigrants and almost 620,000 Moroccans; for the first time they were more numerous than the Portuguese (see Borrel, 2006) [*Editor's note*: In France, a very large majority of immigrants has acquired French nationality ('immigration for demographic reasons', to 'manufacture French people', and not just for labour needs); the children of immigrants who are born in France automatically become French when they turn 18 years old. In France, *jus solis* and *jus sanguinis* are – still – in force, that is, one becomes French due to birth in the national territory or to being the child of at least one French parent; concession of nationality to a foreigner remains at the discretion, not of the judicial authority, but of the police authority. Both people who turn French and those born on French soil are – obviously – no longer recorded as foreigners. After Nazism and by virtue of an assimilationist tradition, there are no statistics on the foreign origins of French people, but estimates show that at least a third of the people with French nationality has foreign origins and perhaps they are even more if one traces them back to five or six generations ago; their origins are mainly Italian, from Maghreb countries, Polish, Spanish and Portuguese. There is information on the 'French by acquisition' only in certain statistics, that obviously exclude those who are 'French by birth' – even if they are children of foreign parents].

of the analysis of the history of immigration, that of a 'post-colonial' society that preserves, *nolens volens* [whether it wants to or not], a devaluing, suspicious and often discriminatory attitude towards populations whose origins lie in its former colonies (Fassin and Fassin, 2006). All of this makes it possible to understand the persistence, over the last thirty years, if not of a more or less explicit xenophobia, at least of an attitude towards populations with immigrant origins that is marked by *suspicion*. A suspicion of 'regressive' violence (as is witnessed by the frequent use of the term 'barbarism' in describing certain criminal events), suspicion of cynicism ('they take advantage of the system', of social benefits etc.), suspicion of 'poor integration', suspicion of rebellion or subversion.

In the 1974–85 period, the French situation took on an extremely conflictual characterization due to the economic crisis and the political decision to 'stop' immigration and, conversely, of combating illegal immigration that was previously encouraged (Weil 1991). After the left came to power (1981) and then the failure of its economic recovery (1982–83), there was the emergence of the *Front National*, the far-right party that has progressively become the backer of the resentment of working-class sectors 'of French origins' that were struck by the crisis (Mayer, 1999) and imposed an 'immigration issue' on the public debate that, since then, has never ceased to be a concern (Gastaut, 2000). At the political level, this has translated into the taking hold of a concern about illegal immigration and into the legitimation of the 'struggle' against it, amid suspicion that it is intrinsically dangerous.[3] A 'governmentality through concern' has hence re-established itself through the figure of the foreigner/immigrant.[4]

At the same time, the 'immigrant workers' and their families have been struck even harder by unemployment than working-class families 'of French origins'. They have hence found themselves 'in imposed residence' in the large council housing agglomerates found on the outskirts of cities, where all sorts of instability were concentrated. After the failure of an attempt to set up a social movement (the 'Beur movement'), immigrants found themselves without any sort of social and political recognition. From then until the turnaround of the 1980s and 1990s, two phenomena took shape: on the one hand, the resurgence of urban revolts, and on the other, 'identitary' assertion through the Muslim religion by some of the French children of these 'immigrant workers'. Throughout the 1990s to date, these two issues – the revolts and the Muslim religion, particularly through the issue of the 'Islamic scarf' at school – have not ceased to stir up the political–media debate.[5] Finally, the 2001–05 period led to a dramatic shift in these two matters due to two important events. Firstly, the attacks of 11 September 2001, which sparked

---

3   See, for example, analysis of political speeches from the period of the vote on the 'Debré Law' in 1996 (Lessana, 1998) and on those in 2007 following the election of Sarkozy as President of the Republic and the creation of a 'ministy of immigration and national identity' (Slama, 2008; Rodier and Terray, 2008).

4   Bigo (1998a); Lochak (2006, 2007).

5   Rey (1996); Tsoukala (2002); Bowen (2007).

fears and legitimated ideas of a 'clash of civilizations' – first supported only by xenophobic intellectual currents[6] – up to the point where they trivialized genuine 'Islamophobia'.[7] Once the link between the 'rise of Muslim integralism' in the world and delinquency by youths in the French *banlieues* had gained credit, one then came to a veritable *moral panic*, as in the 'turnstiles' *affaire* in 2001–02[8]. A veritable figure of the 'internal enemy' then progressively emerged.[9] In relation to all of this, the theme of the 'excessive delinquency of youths with immigrant origins' was very present in the 2001–02 elections, picking up a relative consensus beyond the traditional right–left division.[10] Subsequently, the three weeks of revolts in October and November 2005 had an international resonance. In French public debate, they fostered publicity for opinions that were sometimes overtly xenophobic, which were previously concealed due to the fear of their holders being accused of racism.[11]

Thus, after the presidential elections of 2002, while the theme of security had lost ground among the concerns of the French (the economic themes of unemployment and purchasing power prevailed), that of immigration returned to the centre ground in the 2007 election.[12] In fact, opinion surveys indicate that quite a large consensus emerged that interpreted the revolts in terms of an 'integration

---

6   Cesari (1997).

7   Geisser (2003); Deltombe (2005).

8   See Mucchielli (2005). The expression 'turnstiles', picked up from the popular dialect (*argot*) by journalists, concerns collective rapes. In 2001 and 2002, the media suddenly took over this issue, speaking of it almost always as if it were a new phenomenon, greatly increasing and specifically involving 'youths of immigrant origins', inhabitants of the *banlieues* (suburbs). The cited research tested and empirically belied these three 'assumptions'.

9   Bigo (1998a).

10   Mucchielli (2003).

11   See Gèze (2006); Mauger (2006). Let us recall that Sarkozy, who was then the interior minister, spoke of the presence of numerous 'foreign delinquents' among the rebels, as he did of (totally imaginary) 'Muslim extremists'. In doing so, he was followed by many politicians as well as journalists (for instance those of the weekly magazine *Marianne*, who described the revolts as acts of 'barbarism', but also the editorialists of *Point* and *Nouvel Observateur*); militant associations (like the Union des Familles Laïques, spoke of 'leaders of political Islam'); intellectuals (like R. Redeker, criticized the 'nihilism' of the rebels, seeing them as 'the expression of an essentially cultural problem'; as for A. Finkielkraut, he saw them as 'a revolt of an ethnic-religious character' by 'youths who identify with Islam'). Some among them (B. Accoyer, president of the UMP group in the chamber of deputies [lower house of parliament], G. Larcher, then the employment minister, Philippe de Villiers, a French far-right leader, as well as H. Carrère d'Encausses, the permanent secretary of the Académie Française) linked the revolts to the polygamy of 'these people [who] come directly from their African village'. Mucchielli (2002).

12   See Tiberj (2008). The candidate Sarkozy announced his intention to create a 'ministry of immigration and national identity'.

problem' encompassing a degree of revival of xenophobia.[13] Vincent Tiberj (2008) has shown how this development gave rise to a demand for security (or order) and for 'ethno-centric reassurance' that Sarkozy managed to capture for his benefit, that is, as one of the keys for his victory.

Hence, the related themes of security and foreigners (or immigration) have practically never ceased to return to the centre of the political debate in France since the 1970s. And this is why, almost twenty years after the first study of statistics on foreigners in delinquency and in the penal system (Tournier and Robert, 1991), it is important to return to this data, update it and discuss its interpretations again. First, however, we will offer a glimpse of recent victimization surveys to ascertain whether this instrument of analysis, rather different from statistics produced by the police and justice system, throws up some differences between French people and foreigners (I). We will then analyse police statistics since the start of the 1970s (II). Subsequently, we will compare police data with judicial data (III). Finally, we will look at the situation of foreigners in prison (IV) and in administrative detention structures (waiting zones and detention centres) (V).

Victimization: Are Foreigners Victims More or Less Often than Nationals?

Victimization surveys, apart from providing information on cases that are ignored, makes it possible to describe victims on the basis of their demographic and social characteristics. In France, the first one was carried out on a national scale by CESDIP researchers in the mid-1980s. This research centre then perfected the survey technique that was employed later at a regional and municipal level (Robert, Pottier, Zauberman, 2003: 5–24). After 1996, INSEE inserted a questionnaire on victimization in its annual survey on the living standards of families (EPCV), with a representative sample of around 11,000 people.[14] In spite of some untimely changes in the questionnaire (in 1999, 2006 and 2007), today, a substantial series of such annual surveys are available.[15]

---

13   Thus, the positive answers to the question: 'There are too many immigrants in France: do you agree or not?', were clearly more than 50 per cent.

14   The PCV surveys by INSEE (the French national institute for statistics) do not select interviewees and do not interview them by telephone, but on the basis of the INSEE's housing database and through face-to-face interviews. The questionnaire is translated into several languages. However, it is difficult to know enough about the actual representativeness and reliability of answers. [*Editor's note*: These are similar to the annual surveys that are now carried out by Istat in Italy. The corresponding Istat survey is conducted using 60,000 families every five years, but it is only a telephone survey and does not record any information on the interviewee's nationality.]

15   See Robert, Zauberman, Nevanen, Didier (2008). This survey technique is tending to become generalized. Epidemiologists from the National Health Institute and the National Institute for Health and Medical Research (INSERM) and from the National Institute for

To start with, we calculated the incidence according to the nationality of the people interviewed. The only forms of victimization concerning individuals that are dealt with by the EPCV survey are attacks and personal theft.[16] Those interviewed who are of foreign nationality are a small part of the total (around 6 per cent). Because as large a sample as possible is required in order for the results to make any sense, we have chosen to use the sum of the EPCV surveys from 1996 to 2004 (whose questionnaires are sufficiently similar to justify their being grouped together).

Reading Table 10.1, one will note a greater incidence than average among people whose nationality is from 'Africa excluding the Maghreb' and a lower one among people whose nationality is from the 'Maghreb', '15-country Europe' and the 'Rest of Europe'. The incidence of personal theft is highest among people whose nationality is from 'Africa excluding the Maghreb', the 'Rest of Europe' and the 'Rest of the World'.

Calculating the incidence according to interviewees' countries of birth, as indicated by Table 10.2, we find the same differences. People born in Africa (excluding the Maghreb) run a higher risk of being attacked, whereas people born in Europe or in Maghreb countries run a lower risk of being attacked. Moreover, people born in Europe (excluding the 15 EU countries), in Africa (excluding the Maghreb) and in the rest of the world, run a higher risk of suffering personal theft than the average of interviewees.

Victimization rates may vary depending on socio-demographic characteristics or the places of residence of the people interviewed. The variations noted depending on the nationality of those interviewed or their countries of birth may hence be a consequence of other characteristics of these populations. An analysis of the 'logistical regression' for the purpose of explaining having or not having been a victim during the previous two years could distinguish the criteria that are at play in the variation of rates, enabling a study 'in equality of all other circumstances'.[17]

Prevention and Education for Health (INPES) use it. It has also been used in the framework of research on violence in a school setting.

16   As opposed to victimization concerning families, such as car theft and thefts involving break-ins.

17   [*Editor's note*: the customary expression in French sociology is: *toutes choses égales par ailleurs* which, in Latin, corresponds to *ceteris paribus sic stantibus* (formulae that are characteristic of a Durkheimian tradition, 'all other circumstances being equal').]

Table 10.1 Bi-annual indices of attacks and personal theft by nationality

	French-born	Turned French**	Euro 15	Rest of Europe	Maghreb Africa	Africa excl. Maghreb	Rest of the World	Total
Size of the sample (n)	80,723	2,543	1,921	450	1,456	361	921	88,553
victims of attacks in %	6.51	5.51	3.25	4.33	4.80	9.17	7.01	6.38
victims of personal theft in %	4.95	5.48	4.91	6.39	4.04	8.74	6.26	4.99

* The people interviewed are asked the following questions: 'Over the last two years, have you been a victim of an attack or or acts of violence, including by people who you do not know?' and 'Over the last two years, have you been a victim of a different kind of theft than theft with a break-in or car theft?'.

** Foreigners who obtained French nationality.

Source: Authors' elaboration based on EPCV surveys (1996–2004).

Table 10.2 Bi-annual indices of attacks and personal theft according to countries of birth

	French-born	Euro 15	Rest of Europe	Maghreb	Rest of Africa	Rest of the World	Total
Size of sample (n)	78,656	3,143	859	3,654	812	1,429	88,553
victims of attacks in %	6.51	3.79	4.91	5.31	9.42	7.34	6.38
victims of personal theft in %	4.94	4.71	6.19	4.37	8.95	7.00	4.99

Source: Authors' elaboration based on EPCV surveys (1996–2004).

As can be inferred from the measure of the influence of the different variables[18] on the fact of having or not having been a victim attacks (analysis of the logistical regression),[19] in equality of all other circumstances, women have a lower probability of being victims of attacks than men. The person's age has an effect, but decreases as age advances: people who are 75 years old or over, risk being attacked up to five times less than 15–25 year-olds. This risk also varies depending on individuals' employment, with the unemployed more often victims on average than people who work; farmers, factory workers, pensioners and other people who are not active are victims less often than office workers. Individuals belonging to families made up of couples with children are victims less often than those belonging to other types of families; inhabitants of the Paris region and cities are victims more often than rural people. Finally, and this is what we wish to know, *the most important rate of attacks among people whose nationality is 'African excluding the Maghreb' that was highlighted through the analysis of indices disappears when one takes into account the other variables*; hence, it seems to be an artifact of the combination of other characteristics of the population.

Always in a condition of equality of all other circumstances, the measure of the influence of the different variables[20] as to whether or not someone has been a victim of personal theft (logistical regression analysis)[21] makes it possible to note that women have a lower probability of being victims of personal theft than men. As in the case of attacks, the person's age also has a considerable impact on their risk of being victims of theft, with the over-25s running the risk of being victims at least two times less than 15–25 year-olds, but the progressive decrease as age advances can no longer be observed in this case. The risk of theft also varies according to the social-professional category to which people belong: craftsmen, shopkeepers, members of the liberal professions, cadres, people from the higher intellectual professions, farmers and members of intermediary professions are victims more often than office workers; pensioners are victims less often, while other non-active people are victims more often; individuals belonging to families made up of couples with children are victims less often than members of single-parent families; inhabitants of the Paris region are victims more often, and those in rural towns are less often the victims of theft than city dwellers. Finally, inversely

---

18   We only include significant results; we have sought to introduce other variables: type of habitat, income, countries of birth, but these have not appeared to be significant.

19   Such a model has a percentage of 'good predictions' of just 66 per cent, obviously there are several variables missing that would contribute to explain the risk of being attacked.

20   Again, we have only reviewed the more significant results here; we have also sought to introduce other variables: type of housing, income, position in relation to activity (active/not active), nationality, residence in ZUS (sensitive urban areas), but these have not appeared to be significant.

21   Again, this model has a percentage of 'good predictions' of only 66 per cent, numerous variable are obviously missing here that would contribute to explain the risk of suffering personal theft.

to what we noted in the case of attacks against persons, *the highest rate of personal thefts among people born in 'Africa excluding Maghreb countries' and in the 'rest of the world' persists in equality of all other circumstances.*

In short, the victimization study for the French and for foreigners shows that French nationals are more protected than some categories of foreigners or of people who have turned French but were born abroad, particularly in the case of people from black Africa and Asia. In effect, the latter are most often victims of personal theft (of which only a small part – from 10 to 15 per cent depending on the years and wording of the questions – are committed using violence).

The Impact of Foreigners on Delinquency according to Police Statistics

Elementary Methodological Precautions

Those that are currently and mistakenly termed 'statistics on delinquency' in the public debate are in reality the statistics recording delinquency that is known about and investigated by the police and *gendarmerie* services,[22] however, excluding traffic offences, certain offences recorded by other administrative bodies (such as tax fraud) and fines.[23] Such statistics have been published in a homogeneous and reliable way since 1974. The counting of those who are referred to as 'accused people' (for whom this source presents a break-down between men/women, French/foreign and minors/adults) depends on verification upstream; for a majority of crimes, the authors are not discovered; moreover, clear up rates vary considerably depending on the type of offence: from 7 to 8 per cent for theft in a car or motorbike theft, to over 100 per cent for offences against drug legislation and … offences against the policing of foreigners.[24] The clear up rate also depends on the reported offences [translator's note: by citizens] as well as on proactive work [translator's note: or of prevention] by the police, particularly controls in the street. It is quite

---

22   [*Editor's note*: These are statistics that, in agreement with Kitsuse and Cicourel (1963), must be considered a measurement of police productivity, namely, accusations and arrests that police carry out by generally pursuing 'easy preys' in accordance with directives from the hierarchy, political authorities and so-called public opinion. The *gendarmerie* corresponds to the *carabinieri corps* – the Italian police force with a military status –; in France there are only two State police forces and there has been a proliferation of municipal police forces, as well as private ones, only over the last few years].

23   Robert, Aubusson de Cavarlay, Pottier, Tournier (1994); Aubusson de Cavarlay (1996, 2006).

24   See Matelly and Mouhanna, 2007. [*Editor's note*: these clear up rates – that is, of crimes whose author was identified – are similar to those in Italy. The ratio between crimes and people charged in the case of drug offences is similar in all countries and can be explained because the pusher is often a drug addict as well, and arrests for drugs often take place in groups, notoriously in the case of police raids in public gardens or marginal urban areas.]

well proven that such controls target foreigners, primarily on the basis of their physical traits.[25] It is what is currently known as 'feature-based control' (*faciès*) or, more recently, 'ethnic profiling' (Lévy, Goris, Jobard, 2009 – note: also see Harcourt's chapter in this volume). This practice has become even more frequent during the last few years due to two reasons. The first is that, since 2002, the arrest of irregular foreigners has been one of the means that police officers and *gendarmes* have found to satisfy the political injunction to increase arrest rates.[26] The second is that since 2007, with the creation of the ministry of immigration, the French government decided to organize a real 'hunt' against irregular foreigners, with targets that included figures imposed upon police officers and *gendarmes* for the purpose of 'attaining numbers' in this field as well.[27]

For all these reasons, it cannot in any case be considered that the people accused by the police constitute a representative sample of verified delinquency, *a fortiori* of real delinquency. Furthermore, in evaluating the weight of foreigners among the people accused, one must recall that certain offences only apply to foreigners. It is a matter of so-called 'administrative delinquency' (Mucchielli, 2003), namely, offences against the 'policing of foreigners', but also crimes involving false identity documents and the crime of illegal employment. To calculate the proportion of foreigners among police proceedings, such crimes must hence be excluded. Finally, it must be recalled that the foreigners accused are not necessarily people who reside in the national territory. France is also a country with a large amount of movement of people and goods, and one of the world's leading tourist destinations.[28] Moreover, certain forms of delinquency (particularly any kind of trafficking) are by definition cross-border and some foreigners may hence be arrested in France for crimes committed elsewhere even when they do not live there.

Evolution of the Impact of Foreigners on Recorded Delinquency

Figure 10.1 clearly shows that the shape of the curve of the total of foreigners charged is identical to that of foreigners subjected to proceedings solely for offences against the policing of foreigners. In other terms, the delinquency of foreigners and its evolution are primarily and most of all the result of repression against 'illegal' immigration.

---

25   Lévy and Zauberman (2003); Lévy, Goris, Jobard (2009).

26   Mucchielli, http://champpenal.revues.org/document3663.html

27   See Lévy, Zauberman, 1998; Slama, 2008. [*Editor's note*: some have called this input the introduction of the *sarkomètre* – sarkometer.]

28   In 2007, 82 million tourists stayed in France (1.3 times the French population), of whom 45 million for stays that lasted at least four nights (*Les chiffres-clefs du tourisme*, Paris: Ministère du Tourisme, 2008).

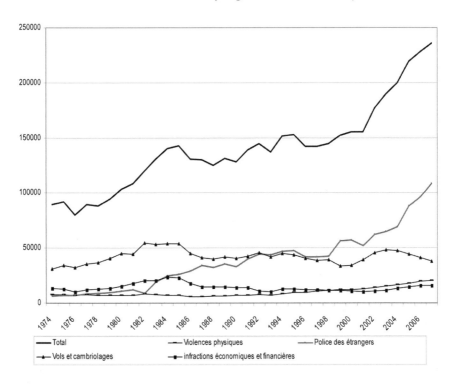

Source: Data from the Ministère de l'Intérieur, re-worked by the authors.

Figure 10.1   Evolution in the number of foreigners among the people investigated (1974–2007)

As for the rest, crimes against property (theft and theft with a break-in), those against people (acts of physical and sexual violence) and economic and financial offences vary only slightly (fraudulent activity, counterfeit goods, stolen cheques, fraud and other offences against legislation on prices and competition, on transport etc.). Crimes against property are stable in the overall period, as are economic and financial offences. The only ones that increase, particularly after the mid-1990s, are acts of physical violence. But it is not something that applies to foreigners, it is a general trend that can be explained through the deep processes of 'penalization' and transformation of the norms on violent acts.[29]

---

29   Mucchielli (2008b).

Table 10.3   Evolution of the percentage of foreigners among people charged (1977–2007)

Offences	1977	1987	1997	2007	evolution 77–07
Theft	16.2	14.4	14.2	14.1	- 13 %
of which car and motorbike theft	13.7	11	8.6	6.1	- 55 %
of which theft in a car	18.3	14.3	10.6	9.7	- 47 %
of which theft in a shop	17.3	19	23.9	21.8	+ 26 %
of which break-ins or in a flat	14.9	11.6	10.4	11.6	- 22 %
of which using violence without a firearm*	23.9	18.8	16.6	13.6	- 43 %
Physical violence	17.1	13	12.7	13.1	- 23 %
of which different types of murder	18.4	15.6	15.1	16	- 13 %
of which CBV (intentional blows and injury)	24	17.4	15.8	13.9	- 42 %
of which sexual violence	29.8	18.5	12.4	13.4	- 55 %
of which other sexual crimes	15.7	13.3	8.6	21.4 **	-
Public order crimes					
of which destruction, damage to private goods	13.5	12.2	11	7.6	- 44 %
of which destruction, damage to public goods	9.4	9.6	8.9	4.8	- 49 %
of which drug trafficking/dealing	62.5	39	21	22.7	- 64 %
of which drug use	10.5	15.6	8.8	6.9	- 34 %
of which IPDAP (off. vs. public authorities)	13.2	12.8	14	10.5	- 20 %
Administrative delinquency					
'Policing of foreigners'	96.3	96.8	97.5	97.2	=
False identity documents	79.2	68.7	71.2	77.1	=
Illegal employment	-	-	23.5	31.5	
Overall	23.5	16.8	17.2	20.9	- 11 %
Number of foreigners charged	136,749	130,070	142,053	235,767	x 6.4
Total, calculated again***	13.8	12.7	12.7	10.7	- 22 %
Number of foreigners, calculated again	78,619	93,437	93,261	119,149	x 1.5
Total number of people charged	582,770	775,756	797,362	1,128,871	x 2

Source: Ministère de l'Intérieur, calculations by the authors.

* = *except* for the year 1987, when the published figure corresponds to 'theft using violence with any sort of weapon'; ** = a figure that has surprisingly been rising quickly since 2002; *** = total excluding 'administrative offences'.

Table 10.3 shows the proportion of foreigners in comparison with the totality of people charged with offences, according to the main categories of offences, comparing it for every decade starting from 1977. Hence, we can suggest the three following observations.

a. During the last thirty years, the portion of foreigners within the overall delinquency has decreased, but the trend had nonetheless reversed in the middle part of the period. In reality, this is due, again, to the repression of 'illegal' immigration. Excluding 'administrative delinquency' (offences that almost exclusively concern foreigners or in which they are, almost by definition, over-represented: offences against the policing of foreigners, illegal employment, false identity documents) from the calculation, a constant decrease in the proportion of foreigners among people who are charged can be appreciated, until it falls to 10.7 per cent in 2007.[30]

b. Apart from some rare exceptions such as theft in shops (quintessential poor people's delinquency), the portion of foreigners among the people who have been charged has decreased over thirty years in every category of crime. The most substantial decreases concern inter-personal violence, offences against drug legislation (especially trafficking) and destruction-damage.

c. While it had increased slightly between 1987 and 1997, the number of foreigners reported increased greatly between 1997 and 2007. Hence, something has happened in the most recent years. We will see that it is what we may call the 'Sarkozy effect'.

The Role of Foreigners in the 'New Management of Security' (after 2002)

As a previous research work shows (Mucchielli, 2008a), on his arrival at the interior ministry, Sarkozy sought to impose a 'new management of security' on the 237,000 French police officers and *gendarmes*. The goal was twofold: on the one hand, to lower the official figure for recorded delinquency, on the other, to

---

30   [*Editor's note*: The French situation thus appears different from the Italian, Spanish or even Greek ones, that is, different from that of southern countries, primarily because France is a country of 'old' immigration in which, despite the approach adopted by governments in the last decade and particularly by Sarkozy, certain guarantees remain strong, at least for regular migrants (less precariousness as regards the keeping of one's residence permit). However, if it were possible to 'delve' further into official statistics, it would be easy to discover that a majority of the French who are reported, arrested and imprisoned is made up of French youths, born in France, but from parents with foreign origins, often from Maghreb countries and particularly Algerians. This is what arises from testimonies given by prison workers; unfortunately, ethnographic research on police practices and those in prisons are quite rare in this country.]

cause the indicators for 'police performance' to increase (clear up rate as to the authors of crimes, number of people arrested and number of people accused, that is, reported to the judicial authority). To reach this goal set in advance and under the control of the entire hierarchical chain of command (with sanctions affecting professional advancement for officials and encouragement, even through awards for merit earned), police officers and *gendarmes* were induced to deal less with matters that had a 'low clearance rate' (i.e. the many types of theft) and to concentrate on crime that brought 'higher yields' in terms of the identification of the author. In this context, multiplying controls in the street and in places frequented by foreigners (sometimes including police headquarters where foreigners seek to obtain permits and are called to turn up for 'trick call-ups'), as well as in the offices of associations and even hospitals that are now considered 'public places',[31] the forces of law and order have strongly intensified their hunt against migrants in an irregular situation.[32] They have also heightened the persecution of drug users as well as that concerning interpersonal disputes of limited seriousness (insults, threats, minor violence) whose authors are easy to pursue because they are explicitly reported by the victims.

Table 10.4 allows one to measure the impact of this policy on the repression of 'illegal' immigration and, consequently, its contribution to this 'new management'. Then, one can see that a 70.5 per cent portion of the growth in the number of foreigners reported between 2001 and 2007 is accounted for by 'illegal' immigration. Furthermore, it can be calculated that just the increase in the number of foreigners reported since 2002 represents 21 per cent of the entire increase in people reported. In other terms, the hunt against 'illegals' has considerably contributed to the general improvement of the 'police performance' during that period. Some equivalent calculations could be made with regards to clearance rates and the number of people held and arrested. That is, foreigners appear to be a category of people who are particularly profitable for police statistics, just as, moreover, is the case for that of drug users (Mucchielli, 2008a).

---

31   This unprecedented hunt has only partly been stopped at the gates of schools, thanks to the mobilization of the 'Network for education without borders' (www. educationsansfrontieres.org).

32   This is the purpose of Circular JUSD0630020C of 21 February 2006, jointly issued by the interior and justice ministries, concerning: 'Conditions for controlling the identity of a foreigner in an irregular situation, for holding a foreigner in an irregular situation, penal responses' (17 pages), that aims to 'invite prosecuting magistrates to fully invest this shared field of action and to define certain directions in the penal response' as well as 'reminding police chiefs of the need to issue orders for accompaniment to the border while specifying certain rules of procedure, notably as regards the specific circumstances of identification in one's residence or in police headquarters'. The practice of 'trick call-ups' to police headquarters has twice been condemned by the Court of Cassation, whose latest decision (25 June 2008) lays out that: 'the administration cannot use a call-up [of a foreigner] to police headquarters to examine their administrative situation requiring their presence, to proceed to identify them with a view to holding them without breaching French law as well as the European Convention on Human Rights'.

Table 10.4   Evolution in foreigners reported between 2001 and 2007

	2001	2007	evolution in %	% in the evolution*
Offences vs. policing of foreigners	52,130	108,675	+ 108	70.5
Theft in a shop	13,791	12,447	- 9.7	- 1.7
Intentional bodily harm	12,212	19,701	+ 61.3	9.3
False identity documents	6,389	4,454	- 30.3	- 2.4
Receiving stolen goods	5,586	6,638	+ 18.8	1.3
Drug use	4,508	8,015	+ 77.8	4.4
'Other crimes'	4,115	6,377	+ 55	2.8
IPDAP (see above)	3,992	4,435	+ 11.1	0.6
Fraud and confidence tricks	3,834	6,172	+ 61	2.9
Threats or blackmail	3,416	5,198	+ 52.2	2.2
Illegal employment	1,859	3,489	+ 87.7	2
'Other sexual attacks'	564	3,341	+ 492	3.5
Others (various)	43,148	46,825	- 7.9	
Total of foreigners reported	*155,544*	*235,767*	*+ 51.6*	

Source: Ministère de l'Intérieur, produced by the authors.

* *the c*alculation is: (nb 2007 – nb 2001 of the offence) x 100 / (nb 2007 – nb 2001 of the total).

The Role Played by Foreigners in Delinquency according to Judicial Statistics

Judicial statistics provide a review of the guilty verdicts passed by the totality of the French courts, on the basis of (partially) checking through the register. These statistics have been published on a yearly basis since 1984, and they provide a detailed breakdown of the offences, gender, age and nationality of people who have been found guilty.[33] In Table 10.5, on one side we compare the composition of delinquency by French nationals who have been charged with that of foreigners,

---

33   Unlike police statistics, they include traffic offences and 5th class fines (the more serious ones, the others are tried by police courts).

and on the other side, the incidence of foreigners charged for each kind of offence (the last column to the left).

Comparison of the two structures throws up an almost perfect likeness, from a judicial perspective, in the distribution between crimes, offences and fines. Foreigners merely appear to be sentenced slightly less for crimes and offences and somewhat more as regards fines. In the breakdown of offences (that represent 94 per cent of overall guilty verdicts), one immediately finds over-representation of foreigners among the 'administrative offences' categories (offences against the policing of foreigners, false claims in documents and illegal employment). Otherwise, in comparison with nationals, foreigners are more often charged for theft, in equal measure for physical and sexual violence,[34] and less often for the majority of other offences, including those against the traffic code. In a political context (especially in 2006, that is, the year when most of the participants in the revolts of 2005 were tried) in which foreigners were often accused of lacking respect for the State and of contributing to social disorders,[35] it must be noted, on the contrary, that their delinquency is less marked than that of nationals as regards offences against public officials (meaning especially police officers), as is also the case for destruction-damage. In sum, there is an almost perfect likeness between the composition of foreigners' delinquency and that of nationals.

Table 10.5   **Comparison of the composition of delinquency by foreigners and French nationals in judicial statistics (2006)**

	foreigners charged	% of total foreigners	French charged	% of total French	% offences by foreigners
Crimes (serious)	372	0.5	2,870	0.6	11.5
Offences	72,670	94.1	471,441	95.2	13.4
Fines (5th class)	4,165	5.4	20,619	4.2	16.8
Total	77,207	100	494,930	100	13.5
Total exc. 'administrative offences'	*69,486*		*488,586*		*12.4*
Breakdown of offences	*72,670*	*100*	*471,441*	*100*	*13.4*
Road traffic	25,372	34.9	194,506	41.3	10.6

34   However, with clearly less sexual attacks on minors compared to nationals.

35   See note 3 above, notoriously, the declarations by Sarkozy concerning the November 2005 revolts.

	foreigners charged	% of total foreigners	French charged	% of total French	% offences by foreigners
Theft and receipt of stolen goods	14,157	19.5	89,230	18.9	13.7
Intentional bodily harm and violence	6,722	9.3	45,062	9.6	13
Policing of foreigners	4,651	6.4	427	0.1	91.6
Drugs	3,792	5.2	29,821	6.3	11.3
Fraud	2,036	2.8	12,064	2.6	14.4
IPDAP (see above)	1,800	2.5	15,871	3.4	10.2
False claims in docs.	1,612	2.2	2,779	0.6	36.7
Irregular employment	1,458	2	3,138	0.7	31.7
Destruction, damage	1,341	1.8	18,081	3.8	6.9
Attacks vs. morality *(incl. against minors)*	1,329 *(278)*	1.8 *(20.9)*	8,750 *(4,483)*	1.8 *(51.2)*	13.2
Involuntary violence	961	1.3	10,886	2.3	8.1
Others	7,439	10.3	40,826	8.6	15.4
Weight of 'administrative offences'	*7,721*	*10.6*	*6,344*	*1.4*	*54.9*

Source: Ministère de la Justice, 'Sentences' series.

Through Table 10.6. we attempt to compare data from police statistics (people charged) and those from judicial statistics (people found guilty), observing the proportion of foreigners in the different categories of offences according to the two sources and for the same year (2006, the last one for which the administration of justice services have published data). It can be noted that the police overestimate the weight of foreigners in delinquency because they prosecute many offences against the policing of foreigners (they will later be dealt with through an administrative rather than judicial course). Once such offences have been excluded, the part played by foreigners in recorded delinquency is nonetheless globally similar (around 12.5 per cent for both populations). In the breakdown, one can likewise observe an overestimation by the police in the majority of types of offences;[36] the most important gap concerns violence in general and sexual violence in particular. Here, one may conjecture that police investigate many events of limited seriousness that courts shelve or treat in alternative ways other than committals to trial.

Table 10.6 Comparison of the composition of delinquency by French nationals and foreigners in police and judicial statistics (2006)

	% foreigners guilty verdicts judicial	% foreigners involved in proceedings police
Theft and receipt of stolen goods	13.7 %	15 %
Fraud, confidence tricks	13.4 %	14.7 %
Destruction, damage	6.9 %	7.5 %
Intentional bodily harm and violence	13 %	14.7 %
Attacks against morality	13.2 %	20.5 %
Verbal threats	11.2 %	13.7 %
Drugs	11.3 %	8 %
Policing of foreigners	91.6 %	97.7 %
IPDAP (see above)	10.2 %	11.5 %
Total	*13.5 %*	*20.7 %*
Total excluding administrative offences	*12.4 %*	*12.6 %*

Sources: Ministère de l'Intérieur and Ministère de la Justice.

Now, let us see the types of sentences passed by courts against foreigners and how they are carried out.[37]

---

36 An exception is represented by offences against drug legislation, and more precisely only drug trafficking (in which foreigners represent 23.5 per cent of people accused by the police and 33.7 per cent of the people found guilty (the difference can be explained through the fact that judicial statistics draw a distinction between 'trafficking (import/export)' that, here, we have instead added to the other two sub-categories: 'trade-transport' and 'offer-sale'.

37 Unfortunately, data that crosses nationality with judicial procedures and decisions prior to final rulings are not yet available.

The Sentences Inflicted on Foreigners and the Evolution of their Imprisonment

Furthermore, judicial statistics on guilty verdicts make it possible to observe the (main) sentences passed against foreigners and to compare them with those inflicted on nationals. Thus, on the one hand Table 10.7 summarizes the available information on the number of foreigners on the basis of the types of sentences and the proportion of foreigners for each kind of sentence, and on the other hand, in particular, it enables a comparison of the structure of the sentences inflicted to members of both populations.

About Foreigners Who are Always Punished More Heavily for the Same Offence

As Table 10.7 shows, even when the composition of their delinquency is similar to that of nationals, overall, foreigners are more heavily punished than nationals. In effect, they are more often sentenced to serve prison terms. To be precise, they are sentenced more often to imprisonment or to a partial sentence suspension, and less often to complete sentence suspension, while longer sentences are also passed against them.

Finally, they are sentenced to pay fines slightly more often than nationals. On the other hand, they are sentenced to serve alternative sentences or educational measures less often. Hence, in 2006, we again find a situation that has been noted various times over the last few years.[38]

---

38   Tournier (1997) [a version of this text is available in Palidda (1996)]; Mary and Tournier (1998), these use judicial statistics from 1991. Also, see the 'civic observation' undertaken by militants from Cimade (*Les prétoires de la misère. Observation citoyenne du Tribunal correctionnel de Montpellier*, 'Causes Communes' collection, not part of a series, January, 2004), insofar as it is resembles a real research work (based on the observation of 50 days of hearings in the TGI – *tribunal de grande instance* –of Montpellier and the judicial treatment of 480 people stopped, of whom 25 per cent were foreigners). This research also stresses that foreigners are more often subjected to trial using a procedure of immediate appearance and that, with the same offences and criminal records, they are punished more heavily than French nationals. [*Editor's note*: The same kind of result was obtained through the research carried out by Palidda and Quassoli for the Migrinf project (fp5) in 1995–98, results that were partly published in Quassoli (1999, 2002).]

Table 10.7   Number and proportion of foreigners, based on the main sentence in 2006

Nature of the main sentence	foreigners found guilty	% foreigners of the total found guilty	composition of sentences for foreigners	composition of sentences for total found guilty
Imprisonment	43,134	13.5	55.9	51.9
Of which imprisonment	*169*	*13.4*	*0.2*	*0.2*
of which confirmed	*20,394*	*17.2*	*26.4*	*19.3*
- for less than 1 month	*406*	*12.2*	*0.5*	*0.5*
- 1 to 6 months	*11,619*	*16.3*	*15*	*11.6*
- 6 months to 1 year	*3,899*	*16.5*	*5*	*3.9*
- 1 to 5 years	*3,952*	*21.8*	*5.1*	*3*
- more than 5 years	*518*	*23.1*	*0.7*	*0.4*
With complete susp. sent.	*22,571*	*11.4*	*29.2*	*32.3*
Fine	25,889	13.2	33.5	32
Alternative sentence	5,835	9.5	7.6	10
Educational measure	1,513	5.2	2	4.8
Educational punishment	42	5	0	0
Sentence exemption	794	10.3	1	1.3
Total of sentences	77,207	12.6	100	100

Source: Ministère de la Justice, 'Sentences' series.

How is one to understand – with the same offences – this greater strictness with regards to foreigners and, in particular, the more frequent use of detention?[39] The customary explanation claims that it is not a form of discrimination based on reasons of an ideological kind, but rather, a sort of vicious circle based on a situation of instability that is simultaneously judicial and social for many foreigners. Regardless of whether they have a regular residence permit, foreigners investigated for offences committed on French territory, *by definition*, offer 'guarantees of representation' at trials less often: home address, family situation, employment

39   [*Editor's note*: This type of results is also obtained by analysing similar cases in Italy – see, in particular, Quassoli (1999).]

(Tournier and Robert, 1991: 87, Mary and Tournier, 1998: 17). In simpler terms, in many situations, when they are subjected to the police or *gendarmerie*'s services, the PMs (investigating magistrates of the *court* who decide the approach adopted in proceedings) may fear that the foreigners may not turn up at a later summons by the court.[40] Hence, they resort more often to the procedure of immediate appearance, during which magistrates opt more often for provisional detention, something that the final sentences generally take into account for the purpose of 'covering' (justifying) the length of this detention.[41]

Other research works have highlighted that, regardless of whether they are foreign or have turned French, 'youths with Maghreb country origins' seem to be victims of a distinctive punitivity. This is what at least three original studies suggest. In a now dated work on procedures for people caught *in flagrante delicto* (in the act) in Paris, Lévy (1987) had shown that, in equality of offences and judicial records, but also of 'guarantees of representation' [references provided to have access to alternative sentencing or to probation], magistrates commit men of a 'Maghreb type' for trial more often. More recently, using local judicial data in an innovative way, Pager (2008) has shown that, with an equal volume of offences and unemployment rates, there is a correlation between courts that issue more prison measures and sentences and the departments (provinces) in which young men of Maghreb country origins are more numerous. However, this is not to say that the discriminatory mechanisms are to be found at the judicial stage. The research by Jobard and Nevanen (2007) devoted to the judicial treatment of offences by public officials also confirms the judicial inequality, but traces back a sort of vengefulness with clarity to the police proceedings phase that specifically targets men 'of Maghreb country origins'. We will return to this point in the conclusions.

Nonetheless, there is a decrease in foreigners' share of the prison population.

---

40   Call-ups addressed to them in writing to an address that is not necessarily theirs, or which magistrates may deem temporary or false [exactly the same thing happens in Italy; see Quassoli (1999); as well as Petti (2004)].

41   See Guillonneau, Kensey, Portas (1999: 1–4); Aubusson de Cavarlay (2006). We have seen that foreigners represent more than 90 per cent of the people found guilty for offences against legislation for the 'policing of foreigners'; now, such offences have given rise to a measure of provisional detention in 27.5 per cent of cases in 2005 (Commission de suivi de la détention provisoire, 2007: 35). The Commission Nationale Consultative des Droits de l'Homme (National Commission for Consultation on Human Rights) has also reported that foreigners have been those most often subjected to provisional detention: 41.7 per cent among imprisoned foreigners compared with 31.3 per cent among nationals in 2004 (CNCDH, 2004: 4). [*Editor's note*: the same sort of result was obtained in MIGRINF research (for the fp4) and later Emilia-Romagna region project in the years 1994–99 (Palidda, 1999). We recall the public protests by Milan prosecuting magistrates against the misuse of arrests that caused a high percentage of them not being validated and a waste of resources for the court –see the results that were partly published in Palidda, 1999; 2000; 2001.]

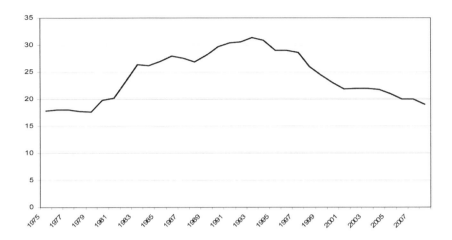

Source: Direction dell'Administration pénitentiaire.

Figure 10.2   Evolution of the weight of foreigners on the prison population 1975–2008

Figure 10.2 shows that in spite of everything that has been said so far, the evolution of the imprisonment of foreigners has moved downwards since the mid-1990s (after an inverse movement during the previous period). On 1 January 2008, foreigners were 19.1 per cent of the prison population, whereas in 1993 they had reached 31 per cent.[42] This decrease can mainly be explained through the lessening of guilty verdicts for offences against the policing of foreigners and, to a lesser extent, those concerning offences against drug laws and simple theft. This trend is also accompanied by a progressive change in the origins of imprisoned foreigners. While in 1993 people from Maghreb countries represented around 57 per cent of detained foreigners, that proportion fell to 36 per cent in 2006 (Hazard, 2008). Conversely, there are increasingly more cases of foreigners from Asian and eastern European countries (particularly Romanians).[43]

---

42   *L'administration pénitentiaire en chiffres*, Paris: Ministère de la Justice, 2008. [*Editor's note*: This figure is even more surprising if compared to that recorded in Italy and generally in southern European countries, as well as in countries that, unlike France, have not had an 'assimilationist' past. In effect, the holding in custody of foreigners takes place mostly under the 'new' forms of detention, but there is also a figure that official statistics do not show, and that the authors cannot comment upon here due to a lack of specific data: as shown by some testimonies, a majority of French inmates have foreign origins, particularly from Maghreb countries.]

43   It is not surprising that the dominant social characteristic of this population remains its deficit of economic and social integration (half of the detained foreigners were not active

In an age in which the criminalization of foreigners is experiencing a strong revival, while the overall prison population has been unceasingly growing since 2001 and police proceedings for offences against the norms on foreigners (ILE) have also risen sharply since 2002, one may find the fall in the number of foreigners surprising. Analysing the reasons for being sent to prison, it can nonetheless be verified that this decrease can be mainly explained through a fall in the number of cases resulting from ILEs (Hazard, 2008 :1-4). To understand this apparent paradox, one must look at the punishment of irregular immigration.

Evolution of the Different Forms of Administrative Detention

For some time, imprisonment after a judicial decision has no longer constituted the only, nor the main means for the repression of 'illegal' immigration. Hence, we will look at the two other kinds of detention: 'holding in waiting zones' and 'in administrative detention', that is, the most common treatment used for 'illegal' immigration since 1990.

Holding People in Waiting Zones

Waiting zones were established by the law dated 6 July 1992 that legalized (and made more transparent) a previous administrative practice. Such zones were set up to hold foreigners who arrived at the borders (by land, air, sea or rail routes) and were not authorized to enter French territory; some of them apply for political asylum. The waiting zone is hence used to receive them for the necessary time or to make them leave again, or even to examine their asylum application. Control is firstly exercised by the border police (PAF), who can hold someone for up to 72 hours, after which a judge can order an extension. In total, foreigners (individuals or families with children) can be held for up to 20 hours in waiting zones, on the basis of a judicial decision. Once this term has passed, if the police have not expelled them, they must let them into French territory but can immediately control them again, put them back into detention and bring them before the court for 'avoiding the execution of a refusal of entry measure', a crime that is liable to incur several months' imprisonment (and is generally accompanied by a ban from French territory). Even though the main waiting zones (the most important one is in Roissy-Charles De Gaulle airport, with around 170 places) are well known,

---

before imprisonment, added to around 30 per cent who were unemployed, that is, in total, 80 per cent. Obviously, the part played by illegal employment is not known). [*Editor's note*: As shown by some research works in Italy and in other countries, the mechanism of 'replacement' is confirmed here: the last arrivals are always worse off in every field, from housing, to illegal employment, to illegal activities and in turning into 'easy prey' for police productivity and racism alike – see Palidda, 2008a.]

ANAFE[44] estimates that there are more than a hundred that are sometimes not active and impossible to control (those for detention in police stations, or also in hotel rooms that are seized *ad hoc*). All of this takes place in living conditions that are often degrading and which associations as well as occasional observers have never stopped criticising (Loisy, 2005; Mermaz, 2001).

The number of foreigners detained in waiting zones grew from 1992 to 2001, a year in which it reached around 23,000 detentions. Since 2002, the figures (around 16,500 people detained in 2006) have decreased thanks to bilateral agreements and police and administrative practices that seek to dissuade migrants 'upstream'.

Administrative Detention

Foreigners accused by the police and punished by the public administration or courts for the sole offence of contravening norms on the policing of foreigners,[45] can be interned in *administrative detention centres and places* awaiting expulsion from French territory. Until 1981, foreigners undergoing expulsion proceedings were detained in prisons. When the left came to power in 1981, it sought to mark a break with the previous administration, creating a form of administrative detention that was independent of the prison administration. The law of 29 October 1981 hence created administrative detention for a maximum duration of seven days, but it did not organize its implementation at all and, in particular, in did not define specific places for it. In practice, these places are generally run-down, often under the control of the prison administration service or the state police, and some of them are none other than old internment camps from the Second World War.[46] In 1984, Administrative Detention Centres (CRA) were created in large cities and

---

44   National association for assisting foreigners at borders. ANAFE is a '1901 law association' established in 1989 for the purpose of ensuring an effective presence among foreigners who are not allowed entry at borders or await a decision on admission in order to apply for asylum, and hence to be able to exert pressure on public authorities so as to ensure that the fate reserved to such foreigners respects French law and the international conventions ratified by France. Plenty of information is available on its website: www. anafe.org

45   Over 80 per cent of the removal measures that are the reason for these detentions in CRAs are orders issued by the police chief to be accompanied back to the border due to irregular stays in France (and do not follow a guilty verdict for any offence). If arrests with a view to re-admission into third countries are added, such crimes (against the policing of foreigners) represent around 90 per cent of detentions in CRAs. Finally, one must also add the part of banning orders from French territory that Cimade is unable to provide figures for; this means that internments in CRAs due to mere offences against the 'policing of foreigners' make up 90–95 per cent of the total (Cimade, 2007).

46   [*Editor's note*: In such camps, even ordinary Italians who were immigrants in France and had not yet disowned their nationality were detained – on camps, see Various Authors, 2006.]

assistance for detained people was entrusted to a national association, Cimade.[47] Finally, the decree of 19 March 2001 regulates living conditions in the CRAs, setting the most elementary judicial and material norms.

For 15 years, in several instances, governments have extended the maximum duration of detention. In 1993, it was raised to 10 days, then to 12 in 1998, with its official goal always remaining that of enabling conditions to carry out expulsions. However, the law of 26 November 2003, the so-called Sarkozy law, was a real watershed, suddenly increasing the maximum length of detention from 12 to 32 days. This considerable extension was also accompanied by an increase in the number of available places that the decree of 12 July 2007 envisaged to raise to around 2,000 by the end of 2008, in the 26 CRAs (of which ten are certified as suitable to receive families with children).

Figure 10.3 illustrates this evolution. From 2003 to 2007 the number of available places grew from 739 to 1,724 (a 133 per cent increase) and the number of people detained in a year passed from 22,220 to 35,923 (a 62 per cent increase).

Moreover, the judicial and practical situation of Places for Administrative Detention (LRAs) remains more than problematic. LRAs are generally big isolated halls in police stations (or also of the air border police, that is, in airports) or even simple cells. In this case, we are dealing with provisional detention for a maximum of 48 hours, but it is not regulated by law as is the case for CRAs.[48] Taking into account the brevity of detentions and the fact that their visit is not required by law, Cimade workers do not intervene systematically there, and are only able to provide an estimate of the annual flow of interned people: between 10,000 and 15,000. Overall, administrative detention could hence concern an annual flow of around 50,000 internment measures.

---

47   Cimade, the 'ecumenical service for mutual aid', is a Christian anti-racist association established in the 1930s. For around the last twenty years, it has been the only association authorized to enter detention centres for the purpose of providing a mission of 'legal and social assistance' to detainees. Thus, it constitutes the only guarantee of a minimum of transparency on detention conditions. However, a decree dated 22 August 2008 intends to break its monopoly by creating regional 'allotments' and specifying that operators will be bound to maintain 'neutrality' and 'confidentiality', which will effectively impede the publication of this association's annual and national reports, which the government certainly deems to be excessively critical. The real threat is that this apparent 'opening to competition' may in fact lead to securing total acquiescence about detention (see www. cimade.org).

48   This has already been reported by associations, but also by the Court of Auditors in its 2006 report, as is also the case of a European Parliament report (European Parliament, 2007: 89).

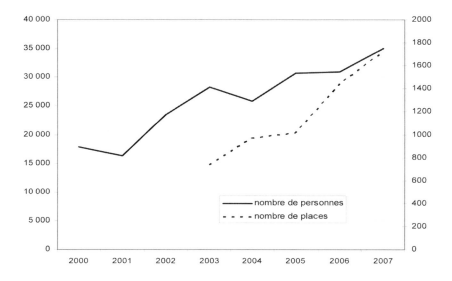

Source: Cimade (annual reports). Reading: the right scale corresponds to the number of places, the left one to the annual flow of people. Note: this data is collected by members of Cimade.

Figure 10.3   Number of available places and flow of people in adminstrative detention (2003–2007)

According to Cimade (2007: 6), this continuous extension of internment and of its length is such that administrative detention may be considered 'a form of imprisonment'. So much so, that people who are sometimes impossible to expel for legal reasons are often placed in administrative detention several times during the same year.[49] In conclusion, the policy that has been practised since 2003,

---

49   Cimade writes:

> In the Marseille CRA, out of 3,132 detainees in 2007, at least 260 had already been interned in the same CRA (at least 80 during the 3rd quarter and 98 in the last one). One foreigner was interned as many as five times during that year after his last 32-day detention. Three others returned four times, 13 for as many as three times and 160 twice, always in the same year. The others, 83 people detained just once in 2007, had already been interned repeatedly in the previous years. In principle, the Constitutional Council's 'reserve of interpretation' of 22 April 1997 authorizes just one repetition of placement in detention on the basis of the same expulsion measure. In practice, we find that it is not rare for police chief's offices to detain a foreigner several times on the basis of the same decision. On the other hand, it also happens that a foreigner who is heard more than once in the same year has a new expulsion decision issued against him and is hence subjected to a new denial of freedom. This distortion of procedure turns detention into a

combined with the expulsion quotas that have been set for every city police chief's office, moves towards a transformation of the nature of administrative detention:

> the latter, having reached an industrial stage by now, is no longer an exceptional measure and limited to the time required for organising a foreigner's expulsion, but it slowly turns into a means of repression and banishment of foreigners deemed undesirable.[50]

Furthermore, administrative detention is carried out in conditions that have been criticized as degrading on many occasions, not just by associations, but also by the State Auditors' Court (2004, p. 417 and following[51]), and that have not ceased to worsen over the last few years due to overcrowding, as is also the case in prisons.

Thus, in reality, the decrease in the number of foreigners who are imprisoned every year (from 26,948 to 17,232 from 1993 to 2007, that is, a 36 per cent decrease) conceals a continuous increase in the administrative forms of detention. With around 50,000 people placed in administrative detention and over 16,500 in waiting zones, the flow managed through these forms of detention is, by now, at least four times greater than that in the prison system.

> repressive measure [*Editor's note*: not a penal one]. Hence, internment is practised to organize the removal of a foreigner in an irregular situation but constitutes a 'punishment' applied to a person that the Administration is unable to expel. The same logic operates at the end of the first 32-day period of detention, when the police chief's offices, deeming that the foreigner has lied or not provided them the elements that would enable their identification and the issuing of an LPC (consular travel permit) by their country of origin, choose to refer him to a penal jurisdiction for 'obstructing a removal measure'. In such cases, the foreigner is more often condemned to serve a prison sentence accompanied by a ban from French territory (ITF). At the end of his imprisonment, he is put back into a detention centre. He may even be subjected to an ITF as his main punishment. In this case, at the end of the hearing, he is immediately taken to the CRA. In the majority of cases, being led back there is no more effective after this second term, and the foreigner is hence either released or referred again. Thus, numerous foreigners experience a denial of freedom that goes well beyond the 32 days that are theoretically envisaged by law. Trapped within a cycle composed by many detentions or of leaving-and-returning from detention to detention, there is no way out for them. (Cimade, 2008: 10)

[*Editor's note*: All these tragic changes of circumstance that have sometimes led to total desperation, self-harm or revolts in such centres have been taking place for over a decade and continuously occur, also in Italy and in other countries – among others, see the accounts of them in publications by ASGI, MD, Fulvio Vassallo Paleologo, and also on the websites of these associations.]

50   Cimade (2008); see also the analyses by Tsoukala (2009).
51   Cour des Comptes (2004).

Conclusions

The portrayal of the dangerousness of foreigners is undoubtedly one of the oldest social fears and one of the oldest resorts of political demagogy (Noiriel, 2007). From the mid-1980s, with the emergence of the *Front National* (Le Pen) on the political scene, the persistence of its electoral weight and of the importance of its xenophobic opinions,[52] this representation has acquired new vigour and has had such an impact in the political field that it has made debates on immigration and nationality something recurring. This criminalization of migrants has been further strengthened at a European level since the start of the 2000s, in the context of the 'war against terrorism' after the attacks of 11 September 200.[53] It is in this context that we have sought to update the analysis of available data on delinquency, victimization, criminalization and the penal treatment of foreigners. We have thus ascertained that: 1) foreigners and nationals have overall types and levels of victimization that are similar (with a slight over-victimization for certain foreigners), 2) the evolution of delinquency by foreigners investigated by the police forces is composed, first of all and mostly, by offences against the policing of foreigners, that is, 'crimes' of 'illegal' immigration; 3) if this 'administrative delinquency' is excluded, the part played by foreigners in overall delinquency has been decreasing for thirty years; 4) the composition of foreigners' delinquency is not dissimilar from that of French nationals; 5) however, foreigners are more severely punished than French people, for reasons that primarily concern the precariousness of their living conditions; 6) in spite of this, the proportion of foreigners in prisons is decreasing, something that can be explained through the development of forms of administrative internment and the speeding up of expulsions ('accompaniment to the border').

Hence, if foreigners occupy a relatively important part in the administrative and penal systems and particularly cause considerable work for the penal institutions, this is primarily because the public authorities repress 'illegal' immigration. As for the rest, the 'penal' delinquency of foreigners, like their victimization, cannot be distinguished from that of nationals. In reality, their over-representation in the delinquency investigated by the police and *gendarmerie* plausibly concerns two main factors that are quite strictly interconnected.

The first of these factors is their frequent precariousness, from every point of view (legal, economic, social, relational), which constitutes a risk factor in certain types of delinquency. Regardless of how limited they may be, the available indicators speak clearly. To highlight only a few of the socio-economic ones provided by the INSEE here, the unemployment rate for foreigners is more than two times higher than that for nationals (16.3 per cent compared with 7.5 per cent in 2007), and that of third-country (non-EU) foreigners is three times higher (22.2 per cent in 2007).

---

52   Which, every year, measure the surveys published in the reports by the Commission Nationale Consultative des Droits de l'Homme (CNCDH, 2004, 2008).
53   Melossi (2003); Palidda (2008a); Guild (2008).

This is notoriously a consequence of legislation that prevents their access to several million jobs due to discriminatory employment practices that are now recognized and measurable.[54] And this difference is not something that time reduces. This precariousness of living conditions is one of the aggravating factors for certain forms of delinquency that are forcefully repressed by penal institutions[55]. Thus, although the part thcy play in rccorded delinquency decreases overall, foreigners are very heavily over-represented in police statistics on 'shoplifting' (22 per cent of the people charged in 2007) and 'pickpocketing' (41 per cent of the people charged in 2007), quintessential poor people's crimes. Finally, if we add up the number of foreigners accused for the five police categories of 'shoplifting', 'pickpocketing', 'simple theft against private individuals in a public space', 'bag-snatching in the street' and 'theft in a parked car and of accessories of vehicles with number plates', we obtain a total of 21,049 foreigners, equivalent to 18 per cent of the total number of foreigners accused without taking 'administrative delinquency' into account. The weight of this petty predatory delinquency in the street is therefore important. If, to finish off, we add the foreigners accused of the use and sale of drugs[56] and those prosecuted for 'insult, rebellion and violence against public officials', we reach a total of 34,623 people prosecuted as a result of controls in the street, that is, around 30 per cent of the total number of foreigners accused outside of the field of 'administrative delinquency'.

This introduces the discussion of the second factor of over-representation of foreigners in prosecuted delinquency: over-exposure to police controls in the street. As has already been stated by Robert and Tournier (1991: 85–6), non-European foreigners constitute

> a population that has high visibility: heavily struck by unemployment, overladen with low-skilled [people], often precariously housed, migrants have living conditions that expose them to being observed. For many of them, their physical appearance and sometimes their clothing enhances their visibility… is a policing of appearance that leads to detention. Moreover, the suspected authors can certainly not oppose the police investigation.

Such a claim is confirmed by research works on the practices and mentality of the police, summed up by two other researchers:

---

54   The poverty rate is far higher among foreign families as well: while 8 per cent of the totality of children lived below the poverty threshold in the late 1990s, this rate for children of parents who are not EU nationals was above 30 per cent, that is, a ratio of almost 1 to 4 (Dell, Legendre, Ponthieux, 2003).

55   Robert, Aubusson de Cavarlay, Pottier, Tournier (1985); Jackson (1997); Various Authors (2002).

56   To distinguish these from trafficking, which, on the one hand, involves foreigners that often do not live in France, and on the other, a majority of whom are undoubtably accused at the end of judicial police inquiries rather than controls in the street.

All the researchers who have closely observed police practices, both in France and abroad, come to the conclusion that it is a matter of a generalized racist discourse that constitutes a veritable norm for police officers to which it is difficult, as a low-level police officer, to escape from and even more to oppose. The character of this police racism as being the norm, firstly turns it into an element of policing culture, separate from customary racism or that of the social layers from which the police officers are drawn, and does not have the character of an ideological or doctrinal construct. ... one does not enter the police due to being racist, one becomes so through the process of professional socialisation. In other terms, the habit of judging individuals on the basis of their supposed ethnic characteristics is acquired in practice, during the course of professional socialisation. ... racist representations have an operative character, insofar as they allow to differentiate among individuals. In practice, by directing police surveillance, they contribute to the mechanism of creative prediction. In some ways, they constitute work tools and form part of an overall body of practical knowledge that shape the backdrop, the reference for policing work. Resorting to ethnic features has a functional character for police officers, as do age and gender, insofar as the policing of the streets primarily refers back to a conception of normality that is conceived as the conformity of a type of population, of a space and of a given moment, to the norm. Any deviation between these three parameters primes police suspicion and may lead to an intervention. (Lévy and Zauberman, 1998: 293–4)[57]

It is always this sort of 'ethnic profiling' that drives a part of the interventions by the police in the street, in France like in other countries, *a fortiori* in the 'post-11 September 2001' context,[58] towards an era of 'new' predictions on the dangerousness of 'actuarial justice' (Harcourt, 2007) and under the rule of the 'new immigration policy', French-style. And it is to be feared that all of this may merely make discriminatory police practices that specifically target migrants coming from the former colonies regain relevance, starting – now as always – from young men of Maghreb-country origins with whom France appears to have a sort of unwitting account to settle ever since the Algerian War.

---

57   A more developed and updated version can be found in Lévy and Zauberman (2003).

58   Goodey (2006); Harcourt (2007).

Chapter 11

Criminalization and Victimization of Immigrants in Germany

Hans-Joerg Albrecht

Introduction: Immigration and the Problem of Social Cohesion

Immigration and its links to crime and victimization continue to receive widespread and ambiguous attention in Germany. When two immigrant youths in December 2007 assaulted and seriously injured an old person in a Munich subway station a nationwide debate ensued on how to deal with juvenile immigrant chronic offenders. The Munich subway case figured also prominently in the January 2008 election campaigns in the state of Hesse[1] (although the outcome of elections demonstrated clearly that the conservative Christian-Democratic Union party could not profit from emphasizing immigration and violence [2]). Beside demands for toughening youth criminal law, requests for stricter enforcement of deportation orders were voiced; the debate then centred around questions of integration of immigrants, in particular also the question of what efforts with respect to integration should be exacted from immigrants and immigrant communities. Some weeks later a fire destroyed an apartment building in Ludwigshafen, a middle-sized city in the southwest of Germany, leaving nine people of Turkish descent dead and several others seriously injured. In the wake of the deadly fire it was quickly assumed that right-wing extremists may have been responsible for setting fire to the apartment building. Parallels were drawn to the deadly fire bombings of Turkish-owned houses in the first half of the 1990s (Moelln and Solingen) which fell into a period of dramatic increase in hate violence shortly after reunification and of political conflicts on asylum and restrictions on asylum.[3] While responsibility for the deadly incident remains unclear today, the case has resulted in heavy coverage in Turkish media, in Turkish investigators being sent to Germany for working with German police as well as in being placed high on the agenda of a rather uneasy meeting between the German chancellor and her Turkish counterpart in

---

1   www.focus.de/politik/deutschland/jugendgewalt/unions-wahlkampf_aid_
232321.html; www.ad-hoc-news.de/Politik-News/de/14789577/(Zusammenfassung+Neu+
Reaktionen)+Parteien+streiten+um

2   www.forschungsgruppe.de/Studien/Wahlanalysen/Kurzanalysen/Newsl_Hess_
Nied08.pdf

3   Esser (1999).

February 2008. [4] On the occasion of his visit the Turkish Premier appealed to his countrymen and advised them not to forget their being Turkish. These appeals sparked in turn furious public comments alleging the purposeful creation of obstacles to integration of immigrants of Turkish descent.

These cases provide ample evidence that the social problem of immigration has diversified along various perspectives among which the question of social integration of immigrant minorities certainly stands out. The process of immigration so far has led in Germany (and elsewhere in Europe) to the re-emergence of questions of cultural, ethnic and religious divides in society and ultimately to the question of how social and political integration can be achieved under conditions of ethnic and religious diversity (and modernity). The ongoing discussion on the rise of a 'parallel society'[5] points in particular to Muslim immigrants who are perceived to detach themselves from mainstream society.

Evidently, the particular German approach to political integration, that is, a federal state with a careful balance between the federal and the state level, is not well-suited to respond to problems of social cohesion and integration in face of substantial groups of immigrants bringing with them ethnic, cultural and religious differences. Federalism was, as was the French tradition of secular Republicanism or the British approach of community-oriented pluralism, a fairly efficient approach to identity building and social cohesion in the nineteenth and twentieth centuries, but does not provide for solutions in the new millennium.

It is also clear that the traditional concept of immigration obviously does not fit immigration in Germany. Rather than conventional assimilation or integration immigration generates networks of migration and a pluralism of 'transnational communities'.[6] This is facilitated by efficient systems of transportation and by the fact that immigration to Germany starts from European countries (including Turkey) or neighbouring regions (as, for example, the Maghreb countries and the Near East).

Immigration, Immigration Policies in Germany

Post-Second World War Germany has experienced quite a short history of immigration, with immigration starting around 1960 and significant changes in immigration patterns occurring in the subsequent decades. While the debate in the 1960s and 1970s has emphasized the concept of 'guest-workers' (migrant workers assumed to return to their home countries after a more or less extended period of

---

4   See www.bundesregierung.de/nn_1516/Content/DE/Mitschrift/Pressekonferenzen/2008/02/2008-02-08-merkel-erdogan-pk.html

5   Halm and Sauer (2006).

6   Nell (2004).

work), the 1990s saw a growing recognition that in fact immigration had taken place.[7]

The ethnic composition of immigrants and triggers for migration have changed significantly over the last 50 years. Sending countries from which the migrant work force originated have changed, with South-East European countries (former Yugoslavia and Turkey) replacing South-West European countries (Italy, Spain, Portugal). At the beginning of the 1960s approximately two-thirds of the foreign population came from countries of the present European Community. In the 1990s, their share had dropped to less than 30 per cent. Turkish immigrants and immigrants from the former Yugoslavia today account for almost half of the resident immigrant population in Germany. Furthermore, immigrants from developing countries in Africa and Asia have made up substantial proportions of the immigrant population since the second half of the 1980s.

The status of foreign nationals in Germany differs as different legal standards apply to citizens of European Community countries, Turkish citizens (who are in-between European Community status and Non-European Community status) and citizens of Non-European Community states). German immigration law makes distinctions between tourists (or short-term visitors), foreign nationals joining the labour force (or enrolling at schools or universities), asylum seekers and refugees (to whom the Geneva Convention applies). Complete abolition of schemes set up for hiring workers abroad and severe restrictions on granting permissions for non-EC foreigners to work in Germany then obviously led in the 1990s to larger numbers of foreigners applying for asylum (which until amendments of the German constitution and the immigration law had the effect of a preliminary permission to stay on German territory awaiting the final decision on asylum). A rather unusual immigration phenomenon concerns ethnic Germans whose ancestors emigrated to Poland, Russia or Romania and who are entitled to be re-naturalized (under the condition that evidence on German origins is provided). Some 4.5 million ethnic Germans were re-naturalized between the early 1950s and 2007,[8] the majority of whom have migrated to Germany since the second half of the 1980s,[9] making them the most important (immigrant and ethnic) minority in quantitative terms. Since 1990, ethnic Germans migrating to Germany have come mostly from countries of the former Soviet Union and face increasingly problematic conditions for integration. The number of migrants from the former Soviet Union is decreasing significantly, though, due also to more restrictive admission rules.[10]

A look at the spatial distribution reveals regional differences in the density of immigrants. The majority of immigrants are drawn to the western part of Germany. In 2007 the proportion of immigrants in the population of the 'New Bundesländer'

---

7   Bade (2006).
8   Sachverständigenrat für Zuwanderung und Integration (2004: 62).
9   Bayerisches Staatsministerium für Arbeit und Sozialordnung (2008).
10   Currle (2004: 55–8).

(the former German Democratic Republic, 16 per cent of the total population in Germany) amounted to 2.4 per cent.[11]

Legal and institutional changes as regards immigration have come slowly in Germany, with the traditional concept of policing-oriented immigration laws (Ausländergesetz) and its focus on risk control and prevention replaced only recently by a new immigration law. The amended immigration law (Gesetz zur Steuerung und Begrenzung der Zuwanderung und zur Regelung des Aufenthalts und der Integration von Unionsbürgern und Ausländern) came into force in 2005 and places more weight on naturalization and integration. The title of the new law combines restriction and regulation of immigration on the one hand and integration of European Union citizens and foreign nationals on the other hand. The focus switched (though not completely) from a rather restrictive approach to naturalization to an approach that seeks to facilitate integration through reducing the length of stay before naturalization can be applied for, accepting to a certain extent dual citizenship and providing for more protection against deportation. Part of the overhauling of the normative framework of immigration was the introduction of new institutions, like for example an ombudsman for immigration (Ausländerbeauftragte), the Council of Experts on Immigration (Sachverständigenrat für Zuwanderung und Integration) and a new concern for basic information on the economic, social etc. situation of immigrants.[12] In 2006, The Federal Ministry of Interior founded the 'German Islamic Conference' seeking to initiate a dialogue between Islamic associations and state institutions as well as civil society.[13] These changes have been encouraged by the obvious social problems visible in ghettoization in metropolitan areas and concerns about the emergence of 'parallel societies', but also through human rights perspectives that were particularly expressed in reports of the Council of Europe and United Nations-based institutions as well as by the efforts of NGOs which emphasize the particular problems experienced by immigrants.[14]

The history of ethnic and racial minorities in twentieth-century Germany, as well as that of research on minorities, is overshadowed by the murderous terror regime German fascism exerted in Europe during the 1930s and 1940s.[15] One of the lessons drawn from this period concerns the elimination of information on race and ethnicity from official data systems (and, furthermore, from most questionnaires and interview forms used in criminological research). So, official statistics, be they

---

11   Statistisches Bundesamt: Bevölkerung und Erwerbstätigkeit (2008, Table 3.3).

12   Sachverständigenrat für Zuwanderung und Integration (2004: 396).

13   See www.deutsche-islam-konferenz.de

14   European Commission against Racism and Intolerance: *Third Report on Germany*. Adopted on 5 December 2003. Strasbourg 2004; Report of the Committee on the Elimination of Racial Discrimination: Seventy-second session (18 February–7 March 2008), Seventy-third session (28 July–15 August 2008), General Assembly, Official Records, Sixty-third session, Supplement No. 18 (A/63/18), p. 38.

15   Bade (2006: 3).

crime or judicial statistics, be they general population statistics, cannot account for the racial or ethnic composition of the German population. Only estimates are available: for example, on the size of the group of black or Afro-Germans ranging between 40,000 and 50,000.[16] Panel research on the number of foreign-born residents reveals that some 10 per cent of the population belong to immigrant groups, while official statistics give a 7 per cent share of foreign nationals in the population at large.[17] However, the foreign-born group does not include second or third generations of immigrants, among whom a substantial proportion has been naturalized. Due to a legal amendment of 1998, under certain conditions children born to immigrant foreign nationals automatically adopt German citizenship, and until the beginning of the twenty-first century ethnic Germans immigrating from countries of the former Soviet bloc automatically received German citizenship after arriving in Germany. The variable 'nationality' or 'citizenship' therefore may be used only as a rather crude proxy in analysing immigrant groups.

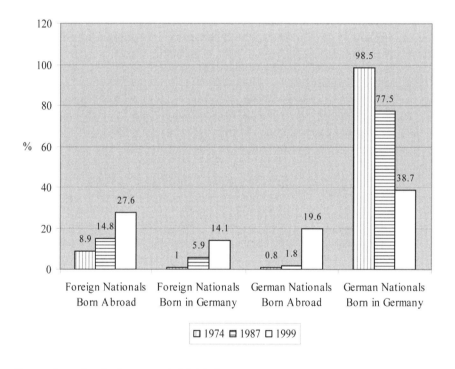

Source: Jugendstrafvollzugsanstalt Adelsheim.

Figure 11.1   Ethnicities in German youth prisons (%)

---

16   Forbes and Mead (1992: 39).
17   Sachverständigenrat für Zuwanderung und Integration (2004: 68).

The problems that arise from the lack of valid data when interpreting official, in particular crime-related statistics, become apparent when looking at changes of inmate composition in German youth prisons (see Figure 11.1). Data from the state of Baden-Wuerttemberg demonstrate that over a period of some 25 years the composition of youth prison inmates changed completely. While in the mid 1970s virtually all inmates were German citizens, in 1999 young German nationals accounted only for less than 40 per cent of prison inmates. If one was relying only on the variable nationality it would go unnoticed that immigrant youth in fact represent the majority of prison inmates today.

Related to these concerns are new approaches in national census studies to account for the size of the immigrant population and the social conditions in which immigrants find themselves. With that, the question is put forward on how and through what criteria an immigrant is defined and how social groups are construed. In particular, the question comes up, who is an immigrant and how long does one remain an immigrant? The first micro census study that looked at the proportion of immigrants in Germany revealed quite interesting data in 2005. In the micro census immigrants were defined as all those persons who migrated to Germany after 1949 as well as those born in Germany as foreign nationals and those born as German citizens with at least one immigrant parent or one parent born as a foreign national in Germany.[18] While on the basis of nationality or citizenship the proportion of immigrants was approximately 9 per cent of the (resident) population in the new millennium,[19] the proportion of immigrants (defined according to the criteria mentioned above) amounted to 18.6 per cent in 2005[20] and 18.7 per cent in 2007.[21] The distribution of immigrants along regions of origin is displayed in Figure 11.2.

However, most information on the social and other characteristics of immigrants is derived from data collection on foreign nationals. Statistical information on the ethnic or racial composition of the population is not available. The complete neglect of ethnic or racial information in official statistics and censuses is a deliberate response to German fascism and the Holocaust which was facilitated by the availability of information on religion and ethnicity but has been criticized recently by the Committee on the Elimination of Racial Discrimination.[22]

---

18   Statistisches Bundesamt: Bevölkerung und Erwerbstätigkeit. *Bevölkerung mit Migrationshintergrund – Ergebnisse des Mikrozensus 2007–*. Wiesbaden 2008: 6.

19   Statistisches Bundesamt: Bevölkerung und Erwerbstätigkeit 2007. Wiesbaden 2008, Table 1.2.

20   Statistisches Bundesamt: Bevölkerung und Erwerbstätigkeit. *Bevölkerung mit Migrationshintergrund - Ergebnisse des Mikrozensus 2005–*. Wiesbaden 2007: 7.

21   Statistisches Bundesamt: Bevölkerung und Erwerbstätigkeit. *Bevölkerung mit Migrationshintergrund- Ergebnisse des Mikrozensus 2007*. Wiesbaden 2008: 32.

22   Report of the Committee on the Elimination of Racial Discrimination: Seventy-second session (18 February–7 March 2008), Seventy-third session (28 July–15 August 2008), General Assembly, Official Records, Sixty-third session, Supplement No. 18 (A/63/18), p. 40.

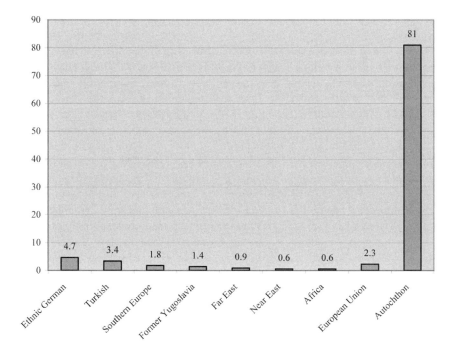

Source: Institut für Bevölkerung und Entwicklung: *Ungenutzte Potenziale. Zur Lage der Integration in Deutschland*. Berlin 2009.

Figure 11.2   Regions of immigrants' origin (%)

According to data available from the National Office for Statistics, foreign nationals are disproportionally affected by unemployment, with unemployment rates of approximately 20 per cent among foreign nationals and 10 per cent among the German-born labour force.[23] In many aspects they display characteristics of the lower working class, seen for instance from housing, social security dependency (which is threefold more among foreign nationals), education and income levels.[24] A particularly precarious situation is found among young immigrants. For them, research on educational achievements and integration in the labour market displays

---

23   Statistisches Bundesamt: *Stand und Entwicklung der Erwerbstätigkeit 2004*. Wiesbaden 2005; see also micro census data on unemployment among immigrants Statistisches Bundesamt: Bevölkerung und Erwerbstätigkeit. *Bevölkerung mit Migrationshintergrund – Ergebnisse des Mikrozensus 2007–*. Wiesbaden 2008: 236.
24   Anhut and Heitmeyer (2000: 22); Tiemann (2004: 37).

significant differences compared to German young people.[25] The emergence of profound social inequality is driven also by a system of education and formation which evidently does not cater to the special needs of young immigrants.[26] Spatial segregation of immigrants is followed by cultural segregation. Such cultural segregation was noticed, for example, with an increase in religiousness in the group of Turkish immigrants.[27]

The current situation of immigrants may partially be explained by social and economic changes in recent decades that in general have worked to the disadvantage of immigrants. The success stories of immigration which are known from nineteenth and even twentieth century Europe and North America concern immigrant groups which managed to work their way up and to integrate (economically and culturally) into mainstream society. So, for example, several waves of Polish labour immigrants settled at the end of the nineteenth and the beginning of the twentieth century in the West of Germany (in particular in coal-mining areas); they melted quite rapidly into mainstream society and became invisible as a distinct group within half of a century. The disappearance of low-skilled work and the transformation of industrial societies into service and information societies dependent on high-skilled workers have contributed to change labour markets drastically and with that the basic framework of traditional mechanisms of social integration (which always was based upon labour and employment). Shadow economies, black markets and low wage jobs, in particular in metropolitan areas, now offer precarious employment opportunities for newly arriving immigrants and the second and third generations of immigrants who have settled down during the last four decades. Political changes in Europe have contributed to affect the legal status of immigrants considerably through changing the statutory framework of immigration as well as enforcement policies. While in the 1960s and 1970s most immigrants entered Germany legally (as labour immigrants or on the basis of family reunification), today the legal status of new arrivals points to illegality or to the precarious status of asylum seekers, refugees and merely tolerated immigrants who are subject to strict administrative controls and threatened by serious risks of criminalization (as a consequence of not complying with administrative rules assigning place of residence). With the transformation of labour markets into places where highly skilled workers are needed, immigrants have come to have an image of being unemployed and dependent on social security. Crime policy agendas are not only preoccupied by crime and victimization but in particular by assumed precursors of crime and deviance such as family problems, unemployment, lack of education and professional training.

---

25   Anhut, and Heitmeyer (2000); Tiemann (2004: 37); Statistisches Bundesamt (2004).

26   Gomollaa and Radtke (2002).

27   Goldberg and Sauer (2003: 7).

Immigration, Crime and Integration

Rates of police-recorded foreign suspects have increased continuously in Germany, reflecting fairly well increasing numbers of immigrants. In 1953, when police statistics had been published for the first time after World War II, the proportion of foreign suspects had been as low as 1.7per cent.[28] Figure 11.3 displays data on the resident foreign population in Germany and on the rates of foreign national suspects from 1961 to 2007. It is evident from these data that foreign nationals are disproportionally represented in police statistics. However, it is also clear that the significant changes in the rates of foreign national suspects are independent of the proportion of the resident foreign population. Although the proportion of foreign nationals in the resident population at large did not change significantly between the beginning of the 1990s and 2007, the rate of foreign suspects drops in the same period by approximately one third. This drop reflects the drastic decrease in the number of asylum seekers from 1993 on (when the German constitution in respect of the right of asylum had been amended and applications for asylum had put under far-reaching restrictions). The decrease is especially marked in the area of petty property crimes (and here in the area of shoplifting) which gives also a significant hint as to the types of crimes where asylum seekers are most active.

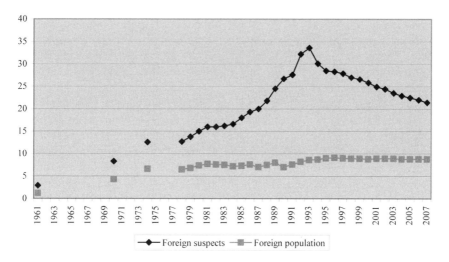

Sources: Bundeskriminalamt   (ed.):   *Polizeiliche   Kriminalstatistik   1961–2007.* Wiesbaden 1962–2008; Statistisches Bundesamt: Bevölkerung und Erwerbstätigkeit. *Bevölkerungsfortschreibung 2007*. Wiesbaden 2008, Table 1.2.

Figure 11.3   Foreign suspects and the proportion of foreign nationals in the population (%) 1961–2007

---

28   Albrecht (1997).

When summarizing the knowledge that is available so far on links between immigration on the one hand and police-recorded crime on the other hand, we may conclude that some immigrant groups exhibit much higher proportions of crime participation or crime involvement than do majority groups. The proportion of immigrant suspects is particularly high in the case of violent crime. However, some immigrant groups display the same degree of crime involvement or even less participation in crime than is observed in the majority group. First-generation immigrants of the 1950s and 1960s obviously have been involved much less in crime than second- or third-generation immigrants and immigrants arriving in the 1980s and 1990s. What most immigrant groups have in common is a socially and economically disadvantageous and precarious position. But cultural differences between socially similarly situated groups can result in quite different crime patterns, different in terms of both the structure and the magnitude of crime involvement. Cultural differences found between immigrant groups concern capacity for community building and for preservation of the cultural and ethnic homogeneity of the immigrant group.

Discussion on immigration and crime during the last two decades has emphasized the particular problems of young immigrants (belonging to the second and third generations). In groups of young immigrants, violence and chronic offending as well as gang activities are assumed to play a significant role. According to Berlin police data, approximately 45 per cent of youth violent crime committed in groups is linked to young immigrants.[29] However, police-recorded crime data come with two problems: they identify immigrants through the variable nationality (which may lead to underestimation of crime participation rates) and cannot account for crimes not reported by victims.

Over the last decade various self-report studies have been carried out with the aim of testing assumptions of disproportional crime involvement among young immigrants. Most of these surveys have been implemented in the form of school surveys (focusing on 15–18 year-olds). While it was found that crime participation rates at large do not differ significantly between young Germans and various groups of young immigrants (Naplava 2002), in particular similar participation rates in property crime and drug use is noted, all studies carried out so far confirm disproportional involvement in violent crime such as assault and (street) robbery, in particular by young Turkish immigrants and by young immigrants coming from the South-East of Europe (former Yugoslavia)[30] Young immigrants of Turkish descent are also more prone to resort to violence in conflict situations when controlling for the extent of inter- and intra-ethnic conflicts (Müller, 2000). The greater import of violence for Turkish boys is explained by strong affiliation to gangs and the particular relevance of honour in Turkish communities (Müller, 2000: 284). Moreover, young immigrants report more experience of corporal

---

29   Der Polizeipräsident in Berlin (2007: 87).

30   Heitmeyer (1995); Tillmann, Holler-Nowitzki, Holtappels, Meier, Popp (2000); Enzmann and Wetzels (2000); Oberwittler, Blank, Köllisch, Naplava (2001).

punishment in childhood (Baier and Others, 2009). If emphasis is placed on the role of honour in the interpretation and explanation of violence among young Turkish males (Gesemann, 2004: 67–8) it should also be considered that this refers to classic themes in research on subcultures and gangs (Miller, 1979; Graham and Wells, 2003). Violence exerted by young males comes with motives such as 'male honour' and a 'desire for violence' (Graham and Wells, 2003: 560). Such motives are embedded in systems of group loyalty and solidarity and the search for social status. However, it seems questionable that a particular Turkish culture of honour and reputation adds to the explanation of violence among young men. Empirical evidence does not yet exist which would confirm that young male immigrants differ from their indigenous counterparts in terms of violence-triggering motives. Affiliation with a gang at least is similarly strong in groups of young Germans, Turkish and ethnic German immigrants who are willing to use violence in solving conflicts (ca. 80 per cent) (Müller, 2000: 291). Moreover, only small differences are found as regards bonds to the family. Violence-prone Turkish and ethnic German youth do agree to a lesser extent than other youth with the idea that immigrants should adjust to German culture and language (Müller, 2000: 287).

In the explanation of youth violence, chronic offending and the increase of youth violence special emphasis is laid on the disappearance of unskilled labour and the growing demand on qualification and training as a requirement for access to the labour market. From that, it is concluded, follow processes of social exclusion and economic marginalization, as well as the growing concentration of problem youth in inner-city disadvantaged neighbourhoods. It is also assumed that there is a long-term trend towards formal control of youth, visible in an increase in formal complaints, and which reflects a deep change in the risk management of children and juveniles (Oberwittler and Köllisch, 2004: 144–7).

Discrimination and Criminal Justice

Theoretical approaches to the issue of discrimination and of biased law enforcement must first of all be differentiated into those assumptions related to immigrant minorities' crime involvement as a serious social problem and furthermore into hypotheses concerning decision-making in policing and in the administrative and criminal justice system. Assumptions about the problem of foreign nationals' contribution to crime can be divided roughly into the theory of scape-goating and the theory of conflicts over resources (employment, housing etc.). Furthermore, administrative agencies' search for 'new' social problems has been identified, as well as the potential function of the social problem of foreigners' crime involvment being used to stabilize political power and rally political support within majority groups.

With respect to the role of police in initiating criminal investigations, it should be noted that the German police are not entitled to formal decision-making on arrest. The German police, when notified about some criminal event, investigate the case and, after investigation process the case to the public prosecutors' office where the actual decision about bringing the case to court (or to arrest in terms of pre-trial detention) is made. Consensus seems to exist on the point that the probability of being processed as a criminal suspect, given a certain number of offences committed, is more or less the same for minority and majority offenders. The probability of being suspected of a criminal offence is extremely low in the case of most offences any way, and police investigations seem to be guided by the characteristics of the offence, especially the seriousness of the offence, in the first place. It has been hypothesized that higher rates of suspects among ethnic minorities could be the consequence of ethnic minority members confronting the police more negatively during encounters than majority members do. But preliminary research based upon an experimental design does not lend support to this assumption. Ethnic minority suspects in general seem even to be more co-operative while being interrogated by police. Going further in the criminal process, the findings do not lend support to the assumption of a greater risk of minority suspects being formally charged and indicted with a criminal offence (Kubink, 1993: 60). However, criticism that foreign nationals are treated in a discriminating way certainly has some merits. In some areas, such as drug law enforcement, law enforcement strategies adopt ethnic profiling and target selected ethnic minorities (involved in various street drug distribution networks). Some studies have dealt with the attitudes and perceptions of the police towards ethnic and immigrant minorities. The questions put forward concern whether discrimination and racism reflects systematic patterns or whether such attitudes reflect a 'black sheep' theory often adopted by state authorities that claims that abusive behaviour is restricted to exceptional cases only (Jaschke, 1997: 191).

Discriminatory treatment and inequality have been raised as issues in the context of explaining the disproportional share of foreign nationals (or immigrants) in police-recorded crime. At the beginning of the 1990s a survey of police officers revealed that a majority among them felt that there were differences between average citizens and immigrants which justify differential treatment. The reasons why immigrants legitimately may be treated differently refer to their immigration status and exploitative behaviour, different values and different behaviour patterns. In general, the data convey the view that police perceive immigrants to be different (Franzke, 1993: 616).

Interpretation of research carried out so far points to structural problems in the relationship between immigrants and the police. Immigrants (in particular immigrants arriving since the 1990s) are placed in disadvantageous conditions. High unemployment rates and the problem of access to the labour market are associated with high participation rates in shadow economies. This is particularly true for illegal immigrants (Albrecht, 2006). High participation rates in drug markets or other informal economies expose immigrants to a high rate of encounters with law enforcement.

Studies have dealt until now with attitudes and perceptions of the police. While data on the use of force in general or police practices as regards stop and search procedures are not available, fatal and other use of firearms is accounted for by information collected by the ministries of the interior. These data do not, however, distinguish between immigrants and other groups as regards victims of police force. Longitudinal data on the use of fatal force by the police reveal that the number of persons killed or injured by police firearms is stable (and tentatively on the decline), as is the use of guns against persons in general.[31] During the last two decades police have used firearms against individuals on an average of 60–70 occasions per year. On average some 10 persons are killed and some 30 are injured as a result of the use of firearms by the police. Although in-depth studies on these cases have not been carried out, it seems that virtually all of the cases of fatal use of firearms emerge from situations that do not have the potential of fueling ethnic tensions.

Studies on trust in the police as an institution reveal that differences between German youth and various immigrant groups are not marked. While West German, Italian and Greek youth declare that they distrust police in general at a rate of approximately 25 per cent, Turkish youth and East German youth express this view at a rate of 37 and 33 per cent, respectively. Trust and mistrust in the police thus might be explained not by the status of an immigrant but by the general feeling of belonging to a marginalized and deprived group in society. The differences, however, are not particularly marked when looking at the groups at large. Differences become more pronounced when introducing variables such as gender, education and place of residence. Mistrust in the police is particularly large in the metropolitan area of Berlin where some 84 per cent of Turkish interviewees declare that they have no or only limited trust in the police (Gesemann, 2003: 211). This certainly indicates a deep ethnic divide as the corresponding rate among German young people amounts to approximately 30 per cent. An explanation may be found in a process of spatial segregation and the emergence of inner-city ghettos and inner-city ethnic communities which – also due to the substantial population of immigrants of Turkish origin – in Berlin have gained significant momentum (Groenemeyer and Mansel, 2003). Mistrust in the police in metropolitan areas may be fueled also by the frequency of (arrest-related) contacts between police and immigrant youth which is especially marked in large cities.

Data from the Freiburg Cohort Study reveal that non-prosecution rates at large do not differ for first offenders and recidivating youth when comparing German, ethnic German and foreign youth offenders in 1985 and 1995. However, there are differences in non-prosecution rates for violent offences. Foreign juvenile offenders are less likely to have their cases dismissed.

---

31   Innenministerium Baden-Württemberg: *Schusswaffengebrauch der Polizei.* Stuttgart, Pressestelle Innenministerium 2005.

Table 11.1   Non-prosecution rates (%) in two birth cohorts

(birth cohorts 1970, 1980 at age 16, male)

	German			Ethnic German			Foreign		
	1st Offender		2nd	1st Offender		2nd	1st Offender		2nd
	1985	1995	1995	1985	1995	1995	1985	1995	1995
Theft	60	82	77	61	85	82	54	81	82
Aggravated Theft	22	37	22	20	49	14	18	27	17
Violence	32	49	37	38	24	9	32	28	18
Total	55	76	60	55	78	60	50	71	66

Source: Data from the Freiburg Cohort Survey.

Quite small effects of immigration status on sentencing can be found. Foreign nationals run a somewhat higher risk of receiving prison or custodial sentences and are somewhat less likely to receive suspended sentences or probation (Steinhilper, 1986). But in general, ethnic and minority variables add only very modestly to the explanation of sentencing variation (Greger, 1987; Albrecht, 1994). This holds true not only for adult criminal sentencing but also for dispositions in juvenile criminal cases (Geißler and Marißen, 1990; Oppermann, 1987; Albrecht and Pfeiffer, 1979). The slight difference with respect to juvenile imprisonment between young German offenders and young foreigners (2.4 per cent vs. 3.4 per cent of all offenders adjudicated and sentenced) found by Geißler and Marißen (1990) is mostly due to sentences for drug trafficking. If controlling for this offence, the difference fades away. It is especially noteworthy that differences in dispositions are virtually non-existent in the case of violent crimes and sexual offences; similar results have been obtained by Oppermann (1987). As ethnicity is a diffuse status variable, it can be assumed that its impact on sentencing is less pronounced or even non-existent in cases where a consistent set of offence- and offender-related characteristics (e.g. seriousness of the offence, prior record) or an obvious need for adopting tariffs in sentencing (petty cases) or administrative convenience point to rather obvious dispositional strategies (Unnever and Hembroff, 1988). Therefore, only an inconsistent particular set of characteristics may be assumed to trigger effects of ethnicity or nationality on sentencing. It has been hypothesized that the relatively small effects of ethnic variables on sentencing outcomes might be due to the fact that substantial numbers of serious personal crimes committed by minority offenders involve a minority victim, too, and that effects might turn out to be larger when including crimes involving minority offenders and victims from the majority group. Up to now this question has not been dealt with adequately.

Immigrants and Victimization

The relationship between immigration and victimization has never been given the attention that active participation of immigrants in crime has received in Germany. While police statistics account for the nationality of suspects, they do not account for the nationality (or the immigration status) of victims. Victim surveys carried out in Germany rarely have systematically included immigrant populations. From the perspective of immigration research, in particular research on illegal immigration, the issue of victimization did not play a role either.[32]

Consideration of the victim perspective with respect to immigrants during the last two decades has been influenced by several issues and different political interests that reflect also to a certain extent immigrants' assumed potential for creating conflicts and violence due to segregation and cultural otherness.

At the beginning of the 1990s it was the issue of hate violence (or xenophobic violence) which attracted attention due to a rise in right-wing extremism and a series of large-scale violent acts toward asylum seekers and other immigrants. A second issue that was placed prominently on political agendas concerns honour killings. A third issue addresses the cycle of violence, with allegations that high levels of domestic violence found in immigrant (in particular Turkish) families negatively affect children and makes them prone to become themselves violent youth and young adults (Baier and Others, 2009). Finally, victims of trafficking have been made a topic of concern. Here, several sensitive social problems are confounded: prostitution, illegal immigration and organized crime (Albrecht, 2007).

The risk of foreign nationals of becoming victims of crime was – on the basis of police-recorded crime – studied thoroughly for the first time in the 1990s in Bavaria (Luff and Gerum, 1995: 48). From this study it is known that the share of foreign national victims accounts for some 11 per cent of all victims registered in police statistics. For various nationalities the rate of violent victimization is two to five times the rate observed for German nationals (Luff and Gerum, 1995: 176). A separate study of four police districts found a share of 54 per cent of foreign national victims of homicide/murder and an elevated rate of foreign national victims of rape and assault (close to 30 per cent of rape and assault victims are foreign nationals) (Luff and Gerum, 1995: 172). It can be assumed also that crime reporting by foreign nationals is strongly influenced by immigration status as illegals account for 0.5 per cent of all crime reported by foreign victims (Luff and Gerum, 1995: 126) and settled labour migrants were overrepresented among victims coming to the attention of police.

---

32   See, for example, Eichenhofer (1999).

Data from the 2005 European Crime Survey provide for the first time information on victimization rates for a national and representative sample which includes immigrants. According to these data (N=2,000, telephone survey), victimization rates are more or less the same for immigrants and non-immigrants across a selection of property and personal criminal offences.

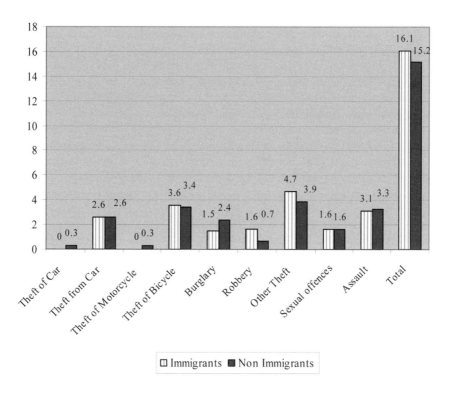

Source: European Crime Survey 2005.

Figure 11.4   Prevalence of victimization (last 12 months) among immigrants and non-immigrants in Germany

Germany has developed and implemented devices aimed at counting racist (xenophobic, anti-semitic) offences and providing thus a basis of assessing the extent of racist crime.

Summarizing the available evidence on racial violence, the following can be concluded. First, the general problem of all police-registered crime data, namely that they are dependent on reporting by victims and by resources invested in investigating (victimless) crime (such as incitement to racial hatred through the internet or other propaganda crime) affects particularly hate crimes where the specific problem of establishing a motive creates additional uncertainties. No police data are available at all on racially motivated violence exerted by certain professions such as the police themselves or prison/correctional staff.[33] Information in this field stems almost exclusively from NGO and media reports.[34] No police data are available on situations of racist violence amounting to pogroms or other forms of collective though not necessarily organized violence.

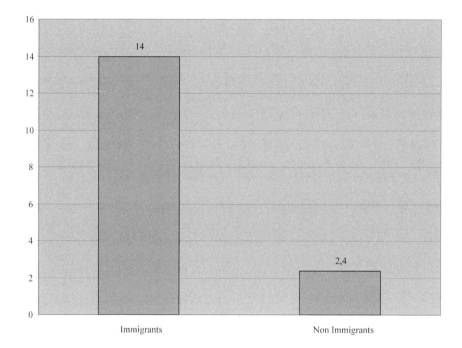

Source: European Crime Survey 2005

Figure 11.5   Prevalence of hate crimes (last 5 years)

The structure of police-registered racist crime reflects the respective definitions as well as data collection procedures. However, in general police statistics show that the majority of racist offences are made up of propaganda crimes and crimes of harassment and threats. What seems clear for Germany is that there was an

33   As regards problems of data collection in this field, see in particular Jobard (2001); and Busch (2000); reports of the Anti-Torture Commission of the Council of Europe have repeatedly pointed to the risk of detained persons being maltreated and abused during detention. See, for example, Comité de prevention de la torture (1991); Feltes (2006).

34   Aktion Courage – SOS Rassismus (1999); Amnesty International Report 2001 – Germany (www.amnesty.org).

increase in racial violence at the beginning of the 1990s. The increase seems to be related to the rise of extremist political parties and organizations as well as of political discourse on 'asylum problems' and immigration. The course of racist violence is evidently subject to a rise and fall of waves of violence which may be explained tentatively by violent campaigns initiated by various extremist groups, the mobilizing effects of international violent conflicts and copy-cat behaviour. Key events in terms of spectacular and extreme violence at the beginning of the 1990s (Rostock/Lichtenhagen and Hoyerswerda, for example[35]) are assumed to have been generated by a media–politics–violence reinforcement process that served to embed xenophobic violence in a framework of legitimating discourses (on asylum politics).[36]

The above-mentioned European Crime Survey 2005 included for the first time variables that aim at identifying hate crime. Respondents were asked for information on the prejudices of offenders. From this survey it can be concluded that official accounts of racial violence seriously underestimate the extent of racial violence. Although victimization rates at large do not differ between immigrants and non-immigrants, a significantly larger share of victimizing events is perceived by immigrants to be motivated by hate.

Racially motivated crime has a stronger impact on feelings of safety, community life as well as on individual adjustment and coping than has ordinary crime. The particular concern linked to such crimes comes evidently from their being committed against individuals solely because they belong to a visible group in society and the potential for the escalation of social conflict as well as for the disturbance of public peace and social order.

Conclusions

Germany has experienced large-scale immigration during recent decades. Substantial numbers of immigrants live in precarious economic and social conditions that expose them to disproportional unemployment rates and other problems. Immigrants are found concentrated in large cities and
integration of immigrants ranks high on political agendas. Recent changes in micro-census studies have resulted in improved knowledge about the size of immigrant groups and the problems that affect them.

On the basis of police statistics high participation rates in crime, in particular among groups of young immigrants can be observed. Violent crime and chronic offending have been made particular topics of political concern.

Self-report studies show in general that young immigrants do not differ from their authochton counterparts with respect to property crime. However, serious

---

35   For an overview see Esser (1999).
36   Ohlemacher (1998); Lüdemann (1992).

violence over time and across various self-report studies has been shown to be more prevalent among some groups of young immigrants.

Perceptions of discrimination are prevalent among Turkish youth in particular. Trust in the police (and other institutions) in general is not that different compared with other immigrant youth and German youth. An exception is the city of Berlin where segregation is most visible and distrust in the police most pronounced.

Although violence rates among Turkish male youth are higher compared with German young people or other immigrants, large-scale violence or large-scale riots have not been observed during recent decades.

Victimization rates do not differ between immigrants and non-immigrants in Germany as a recent survey shows. However, a substantial proportion of immigrants perceive their victimizers to be motivated by prejudice.

Particular victimization issues have been emphasized during the past decades. Among them we find honour killings and forced marriages, human trafficking and hate crimes. Placing the focus on these issues reinforces the problem view on immigration and the public perception that certain groups of immigrants display significant signs of otherness and create a potential of social and cultural conflicts.

Chapter 12

The Construction of Migrants as a Risk Category in the Spanish Penal System

José Ángel Brandariz García and Cristina Fernández Bessa

The proliferation of migration into Spain during the early years of this century has grown, in a short space of time, into one of the most pressing subjects of our contemporary social reality; so a no less urgent preoccupation with the characteristics of the phenomenon in terms of its repercussions for security and social order has brought about a significant change in the penal system. Anxiety on the part of the media, society and the political establishment regarding migrant criminality, reforms in the juridical precedent approach to such situations, and the ways in which that model has been tied in with migration policy generally, particularly in terms of administrative sanctions, are just some of the areas in which the impact of this situation can be seen.

What is intended in this chapter, specifically, is to deal with a small number of questions that are fundamental to understanding crime policy in regard to migrants. The first of these relates to the social conditions and perceptions which make the construction of migrants as a risk category possible; it is hardly a trivial point to consider how it is that the migrant subject should, in a short space of time, have become the main target of the penal system, in a recast version of what in the old days were referred to as the 'dangerous classes'.

A second question focuses on the repercussions a constructed category of risk subjects has for the Spanish penal system. Analysis will show that our current crime policy model exhibits high levels of 'hybridation' between two extremes – guarantees of inclusion (rehabilitation) and the imposed conditions of exclusion (neutralization) – which give rise to mixed solutions, such as selective exclusion and subordinated inclusion. This last point raises further issues in relation to what has become known as the 'political economy of penality' (or of punishment), a trans-disciplinary approach that may well offer new insight into the aforementioned hybridation process.

Offending Migrants: Constructing a Category of Risk Subjects

To say that the penal system operates on a selective basis today seems almost a cliché of criminological thinking – a given, as it were – but one that is often overlooked for that very reason. Research based on theories such as 'symbolic interactionism' and 'labelling approach' has demonstrated that the penal system consistently combines within itself a number of different social dynamics, as a result of which only a small segment of all subjects who break the law ever actually receive the prescribed juridical response to their crime (Anitua 2005: 363–6, Cid Moliné and Larrauri Pijoan 2001: 202–5, García-Pablos de Molina 1999: 792–4).

This selective tendency is inserted in the context of the crime policy strategies promoted by so-called 'actuarial' modes of thinking.[1] At a time when, in line with the *doxa* of actuarialism, any meaningful reduction in criminality is assumed de facto to be almost impossible and the focus falls instead on accommodating feasible objectives to an economy of always limited resources, it seems inevitable that responsibility for social control and defending against criminality should fall to certain groups and sectors of society. It comes as no surprise, therefore, to find that actuarial philosophy, itself designed to manage and redistribute the risks associated with criminality, argues the need to identify the most dangerous groups and to target regulatory and surveillance resources against those sectors of society specifically (Anitua 2005: 509).

In this way, *actuarial* logic consolidates the focus on certain social subjects as number one targets of the penal system. In this context, one of the least important variables is the individual subject's actual propensity to crime (Portilla Contreras 2005: 61–2, 78).

For much of the period of the last few decades the top spot on the penal system's list of prime targets (the equivalent, in a way, of what at the turn of the twentieth century were known as the 'dangerous classes') was occupied by drug addicts, especially heroin addicts (Christie 2004: 62, Miró Miquel 2005: 307–8, Rodríguez 2003: 118–19). During that period drug addicts entered the penitentiary system circuit *en masse*, slaves to an illegal market that generated utterly exorbitant prices which in turn saw them compelled to an existence of either constant petty theft or low-level illegal drug trafficking (Ruggiero 2000: 15–17). While not its principal objective, the massive internment of drug-addicts in this way was one of the outcomes of the so-called 'War on Drugs', the guiding vector of official crime policy for many Western countries during the final decades of the twentieth century.

However, the predominance of drug addicts in the Spanish system has found itself being challenged in the last decade or so. The percentage of illegal substance users and drug addicts among the prisoner population and the number of inmates condemned for crimes relating to drug addiction still remains high.[2] Nevertheless, the past predominance of the category is now declining, owing, in part, to the

---

1   The 'actuarial' approach, that was initially known as 'New Penology', was developed after the founding works of the American scholars Feeley and Simon (1992 and 1994).

2   According to the figures in Aebi and Del Grande (2009: 58), in 2007 the percentage of inmates in Spanish penitentiaries for drug trafficking crimes was 27.8 per cent, while the figure for those sentenced for crimes against property was 43.3 per cent. Perhaps what

changing nature of drug use itself and its related effects. The high mortality rates caused by the AIDS crisis, and the sustained decrease in heroin consumption, have gradually succeeded in moderating the once prominent position of drug addicts among the prisoner population.

The new prime target of the penal system, the paradigmatic subject of its current clientele, is the migrant. If we accept that the heroin crisis was related above all to poor life expectancy, and an element of nihilism also, among the first (home-grown) generation of the Fordist 'welfarism' transformation (Rodriguez 2003: 119)· the migrant's rise to prominence has come about as a result of the steady consolidation worldwide of a post-Fordist system founded upon a labour force which is not regulated according to a dual system – as described in the classical theses of Piore (Castel 1999: 658–61, 715–17) – but to a model of general precariousness. The predominance of migrant subjects is not just or particularly quantitative, but rather qualitative. This is demonstrated in a number of ways: a) in the area of production, in how the composition and regulation of the labour force are affected; b) in the composition of society, where the trend is one of growing complexity; c) in the area of social control, to the extent that the formal juridical management of migrants prefigures a profile which could have repercussions for the future development of systems of control and sanctions (De Giorgi 2000: 17–20 and 2002: 114–15, 131, Rodríguez 2003: 131–2).

The growing primacy of (non-EU nationals) migrants on the list of penal system targets is obvious in a number of ways. The process has been going on for a long time in the U.S., a country which has experienced intense waves of migration throughout its history and where, as a result, there is a long tradition of social (and academic) preoccupation on the issue of migrant criminality.[3]In more recent times, this primacy has reached the countries of the EU. Although its progress and character have varied from state to state – owing, among other circumstances, to the different stages at which migrations have been received – an analysis of the predominance of migrants in the penal system in relation to the new phase in migration policy entered upon in Europe at the start of the 1970s seems appropriate (Melossi 2002: 266).

---

is most significant about these figures is that the corresponding averages for the rest of the European Council states were 17.7 per cent and 31.9 per cent.

3   Melossi (2002: 263–5) draws attention to the long-standing preoccupation in U.S. criminology with the question, dating back to the time of the Chicago School. He points out that it was a century ago in the U.S. that something which has now become almost a commonplace of criminological thinking was first adverted to (and, one could add, to which some consideration should be given in relation to the situation in Spain today): the finding that the crime rate among first-generation migrants is usually lower than that of the native population; it is among the second generation that the problems begin to appear, with the emergence of a certain cultural conflict and related criminal behaviour. See also Pérez Cepeda (2006: 232), who argues that in Spain criminality among regularized migrants is lower than among the native population.

The phenomenon began to emerge in Spain in the early years of the new millennium, as prison figures show. Among the data, there are a few which are particularly revealing: a) in November 2009 the proportion of foreign inmates in Spanish prisons was 35.2 per cent,[4] nearly more than three times their demographic weight; b) 60.5 per cent of the growth in the prison population for the period 2000–2008 was due to foreign inmates, a statistic which is perhaps the strongest single indicator of the centrality of migrants in the Spanish prison system currently;[5] c) in September 2007 the proportion of foreign nationals on preventive detention was 53.9 per cent. Data such as these, especially when combined with the discourse employed by the media[6] and politicians, serve to strengthen the claim that migrant criminality is one of the main crime policy issues in Spain today.

If we are to assume, then, that the controls and sanctions being used against migrants are an indication of the form current – and future – formal control structures are likely to take a brief analysis of some of the key features of that risk management system is surely in order.

Philosophy behind the Construction of Migrants as a Risk Subject Category: The Significance of Juridical Status

Migrants, owing to various circumstances but in particular to their high social visibility and limited interaction with the native population, are easy to cast as a group marked out by otherness (Melossi 2002: 263, Silveira Gorski 1996: 141). The construction of migrants as a distinct sector of society makes it much easier to identify them as the group responsible for much of the current disorder and insecurity, as potentially key players in a narrative of social risk (Dal Lago 2004: 44, Garland 2005: 228–31, 300–302).

It should be pointed out that the social construction in question is also the result of the actual involvement of a certain segment of migrants in criminal circles. Notwithstanding, that involvement has also been determined by both a prohibitionist migration policy that has made normal mobility next to impossible; and a social developmental model which, rather than encouraging the stable insertion of migrants, actually promotes social exclusion and criminalization; not

---

4   Data taken from the official statistics of the Secretaría General de Instituciones Penitenciarias (2010). Older figures, that shown the evolution of these data, can bee seen in the data of the Ministerio del Interior (2009: 252ff.).

5   According to the data of the Ministerio del Interior (2009: 252–3), in Spain during the period 1996–2008 the native prison population increased 31.1 per cent, whilst the foreign one had of growth of 291.4 per cent.

6   In the midst of all the media rhetoric surrounding the issue, it is not hard to see how *artificial surges* of social alarm over migrant criminality have been orchestrated (see Fuentes Osorio 2005: 17–18, Pérez Cepeda 2006: 223–4, Rechea Alberola, Fernández Molina, Benítez Jiménez 2005: 9, 18–20).

to mention the demand created by part of our society for certain services available in this context of illegality (Melossi 2002: 267–8, Mosconi 2005: 147–65). What emerges, then, is that, just as organized crime has always thrived under prohibition of whatever kind, so prohibitionist migration policies have given rise to the social exclusion of migrants today, and to their criminalization and self-criminalization, with the effects being felt by young migrants in particular (Palidda 2001: 214–16).

Still on this question, there is also the point that the classification of migrants as a risk category relates to factors that go entirely beyond a notion of otherness based purely on physical or cultural characteristics. A more important consideration is the issue of their legal status, as that determines the social meaning assigned to them as a group. To put it simply, the juridical status assigned to migrants (that is, non-EU migrants, or migrants from the South and East) attributes them the permanent risk of illegality, setting them from the start in a grey area verging on the criminal (Guild and Bigo 2005: 67, Dal Lago 2004: 49–50, 138, De Lucas 2005: 217, Márquez Lepe 2005: 209, Melossi 2002: 273, Monclús Masó 2005: 331),[7] thus making their classification as a risk category all but a foregone conclusion. The constant suspicion of illegality is an important factor in the construction of a risk category based on ontological profiles: an a priori principle for the purposes of creating a broad-based policy on crime (control strategies, security policies), that will ignore as largely irrelevant the detail of whether the migrant has actually committed an offence or not. After all, as has been shown already, in selecting a particular risk group to fit the preventive logic of actuarial thinking, individual circumstances and a person's actual criminal record barely come into it.

Aside from the connection with criminality, there is also the issue of the migrant's juridical status, which reduces the subject to his or her condition as a worker, in the sense that it is only possible for the subject to remain within the sphere of legality as long as he or she is engaged in some kind of employment and provided that employment is regular. In terms of the issues being examined here, and so laying aside the obvious decline in the availability of stable regular work in comparison with the myriad alternative forms of involvement in the labour market, this blatant constriction of migrants to a defined social function makes them an ideal target for certain control practices (De Giorgi 2000: 60–1, Rodríguez 2003: 112).

The migrant status is surely no longer one which can be classed simply as *non-citizen*. Indeed, if – as noted by Dal Lago (2004) – we are to take for granted that a person is more than the mere compendium of philosophical reflections, that the person is, in fact, the product of his or her insertion in a given context of positive norms (that is, in a legal system); understanding, thus, that it is citizens alone – increasingly – who invest the human being with a social personality: this being the case, we would have to reconsider this 'non-person' category (Dal Lago

---

7   In this sense, Palidda (2000: 233–6) highlights the consideration of immigration as a crime de facto, and connects this juridical status with police abuses in relation to migrants.

2004: 205–8, De Lucas 2005: 205–7, Mezzadra 2005: 94–106) as the product of a system founded upon the logic of exceptionality (Rodríguez 2003: 132, Agamben 1998: 212–15, 221–2, Pérez Cepeda 2006: 232). One last point to note on this idea of the non-person is that migrants are different in this respect from other social subjects in – or in danger of being in – situations of exclusion (homeless people, drug addicts, the poor etc.), as the latter conserve, theoretically at least, a small array of rights from which migrants find themselves cut off.

The issue is much more than a mere difference in juridical status. In the construction of migrants, the crucial factor becomes lack of citizenship; their social image is no longer one simply of otherness, but of permanent potential illegality. It is worth examining what aspects of the juridical regime are most responsible for this.

Firstly, the rigid border controls put in place to prevent entry into a given territory (Articles 25ff. O.L. 4/2000 (11 January) on the rights and freedoms of foreigners in Spain and their social integration).[8] In regard to this aspect, what has been interesting in recent times has been the growing tendency to distance border lines away from the state, placing them in some cases in the migrant's actual country of origin, a policy which has been termed 'externalization of borders' (Andrijasevic 2006a: 8–17, Dal Lago 2004: 153, 271, Saint-Saëns 2004: 62–5). The process, which is beginning to cause major changes in the morphology of control measures against unregulated migration, has been formally promoted within the EU since the end of 2004 (Andrijasevic 2006a: 8–17, 2006b: 150–1, Rigo 2007) and occurs there in different forms.[9] The most obvious of these is externalization in the geographical sense, in other words, the tendency mentioned already by reception-states to establish their controls near border lines, or even along non-land borders, in territory belonging to the migrant groups' states of origin or the states they pass through. A specific feature of geographical externalization has been the construction of internment centres for migrants in their countries of origin or transit, which has, in turn, given rise to the criminalization of, not just entry into, but also unregulated departure from those states.[10]

---

8   According to data from the Ministerio del Interior (2010), in 2009 a total of 12,625 subjects were sent back to their country of origin from Spain, representing a 32.6 per cent decrease on the figures for the previous year. Meanwhile, the Spanish government carried out 13,278 expulsions in 2009, a 25 per cent increase in relation to 2008.

9   Gil Araújo (2005: 131) identifies three different ways in which border controls can be externalized or moved: vertical displacement above (EU) or below (regional and local authorities) the state authorities; geographical displacement towards a different control area (other countries' borders); and externalization of responsibility onto the private sector (transport companies) and the government of the countries of origin.

10   Indeed, perhaps one of the most significant aspects of this process is how it has restricted freedom of movement, not just in relation to entering a country, but by preventing the subject from leaving (e.g. in Moroccan law, Articles 50 ff. L. 2/2003 (11 November), which establish a prison sentence of 1–6 months for anybody attempting to leave the country illegally; for those involved in smuggling people out of the country, the penalty rises to

The situation, though, must be understood as an intrinsic part of the much broader process of deterritorializing and reterritorializing borders, involving the extension of the notion of a border – together with the controls which the concept traditionally implies – to the wider social sphere, as part of the aim of keeping the lives of irregular migrants under constant control (Guild and Bigo 2005: 59, Mezzadra 2005: 148, Various Authors, 2006).[11]

A second factor to consider is the role played by the juridical regime in creating the constant threat of illegality by restricting considerably the basic rights and freedoms available to migrants, since these are made conditional upon the legality of the migration. According to former legislation in Spain, the following rights might not be exercised in the absence of an official permit of stay or residency: right to non-compulsory education, right to Social Security grants and services, right to free legal aid in cases other than expulsion, right to assemble and demonstrate, right to association, right to be a member of a union, right to strike, right to live as a family, have a private family life and come together as a family. Nevertheless, the decisions pronounced by the Spanish Constitutional Court, 236/2007 (7 November) and 259/2007 (19 December), declared it unconstitutional to impose restrictions on the exercise of the right to non-compulsory education, free legal aid, assembly, demonstration, association and membership of a union, and the right to strike. Finally, the mentioned rights are recognized by the most recent reform of the Spanish Immigration Law (OL 2/2009).[12]

The third issue is how the Spanish juridical regime actually sponsors the confused definition of migrants as irregular/illegal/criminal in attempting –unsuccessfully – to merge into one the penal system and the system of administrative sanctions (Asúa Batarrita 2002: 18–67, Baucells i Lladós 2005: 60–1, Monclús Masó 2005: 336–45), and in the process subjecting migrants to exceptionally severe penal-administrative measures, such as internment (Articles 61ff. O.L. 4/2000)[13] and expulsion (Articles 57ff. and 64 O.L. 4/2000). Legal extremities of this kind must surely play a significant part in creating this migrant category in which illegality is confused with criminality (García Vázquez 2005: 423–6, Mosconi 2005: 165).[14] Legal measures of such severity should actually be classed as penal sanctions

---

10–15 years in prison, or life imprisonment, if a migrant dies as a result), even when he or she is a national of that country. This contravenes an aspect of the freedom of movement principle that is usually defined specifically in international human rights documents as a fundamental human right (e.g. Art. 13.2 Universal Declaration of Human Rights, 1948).

11   According to Pretel (2006: 53–4) in Western societies this can lead to the creation of internal borders, in the form of: a) police harassment and the power to impose controls on public transport; b) lack of workers' rights; c) serious difficulties finding housing; d) emergence of racist or xenophobic attitudes.

12   Organic Law 2/2009, passed by the Spanish Parliament on 11 December 2009.

13   On the Spanish internment centres see Silveira Gorski (2002 and 2003: 550–7).

14   In this sense, Monclús Masó (2005: 335) highlights how this confusion between illegality and criminality is affected by having expulsion as both a legal administrative and a penal provision. The double provision is just another example of the intersection already

(making this an example of fraudulent labelling) (Dal Lago 2004: 39, Mosconi 2005: 164, Silveira 2002: 551),[15] and that way would be subject to greater guarantees of application, execution and control than is the case with sanctions of an administrative nature.[16]

In fact, despite the normalcy with which internment and expulsion have become established among the various different European legal systems, the severity of the sanctions cannot be ignored. These are exceptionally serious juridical measures, they include restrictions on the right to defend oneself and be defended effectively before the law.[17] In the case of internment, being to deprive a person of his or her freedom for up to 60 days (*ex* Art. 62.2 O.L. 4/2000). The conditions under which sanctions are usually carried out: again, in the case of internment, meaning precarious circumstances and regularly oversubscribed centres, or centres that have not been properly equipped for the purpose.[18] In view of the serious repercussions these sanctions can have: if we take into account the enormous potential risks involved in repeating the attempt[19] (dangers attested to by the appalling figures for deaths resulting from attempting to enter Spain irregularly),[20] it is not difficult

---

discussed between penal law and administrative (sanction) law, in which the former ends up subordinated to the latter.

15   The internment of illegal migrants is an administrative custodial penalty (in itself a constitutionally suspect concept, in view of Art. 25.3 of the Spanish Constitution), largely equivalent to a custodial prison sentence, the sole difference – its administrative character aside – being that it may last up to a maximum of 60 days (Art. 62.2 O.L. 4/2000). Expulsion, meanwhile, shares much the same morphology as traditional penalties such as deportation and, more recently, exile (Art. 86 Penal Code 1944/1973).

16   Rigo (2007: 144), who observes how the 'administrativization' of the sanction system in regard to migrants is aimed, not at making sanctions less severe, but at increasing the speed and efficiency of juridical response. However, these administrative provisions are formulated in coordination with the resolutions of the penal system, as evinced by the expulsion regulation contained in Article 89 Spanish Penal Code.

17   On the prominent restrictions of the right to defend oneself and to be defended before the law, and on the violation of the *non bis in idem* principle that brings this expulsion sanction, see García Vázquez (2005: 431–3), Monclús Masó (2002: 177–8) and Silveira Gorski (2002: 97–8 and 2003: 549–50).

18   On the issue of the harsh conditions under which irregular migrants in Spain are frequently interned, see: Observatori del Sistema Penal i els Drets Humans (2004) and, among others, the report of CEAR (2009).

19   As De Lucas (2005: 217) and Palidda (2000: 221) have pointed out, rigid border controls compel migrants to pay large sums of money in order to gain entry to their country of destination; places them in the hands of criminal networks, leaving them vulnerable to all manner of pressures and threats during the process of migration; and puts them in danger of theft, injury and – all too often – death during the journey. They also place them at risk of repression at the hands of the police in their countries of origin, transit and destination.

20   According to the Euro-mediterranean Consortium for Applied Research on International Migration (CARIM) (2005), between 1989 and 2002, 8,000–10,000 people died while attempting to enter Spanish territory from Morocco. The Spanish Guardia Civil,

to understand how, for some migrants, expulsion rather than prison might seem by far the more grievous sanction, despite the latter's being, in theory, the most serious sanction contemplated by the legal systems in Europe.

In addition to all the issues highlighted already, however, there is a fourth affecting the construction of the migrant as a risk subject: the increasingly common view of migration phenomena as conditions under which subversive or terrorist activities are likely to emerge, which, in turn, has been used to justify their institutionalization as priority social control areas (Bigo 2005: 76, Gil Araújo 2005: 114, Ruiz Rodríguez 2006: 184–6, Saint-Saëns 2004: 62).[21] Yet, while such an attitude may have been strengthened by the events of 2001 (and, in Spain, by those of March 2004), its history actually goes back further than that.

For over a decade, irregular migration has been defined as an international security problem, a status only shared by organized crime and terrorism (Gil Araújo 2005: 114, 120, Moulier Boutang 2002: 144–5).[22]

---

meanwhile, have evidence to suggest that in the last few months of 2005, 1,200–1,700 people may have lost their lives while trying to reach the Canary Islands from the coast of Mauritania (on this subject, see *El Mundo*, 20 March 2006, quoting the CARIM website, http://www.carim.org/index.php?callContent=1). For the first eight months of 2006, the estimated number of deaths on the same route, according to the Red Cross, was somewhere between 2,000 and 3,000 (see *El País*, 1 September 2006). The Asociacion Pro Derechos Humanos de Andalucía (APDHA) has reported the death of 1,167 persons in 2006 and 921 in 2007 during their migratory journey towards Spain but they estimate that at least 7,000 persons died in 2006 and 3,500 in 2007 as a consequence of European border controls (2008: 33–5). Another particularly deplorable example of this occurred between the end of August and the beginning of October 2005, when massive attempts were made to get across the Spanish border at the autonomous cities of Ceuta and Melilla. At least 14 irregular migrants lost their lives in the course of those attempts, the majority of them as a result of shots fired by border police (see *El País*, 30 September 2005, 7 October 2005, and Aierbe 2006). The scenes were repeated in July 2006, when three migrants died while attempting to jump the border fences at Melilla, most likely as a result of shots fired by border security forces (see *El País*, 4 July 2006).

21   Some authors quoted in this text meanwhile, points out that this circumstance tends to combine in the migrant the roles of the internal enemy and of the external enemy. A specific expression of this linking between migration and terrorism can be seen in artificially constructed sources in autumn 2004 focusing on the alleged existence of Islamic networks in Spanish prisons. See the editions of *El Mundo* for 23 September, 8 October, 24 October, 27 October and 2 November 2004.

22   Meanwhile, Bigo (2005: 76–7), underlines the primacy of migration matters in the international police activities.

The Function of Risk Category: Social Cohesion, Managed Exclusion and Subordinated Inclusion

There is the need created by an actuarial approach to security to identify specific risk groups, as the focus shifts away from guaranteeing security in general terms towards targeting restricted resources to tackle specific risks arising out of defined sectors of the population. The particular control of migrants, according to this logic of managing and distributing risk, is a key aspect of the whole system's *raison d'être*.[23]

At a time characterized by the breakdown of traditional (modern) identity markers (Beck 1998: 95–9, Matthews 2003: 163–5, 316–20, Young 2003: 32, 159–62) and ever-increasing individualism, the negative definition of what certain criminologists have termed suitable enemies;[24] also has an obvious role to play in offsetting this lack of social cohesion and coordination (Bauman 2005: 105–13, Dal Lago 2004: 46–7, Portilla Contreras 2005: 77). Thus the group definition of irregular migrants as a category based on a powerful sense of the subjects' otherness fulfils the essential function of creating cohesion within a society that finds itself in crisis (Dal Lago 2004: 11, 44–50, 237–45, Márquez Lepe 2005: 210, Palidda 2000: 25). Historically – though perhaps with greater urgency nowadays – society has used the characterization of a social subject as requiring control and being logically responsible for the dysfunctions and conflicts within the community as a potent mechanism of social cohesion (Young 2003: 177–9, Žižek 2005: 89).

A number of additional, no less important uses are also apparent. In order to understand these properly, however, we must first of all be aware of the clash created within the regime of sanctions for irregular migrants between exclusion objectives and aims of insertion.

Just as the principle upon which the juridical status of migrants seems be founded is one of potential exclusion, so the most extreme juridical implications for irregular migrants as contemplated by the (penal and administrative) Spanish regime of sanctions (i.e. expulsion, internment, or imprisonment with a view to expulsion and no possibility of getting the sentence suspended) would appear to have incapacitation as their primary objective (Pérez Cepeda 2006: 237). By the same token, any rehabilitationary considerations in this regard are conspicuously absent. That said, in order to understand fully the purpose of this migration policy and the crime policy philosophy behind a mechanism like expulsion (as established by Article 89 Spanish Penal Code), a vital point to realize is that what all this provides for is *selective* incapacitation (De Giorgi 2000: 73–4). Put another

---

23   In this sense, Bietlot (2003: 64) identifies some of the specific functions of these migration management practices: to dissuade future irregular migrants; to transmit messages to society that may help to conjure up a sense of insecurity; even to justify existing public (and private) security apparatuses.

24   This expression is commonly used by Christie (1986: 42–5), but it is usually employed also by other scholars (e. g., see Wacquant 1999: 215–18).

way, internment and expulsion (following imprisonment, or not, depending on the case) are not enacted against all those who should, in theory, qualify to be so dealt with. In fact, the data available to us indicate that, over the last few years, the proportion of expulsions in Spain that have actually been carried out is only just over 25 per cent of those agreed.[25] There are, of course, different reasons for this: juridical (absence of repatriation agreements with different countries of origin); informational (failure to identify the nationality of a particular migrant, or refusal on the part of particular state to acknowledge a migrant as a national of the same); and, above all, material (lack of means required to execute the totality of expulsions) (De Genova 2002: 209). Nevertheless, a further factor to take into consideration must surely be the lack of political will to enforce the full rigour of the expulsion system in the knowledge that such a scrupulous approach would risk blocking or dramatically reducing the stream of irregular migrants into the country where their diverse economic and social contribution is one of the utmost importance (De Genova 2002: 209). In parallel with the kinds of functions outlined above, there is also: the effect the sector has on what is a rapidly aging population pyramid;[26] its outstanding contribution to economic growth;[27] and its

---

25   See *El País*, 20 July 2004, which reported that between 2002 and early 2004 the Spanish government carried out only 27.8 per cent of agreed expulsions. See also further data supplied by Silveira Gorski (2003: 540–56), which show that figures for executed expulsion orders remained more or less around these levels. See also Andrijasevic (2006b: 152) – who reports, in the Italian case, figures around 50 per cent.

26   The study Oficina económica del Presidente (2006: 3–5) shows that the spectacular growth in immigration has caused the Spanish population to rise by 3 million in the period 2000–2005, representing a growth rate of 1.5 per cent annually, the highest since the statistical register began. To put it another way: of the 4.7 million new members of Spanish society in the years1996–2005, 3.6 million of them were migrants. Based on these figures, for the period 2000–2005, Spain was the country in the OECD with the highest percentage growth of its migrant population: 7.1 per cent.

27   A report produced by the Servicio de Estudios de Caixa Catalunya (2006), shows that, without migration, Spanish income *per capita* would have fallen in the period 1995–2005 at a rate of 0.6 per cent *per annum*, representing a decrease similar to or greater than that of other European countries: Germany (1.5 per cent), Italy (1.1 per cent), Sweden (0.7 per cent), Portugal (0.6 per cent), Greece (0.6 per cent). The study Oficina económica del Presidente (2006: 14–16) highlights that the massive influx of migrants into the Spanish market has not caused a rise in unemployment, but rather a sharp reduction instead. Migrants are also shown to have a higher rate of activity than native workers (79 per cent against 68.2 per cent in 2005). The study also indicates that the level of temporary contracts among migrant workers is 61.4 per cent and that their salaries are 30 per cent lower than those of native workers. The paper adds that migrants accounted for 51 per cent of GDP growth for the period 2001–2005. As an indirect effect, it estimates that 30 per cent of the growth in female economic activity among 1996–2005 was due to the presence of migrants. The study highlights that the fall in unemployment was an effect of the increased flexibility which migrants introduce into the labour market, since they tend to be focused in sectors in which native labour is scarce, their geographic mobility is greater and their salaries are lower.

no less outstanding role in improving the public finances[28] (one of the fundamental considerations of successive regularization processes).

It might be assumed, therefore, that a migration policy aimed less at putting a stop to the flow of migrants than at managing it[29] (as evinced by a distinct official reluctance to clamp down on the black labour market) was always destined to encourage the massive-scale employment of migrant labour in conditions of maximum flexibility and exploitation, in keeping with the demands of an increasingly post-Fordist system of production. Likewise, a system of control that targets irregular migrants – in particular, measures such as internment and expulsion – also has a normalizing objective that is (neo-)disciplinary in nature (though not in the least way rehabilitatory, as it focuses, not on the individual subject, but on the collective social group[30]), and aimed at binding migrants to a scheme of employment that pigeonholes them into jobs that are every bit as precarious and exploitative as they are economically essential (Fuentes Osorio 2005: 20, Guillén and Vallés 2003: 318, Dal Lago 2004: 48, 235, 255, 267–9, Palidda 2001: 207–14, Rodríguez 2003: 76–7). What this means, in short, is that migrants are left to feel the full severity of a new 'workfare' regime[31] according to which the labour market is segmented along ethnic lines, with middle to high value-added occupations being reserved, by and large, for the native workers (Dal Lago 2004: 130, 267–70, Rodríguez 2003: 77, 118–22).

---

28   In relation to the public finances, the study Oficina económica del Presidente (2006: 14–16), shows that in 2005 migrants generated 6.6 per cent of the state's income, but received only 5.4 per cent of its expenditure, thus contributing 48 per cent of the surplus in the public finances for that year. Figures relating to the importance of contributions made by migrant workers to the financial sustainability of the Spanish social security system can be also found in *El País*, 29 October 2006.

29   In as far as the prevailing ideology behind migration policies is one of 'border management' and 'migration management', based on the principle of productivity, the 'Fortress Europe' metaphor does not reflect the full complex nature of the how the EU controls the migration process. A further indication of the metaphor's unsuitability is the already mentioned dissemination of the idea of borders –and the controls traditionally associated with them– across the social terrain, with the aim of maintaining constant control over the lives of irregular migrants (see Guild and Bigo 2005: 59, Mezzadra 2005: 148, Various Authors 2006).

30   Using the distinction, suggested by Foucault, between disciplinary measures and government biopolitical measures, it is possible to conclude that the normalizing, neodisciplinary principle operating in this situation does not do so individually, with reference to each separate migrant (with a view to individual rehabilitation), but collectively as a risk group.

31   On the 'workfare' concept, an expression that tries to identify the transformations that have occurred in the welfare systems during the last decades, see, among others Faria (2001: 200), De Giorgi (2000: 87), Matthews (2003: 313), Rodríguez (2003: 84–6), Wacquant (2000: 41–3).

There can surely be no question but that the harsh juridical status of irregular migrants, which makes it next to impossible for them to escape from the cycle of illegal residency and black economy labour, translates into their coercive relegation to the lowest levels of the production system, circumstances characterized by exceptionally poor employment regulation and the implications of that in terms of the virtual non-existence of workers' rights (De Giorgi 2000: 54–5, Rodríguez 2003: 77, Silveira Gorski 2003: 563). Thus irregular migrant workers, subordinated to a process of overexploitation, end up consigned to the lowest rung of a universally precarious labour regime.[32]

The situation cannot be read as one of simple dysfunction, as it might have in an age of Keynesian 'welfarism'. On the contrary, in a post-Fordist regime of production in which high levels of flexibility and adaptability are required of the workforce, it becomes not just expedient but utterly essential that sections of that workforce should be subject to the conditions of extreme precariousness described above. Viewed from this perspective, the whole concept of juridical irregular migrant status, including its control aspects, seems a most extraordinary instrument of subordination, aimed above all else at coactively subjecting groups of that description to highly undesirable labour conditions. Even the exclusionary, segregationist aspects of the juridical regime are constructed as crucial elements of a greater scheme of thinking: that of enforcing disciplined subordination to the kind of labour practices demanded by our present system of accumulating capital (Bietlot 2003: 64–6, Mezzadra 2005: 148, Rodríguez 2003: 77, 118–22, De Giorgi 2000: 55, Dal Lago 2004: 142). It should also be noted, of course, that acts of exclusion are also deployed to avoid the influx of migrants on such a scale as would make it impossible for them to be absorbed, even taking into account the demand for labour. However, to use the language of the experts in the field of governmentality studies, as first investigated in his day by Foucault (1995 and 2000), one might say that the 'control society', as a hybrid, conflictive, changing social management model, also reveals aspects of the disciplinary logic of normalization (Bietlot 2003: 58–64, Deleuze 1995: 273–5, De Giorgi 2000: 24, 48, 96–107, Rodríguez 2003: 124–6).

The Repercussions of Risk Category: The Discriminatory Operation of the Spanish Penal System in Relation to Migrants

The penalties meted out to migrant subjects are a clear demonstration of the tensions and limits of a sanctionary regime which, while designed from the perspective of an abstract subject type (the citizen), in practice operates according

---

32   By way of an illustration, at the public presentation of the study Pereda, Actis and De Prada (2005), it was pointed out that the average salary for a migrant at that time was €870 a month, compared with the €1,741 a month earned by a native worker. On this subject, see *La Voz de Galicia*, 17 February 2005.

to a patently selective and differential system of punishment. At a minimum, in relation to how prison sentences are implemented, the evidence should compel some reconsideration of the existing objective parameters for measuring progress in the area of rehabilitation: analysing these in relation to the actual status of irregular migrants in general, typically what emerges is that outside of the native prisoner population those parameters are largely unworkable.

To start with, the 'typical' criminality of migrants as a group is exaggerated by Spanish crime statistics owing both to the priority targeting of resources against them (Harcourt 2007: 156) – for example, in relation to street crime – and to the ease with which their crimes are typically detected, investigated and demonstrated. The high rate of detection observed in such cases is also a function of the high social visibility of migrants, combined with the pervasion and effectiveness of Spanish police stereotypes (Fuentes Osorio 2005: 20, Dal Lago 2004: 30, Melossi 2002: 267–89, Pavarini 2002: 171–2, Rodríguez 2003: 121–30),[33] as illustrated by various data relating to arrests and identity checks.[34] Stereotypes of this kind are merely a reflection, however, of public opinion generally (Melossi 2002: 279–81, Mosconi 2005: 157),[35] social attitudes also mirrored to an extent in the whole Spanish penal system approach to migrant criminality (Mosconi 2005: 157, Tonry 2004: 209–10).

Secondly, as the statistics would seem to show, a migrant offender is much more likely than his or her native counterpart to suffer preventive detention in

---

33   In this sense the Open Society Justice Initiative (2007) shows a fieldwork study that demonstrates the persistence of these stereotypes among Spanish police practices and the selectivity with which the system operates in regard to migrants; and the European Commission against Racism and Intolerance (2006) has recommended that the Spanish government investigate the presence of selective practices among police services. In Spain, despite the fact that article 5.1.b O.L. 2/1986 (13 March) for the Security Forces and Bodies establishes as its guiding principle of action that police forces should 'act, in the fulfilment of their duties, with absolute political neutrality and impartiality and, consequently, without discrimination of any kind by reason of race, religion or opinion', the Decision of the Constitutional Court 3/2001 admitted selective practices of this kind, at least in relation to actions based on immigration law. However, Spain has been condemned for this Decision according to the Comunication 1493/2006 of the UN Human Rights Committee in the case Rosalind Williams vs. Spain.

34   According to data from the Ministerio Del Interior (2007: 288), in 2006, 88,820 foreign citizens were arrested in Spain, representing 34 per cent of the total 260,500 arrests made that year. The study European Commision Against Racism and Intolerance (2006: 11) states that there is evidence to show that, while foreign subjects account for 30 per cent of people arrested, they represent only 10 per cent of those convicted, which suggests that arrests against migrants may be based on weaker evidence than those against native subjects.

35   As an illustration of the general persistence of these stereotypes, a study by the CIS (the Spanish Centre for Sociological Investigation) for the year 2004 found that 60 per cent of those surveyed associated immigration with criminality (European Commission Against Racism and Intolerance, 2006: 14).

Spain (García España and Pérez Jiménez 2005: 92, De Giorgi 2000: 71–3, Pavarini 2002: 170–1) – a factor, it should be remembered, that usually prejudices the subject at sentencing when it comes to deciding between imprisonment and a sanction of a different type (Tonry 2004: 225). Looking at how preventive detention is regulated in Spain, there would appear to have been at least two legal bases for this circumstance (Ruiz Rodríguez 2006: 188–9). The first of these is the greater social alarm, fomented by media representations, which illegal acts by migrants tend to generate among the public; this popular anxiety was already recognized under Article 503.2 of the Spanish Criminal Procedural Law, the so-called *Ley de Enjuiciamiento Criminal* – LECrim – prior to the reform introduced by O.L. 13/2003 (24 October), as adequate grounds for remanding an individual to preventive custody. The second is the suspicion, based on the subject's social circumstances (possible lack of fixed address, failure of identity documents, precarious employment, lack of income etc.), that he or she represents a flight risk (Art. 503.1.3 LECrim).

A third aspect of the selectivity issue is how, in relation to sentencing, the uncertainty surrounding the social situation of migrants makes it more difficult to implement either non-custodial alternatives or the mechanisms for substituting or conditionally suspending a sentence (García España and Pérez Jiménez 2005: 92, De Giorgi 2000: 71–3, Dal Lago 2004: 31, Pavarini, 2002: 170–1, Melossi 2002: 267, 274–7). In Spain, the use of substitution or suspension mechanisms in cases involving irregular migrants is not officially permitted under current expulsion regulations (Art. 89.1 Penal Code).

Fourthly, conditions discussed earlier, such as precariousness of employment, weak family ties or irregular status, frequently obstruct subjects in the final phases of a prison sentence from gaining access to the different forms of parole (Aguilera Reija 2005: 268, Re 2006: 192, Ruiz Rodríguez 2006: 187–9). In Spain, the access of migrants to such alternatives is again denied under Article 89.1 Penal Code which establishes expulsion across the board, thus excluding any possibility of gaining parole or conditional release.

However, having a criminal record removes any chance he or she may have of regularizing his or her status, leaving the subject with all the negative consequences that situation entails; signally, the permanent threat of expulsion and the lack of any alternative but to seek a living outside of regular paid work (Aguilera Reija 2005: 267–9, Ruiz Rodríguez 2006: 192). One final point to note in this context, during the period of a prison sentence, migrants are denied any possibility whatsoever of receiving a release permit, on the grounds that they are considered a flight risk; this is despite the fact that there has still been no empirical research produced to back up such a theory (Ruiz Rodríguez 2006:189–90).

A fifth and final aspect of the experience of migrants in the Spanish penal system is that theirs tends to be more punishing than the average, owing as much to the lack of external human support as to the subjects' limited understanding of how the system operates (Matthews 2003: 290–300, Re 2006: 130–1).

All of which goes to illustrate a point on which to conclude this brief analysis: the juridical status of migrants and their definition as a dangerous group are not merely risk management responses to the actions and behaviour of migrants. The symbolic exclusionary rationale behind them and the specific practices that go with it also play a part in creating the risk in the first place. In an example of the Mertonian self-fulfilling prophecy, migrant criminality may actually be a result of the way the juridical system operates (De Giorgi 2000: 71–3, Harcourt 2007: 36, 154–6, Rodríguez 2003: 120, 130, Melossi 2002: 267–8, Mosconi 2005: 147, 153, 165).

Chapter 13

The Italian Crime Deal

Salvatore Palidda

The Italian case is similar to others, but it may be emblematic of the raising to extreme levels of prohibitionist and securitarian practices, of their societal effects and of their combination with racist criminalization (as recently reported by the European commissioner for human rights, Hammarberg[1]). This is also why Italy appears to resemble neoconservative America more than other European countries, due to the particular blend of the less noble aspects that have traditionally been present in the country (consider the underground economy, and the hybridization between legal, informal, and criminal economies). Referring to the recent literature analysing the various aspects of the social construction of the condition of immigrants in Italy and racism in depth,[2] I hereby summarize what is essential:

a. More than other European countries, Italy is the country in which a heightened uncertainty about immigration law perpetuates itself; discretion if not utter arbitrariness in the interpretation of norms (rarely in a sense that benefits the immigrant) are commonplace and strengthened by laws that grant disproportionate power to the police and the other authorities in charge of managing the various stages of the migration process; from the application for a visa to the request of asylum, up until obtaining a residence permit and/or asking for its renewal, Italian norms and practices de facto ensure the reproduction of irregularity, which only to a small extent results from entries into the country that are actually irregular.[3]

b. Over thirty years, Italian prohibitionism has contributed to the death of thousands of migrants as they attempted to enter Italian territory, to

---

1 His report, in English and French, is available online: https://wcd.coe.int/ViewDoc.jsp?id=1428427&Site=CommDH&BackColorInternet=FEC65B&BackColorIntranet=FEC65B&BackColorLogged=FFC679 and was cited by several daily newspapers on 16 April 2009.

2 Insofar as legal aspects are concerned, I refer to various essays published in the magazines and on the websites of ASGI and Magistratura Democratica: http://www.asgi.it/, http://magistraturademocratica.it/ For research in social sciences, the literature is quite vast and widely cited in different chapters of this volume.

3 Here I summarize the results of 15 years of researches on immigration in Italy and also some analysis proposed by the Italian Association of Legal Studies on Immigration (www.asgi.it). See Palidda (1996, 1999, 2000, 2005, 2008a, 2009a, 2009b).

the sequence of casualties, sometimes not very visible, that result from unbearable working and living conditions, but also to the wear and tear – a fact that is entirely ignored – of thousands of people who decide to return to their home countries.[4]

c. The majority of regular immigrants who are in Italy today have gone through periods of irregularity. After five regularizations and increasingly punitive legislation, at the start of 2009, the estimate of irregulars varies between 500,000 and 900,000 people. According to recent estimates, irregulars contribute 3–4 per cent of GDP, and the sum of regular and irregular foreigners accounts for as much as 13 per cent of national GDP.[5]

d. As we will see below through the analysis of statistics, the Italian 'Crime Deal' has fed off the criminalization of immigrants, and particularly of those that are most easily classified as 'natural born delinquents', primarily because they are the ones at greatest disadvantage in relation to the possibility of regular and peaceful integration (namely, young Maghrebians, people from the Balkans and Nigerians). However, although statistics are the inflated and rather predictable result of a construction of criminalization in which many actors participate, they disprove the view according to which immigrants have contributed to an increase in criminal offences[6]: from 1990 to 2010, the total number of crimes has actually decreased (almost 12 per cent), while the number of immigrants (both regular and irregular) has increased by 567 per cent.[7] However, according to the dynamics of

---

4   According to the following press review, at least 14,921 people have died since 1988 along the European frontiers. Among them 6,469 were missing at sea. 10,925 migrants died in the Mediterranean Sea, and in the Atlantic Ocean around Spain, and 1,691 lost their lives trying to cross the Sahara desert in order to reach Europe (See the website: http://fortresseurope.blogspot.com/2006/02/immigrants-dead-at-frontiers-of-europe_16.html)

5   According to all of the most important Italian economic organizations (Industry, trade, and banks) the contribution of immigrants to Italian GDP is almost 10–12 per cent, but I think that is useful to add almost 3 per cent (and perhaps more) for the shadow economy. See http://www.europaquotidiano.it/dettaglio/62500/quanto_vale_il_pil_degli_immigrati

6   This claim has also been noted by Bianchi, Buonanno, Pinotti (2008).

7   In 1990 the number of regular immigrants in Italy was almost 785,000, with almost 300,000 irregular; in 2010 the total of the regular and irregular population is almost 5 million i.e. a growth of 567 per cent (estimates of the Fondazione ISMU, 2009). Yet Mr Berlusconi and his allies, the Northern League (the party gaining votes for 20 years with its anti-immigrant demagogy) continues to say 'Less crime means fewer immigrants' (see http://www.lastampa.it/redazione/ cmsSezioni/politica/201001articoli/51689girata.asp) and also 'Milan equal to Africa' (see http://www.lastampa.it/redazione/cmsSezioni/politica/200906articoli/44325girata.asp). For its part, the Interior Minister, Mr Maroni (Northern League) says: 'The fight against illegal immigration must not be polite but nasty and determined to affirm the rigor of the law' (see http://www.corriere.it/politica/09_febbraio_02/maroni_immigrazione_clandestina_cattivi_6cdc5e96-f155-11dd-b48f-00144f02aabc.shtml).

racist criminalization, arrests and imprisonments have grown ceaselessly in spite of the false pardon law[8] (false because those released from prison did not find any support outside, and have become 'easy prey' anew in the hunt by zealous police officers, who want to appear efficient and/or or have embraced the authoritarian-racist cause[9]) (see the Table that follows). Unlike in other countries – even when they are governed by right-wing coalitions[10] – in Italy all this occurs within a context of brazen impunity for the people who enact violent and racist behaviours. Just as nearly all those responsible for the acts of police violence and torture on the occasion of the G8 meeting in Genoa in 2001 have been acquitted and even promoted,[11] a majority of the perpetrators of racist attacks against gipsy encampments or against immigrants is not prosecuted; they sometimes even embark upon careers in politics, media, or in the ranks of local and central government.

As data trends in Table 13.1 show, Italy – like other countries – does not exhibit an increase in crime; the total number of crimes goes down in spite of the likely 'inflation' caused by reporting what would have not been previously considered crime, either by more zealous police forces or by zealous citizens and 'militants of zero tolerance', particularly against immigrants and gypsies. The sharp increase (from 1990 to 2006) in the number of people reported, arrested, jailed and sentenced to prison terms thus appears sensational: an overt intensification of repressive and penal action, to the detriment of social prevention and re-insertion/rehabilitation. This finds no rational justification, if one considers the fact that, in reality, all serious crimes have decreased in number.

---

8   With the Law of 31 July 2006, No. 241 'Granting amnesty' published in Official Gazette No. 176, 31 July 2006 a great majority of the Italian Parliament granted the pardon to more than 26,000 detainees (see Campesi, Re, Torrente, 2009).

9   See Fondazione Michelucci, 2007 (http://www.michelucci.it/node/79); Palidda (2008a).

10   In the UK, as in France and elsewhere, as soon as a police officer is charged with violent acts and violation of rights and democratic guarantees, they are immediately suspended and often fired as well. Among so-called democratic countries, it is only Italy that has never had bodies for effective democratic control and punishment of police abuse, confirming the absence of a liberal-democratic tradition, also thanks to the Italian left whose hierarchy has almost always shared the same authoritarian notions that are espoused by the right and centre.

11   Find all the documentation on www.processig8.org; see also Palidda (2008b).

Table 13.1   Italy: measure of police forces' production (1990–2008)

Year	Total crimes	People accused	% Accused over crimes	People arrested	% Arrested over crimes	Entries in prison	Detainees
1990	2,501,640	435,751	17.4	64,814	2.6	64,722	26,150
1995	2,267,488	644,383	28.4	111,071	5.0	88,415	47,344
1999	2,373,966	700,199	29.5	123,252	5.2	87,862	53,000
2005	2,515,168	644,532	25.6	145,231	5.8	89,887	60,109
2006	2,526,486	651,485	25.7	153,936	6.1	90,714	
2008	2,260,000*	not av.	-	not av.		92,800	61,000
1990–2008	- 11	+ 60*		+ 170*		+ 43*	+ 133.3

Sources: produced by the author on the basis of data from ISTAT [Italian Institute for Statistics], the Interior Ministry and www.giustizia.it [the Justice Ministry website].

*Note: my estimates, since updated information is not available to include 2008 in the total number of criminal offences recorded by police forces (acting on their own initiative or based on allegations made by citizens), but according to statements made by the chief of police himself, there has been a decrease in crime of at least a 12–15 per cent (from 2006 to the end of 2008); however, arrests and the number of prisoners, which in late March 2008 had climbed back to 61,000, i.e. as many as they had been before the pardon law released over 26,000 of them. As in the United States, a reversal in the progress of the relation between number of crimes, arrests and imprisonment, which is the typical trend of zero tolerance, or indeed the 'Crime Deal', is confirmed by data. In 2008, among the 'entries from freedom' into Italian prisons, 46 per cent concerned foreigners. The regions with the most entrants were Lombardy (15,648, of whom 10,021 foreigners), Campania (10,760, of whom 2,201 foreigners), Piedmont (9,933, of whom 6,002 foreigners), Latium (8,649 of whom 4,237 foreigners). More generally, criminal offences have diminished. They have been 7,500 per day on average; pick-pocketing has fallen by 24 per cent, mugging by 21 per cent (below 10,000), car theft by 19 per cent (76,000), there have been fewer frauds reported (-21 per cent, 52,000), 11 per cent fewer robberies (less than 24,000 cases), 8 per cent fewer home burglaries (72,000). Murders remain stable at around 610–620 per year (according to the 2007 Interior Ministry report – the most recent available, they were 1,918 in 1991, the year with most murders since 1968, and in 2006, out of 621 murders, 109 were committed by organized crime).

The ratio between people reported and arrested was 6.7 in 1990 (7.6 for Italians and 2.8 for foreigners), 5.7 in 1999 (6.4 for Italians and 3.3 for foreigners), 4.4 in 2005 (6.1 for Italians and 2.9 for foreigners), and 4.2 in 2006 (around 7 for Italians and 3 for foreigners). In other words, immigrants have a greater chance of being reported, arrested and imprisoned than Italians.

Table 13.2   Italians and foreigners reported, arrested and imprisoned from 1990 to the end of 2005 – detainees before the pardon in 2006

Year	Reported				Arrested				Imprisoned			
	Italians	% of tot.	Foreigners	% of tot.	Italians	% of tot.	foreigners	% of tot.	Italians	% of tot.	Foreigners	% / tot
1990	403,175	92.5	32,576	7.5	53,155	82	11,659	18	22,133	84.6	4,017	15.4
1995	587,193	91.1	57,190	8.9	88,827	80	22,244	20	38,716	81.8	8,628	12.2
1999	606,603	86.6	93,596	13.4	95,185	77	28,067	23	38,000	71.7	15,000	28.3
2005	434,301	67.4	210,231	32.6	71,466	49.2	73,765	50.8	40,273	67	19,836	33

Sources: produced by the author on the basis of data from ISTAT [Italian Institute for Statistics], the Interior Ministry and www.giustizia.it [the Justice Ministry website].

Note: The sharp decrease corresponds to the Pardon Law of 2006; the re-imprisonment of many who had benefited from it reflects the almost complete lack of assistance to those released from prison.

Table 13.3   Criminalization trends in Italy: a comparison between Italians and foreigners

Year	Foreign detainees	Annual increase	% Foreigners on total	Total detainees	Italians	Incr. Italians
1990	4,017		*15.4*	26,150	22,133	
1991	5,365	33.6	*15.1*	35,485	30,120	36.1
1992	7,237	34.9	*15.2*	47,588	40,351	34
1993	7,892	9.1	*15.7*	50,212	42,320	4.9
1994	8,481	7.5	*16.6*	51,231	42,750	1
1995	8,334	-1.7	*17.6*	47,344	39,010	-8.7
1996	9,373	12.5	*19.5*	48,049	38,676	-0.9
1997	10,825	15.5	*24.1*	45,000	34,175	-11.6
1998	11,973	10.6	*23.9*	50,000	38,027	11.3
1999	14,057	17.4	*26.6*	52,870	38,813	2.1
2000	15,582	10.8	*28.8*	54,039	38,457	-0.9
2001	16,294	4.6	*29.3*	55,539	39,245	2
2002	16,778	3	*30.1*	55,670	38,892	-0.9
2003	17,007	1.4	*31.4*	54,237	37,230	-4.3
2004	17,819	4.8	*31.8*	56,068	38,249	2.7
2005	19,836	11.3	*33.3*	59,523	39,687	3.8
2006*	13,152	-33.7	*33.7*	39,005	25,853	-34.9
2007	18,252	38.8	*37.5*	48,693	30,441	17.7
2008	21,891	19.9	*37.1*	59,060	37,169	22.1
March 2010	24.992	13.8	*37.2*	67.046	42,124	13,3

* *year* of the pardon.

Source: produced by the author on the basis of ISTAT [Italian Institute for Statistics] and DAP [Italian prison administration service] data.

Note: From 1990 to 1994, centre-left governments; 1994: Berlusconi gov.; 1995–2000: centre-left governments; from 2001 to 2005: Berlusconi gov.; from 2006 to 2008: centre-left governments; from 2008: Berlusconi gov. 1990: Martelli law; 1995: Dini decree; 1998: Turco-Napolitano law; 2004: Bossi-Fini law; 2009: new security package (Maroni).

Since the pardon, Italian detainees have increased by 43.8 per cent and foreigners by 66.4 per cent (at the end of 2008). The return to imprisonment after the pardon was effectively spurred on first by the Prodi government and then by Berlusconi's return. The interior minister of the Prodi government, Amato, openly stated that he would follow 'the example set by Giuliani's zero tolerance', and the then mayor of Rome, Veltroni, who later became the leader of the centre-left, called for the expulsion of Romanians (see Maneri's chapter), raising protests from the European Commission itself and the Strasbourg Parliament (see Sigona's and Trehan's chapter), following the murder of Mrs Giovanna Reggiani by a mentally ill Romanian/Roma man.

Table 13.4   Incidence of the increase of Italian and foreigner detainees on the total increment of the imprisoned population

Year	Foreigners	Incidence of increase of foreigners on total increment	Italians + foreigners	Italians	Incidence of increase of Italians on total increment
1990	4,017		26,150	22,133	
1991	5,365	14	35,485	30,120	86
1992	7,237	15	47,588	40,351	85
1993	7,892	25	50,212	42,320	75
1994	8,481	58	51,231	42,750	42
1995	8,334	Decrease	47,344 Decrease	39,010	Decrease
1996	9,373	Increase	48,049	38,676	Decrease
1997	10,825	Increase	45,000 Decrease	34,175	Decrease
1998	11,973	23	50,000	38,027	77
1999	14,057	73	52,870	38,813	27
2000	15,582	Increase	54,039	38,457	Decrease
2001	16,294	47	55,539	39,245	53
2002	16,778	Increase	55,670	38,892	Decrease
2003	17,007	Increase	54,237 Decrease	37,230	Decrease
2004	17,819	44	56,068	38,249	56

Year	Foreigners	Incidence of increase of foreigners on total increment	Italians + foreigners	Italians	Incidence of increase of Italians on total increment
2005	19,836	58	59,523	39,687	42
2006*	13,152	Decrease	39,005 Decrease	25,853	Decrease
2007	18,252	53	48,693	30,441	47
2008	21,891	35	59,060	37,169	65
2010 **	24,496	37	66,161	41,665	63

* *year* of the pardon.

Sources: produced by the author on the basis of data from ISTAT [Italian Institute for Statistics], the Interior Ministry and www.giustizia.it [the Justice Ministry website]. ** Data of May 2010 from DAP [Italian prison administration service] – Justice Ministry.

Note: Without explaining here the specific yearly developments, we can observe that the total number of prisoners has slightly decreased in three years, diminishing dramatically just in the year of pardon (the 'parentheses' of pardon lasted about one year). These calculations show that foreigners replace Italians, although the trend is not constant. However, during the 20 analysed years such phenomenon is more evident: in some years there is a decrease in the number of Italians and an increase in the number of foreigners, and as shown in the above Table, the incidence of the increase of foreigner detainees has greatly affected the total increment of the imprisoned population. It could also be said that both centre-left and centre-right governments, especially the latter, have practised the same policy, repressing more and more foreigners, who have always been accused of less serious crimes than those being contested by the Italians and punished proportionately higher than the latter. Interestingly, in spite of the incitement to repress foreigners during the last period of the Prodi government and even more with the return to power of the right – and in particular following the success of the League –the percentage of foreigners has not increased, nor has the incidence of their increase on the total increment of the imprisoned population grown. 'Is there no alien arrested?', 'Have they finished scraping the bottom of the barrel?' 'The police officers are fed up with persecuting the unfortunate of the earth.' These are the comments of some prison managers and police operators. And maybe this is one of the obvious symptoms of the failure of 'zero tolerance' and in particular the clash of the exasperated war on migration.

The current interior minister, Maroni, is leader of the Lega Nord, a party that for years, and now more than ever, has sought to be the leading if not the only anti-immigrant political force, not even attempting to conceal its blatantly racist overtones. Maroni has never lost an opportunity to call for the repression of migrants who, except for when they live lives of submission as slaves in the underground economy (also to the benefit of the small entrepreneurs of Padania

– Lega Nord's imagined homeland in northern Italy's Po Valley), are suspected delinquents.[12] The result is that in two years, the stock of detainees has returned to the levels prior to the 2006 pardon that had released around 26,000 people, but the majority of the new 20,000 detainees that have since gone behind bars is composed by foreigners and by Italians who are serial repeat offenders (a figure that reflects the deterioration in the provision of services aimed at social recovery, particularly in the case of the drop in the number of public SERT centres assisting drug addicts, due to the logic of neoliberalism and privatization, which has subcontracted the treatment of addicts to private rehab communities, which cure the wealthy and throw the poor back onto the streets[13]).

The recent, brazen wave of criminalization in the first decade of the 21st century appears even more disgraceful when looking at the crimes attributed to foreigners. According to data from the DAP (prison service administration, available at www. giustizia.it), the percentage of Italian detainees sentenced to house arrest or other non-prison punishment is 50.5 per cent, whereas that for foreigners is of 37.7 per cent, confirming that foreigners are often held in prisons because they are deemed too unreliable to be given house arrest or placement in a community.

<hr />

12   One of the paradoxes of the Nord League demagogy is the constant demand for expulsion of immigrants: as a matter of fact most immigrants, both regular and irregular, live in Northern Italy and their work – inferiorized, underpaid and racialized –is essential for the economy of this area. Therefore the Nord League's intolerance is a perfect tool for relegating the immigrants to a status without rights. The speeches and statements of Minister Maroni and of the Northern League leaders are accessible in Parliamentary publications. See also Maneri's chapter.

13   The apparent paradox of the Crime Deal finds its full expression in the choices made by many local right and centre-left administrators. While increasingly more resources are devoted to police forces, video-surveillance and even citizens' patrols to secure city centres, nothing is said or done about drug addicts who, in increasing numbers, have gone back to injecting themselves in the streets, particularly because SERTs (public rehab centres) no longer operate, due to the neoliberal logic that has casualized medical and paramedical employment, forcing them to supplement their miserable contracts with others working for private rehab communities, which are preferred by current policy-makers but do not cure the worst off. Consider the situation of social workers or psychologists who have 24-hour contracts and are expected to deal with 80 cases a day! An emblematic example is the demagogy of the mayor of Genoa (Democratic Party) and her councillor-sheriff (Italia dei Valori) who, in the name of hygiene, decorum and morality, have moved forcefully against (foreign) prostitutes living in the alleys of the old city centre. According to some observers this action had some effect on the criminals, but more on encouraging property speculation in the cleared up area. See evidence at http://www.sanbenedetto.org/index. php?option=com_content&view=article&id=572%3Agenova-ripulisce-i-bassi-e-caccia-le-prostitute&catid=17%3Aapprofondimenti&Itemid=80 and also http://circospetto.net/tag/il-secolo-xix/

Table 13.5 Offences attributed to detainees present in penitentiary institutes (at 31 December 2008)

typology of crimes	Italians					Foreigners							Overall total	%
	women	men	Total	%		women	Men	toal	%	%*				
Mafia-style association	87	5,376	5,463	3.9		2	93	95	0.2	1.7			5,558	3.0
drugs law	717	16,663	17,380	12.4		570	11,563	12,133	26.3	41.1			29,513	15.9
weapons law	313	25,379	25,692	18.4		31	1,797	1,828	4.0	6.6			27,520	14.8
public order	31	2,053	2,084	1.5		60	690	750	1.6	26.5			2,834	1.5
against property	1,213	41,464	42,677	30.5		611	11,692	12,303	26.7	22.4			54,980	29.6
Prostitution	16	146	162	0.1		134	704	838	1.8	83.8			1,000	0.5
against the public administration	114	4,568	4,682	3.3		35	2,692	2,727	5.9	36.8			7,409	4.0
public safety	34	1,604	1,638	1.2		4	194	198	0.4	10.8			1,836	1.0
public faith	159	4,179	4,338	3.1		111	1,847	1,958	4.3	31.1			6,296	3.4
public morality	3	166	169	0.1		0	57	57	0.1	25.2			226	0.1
against the family	46	991	1,037	0.7		7	257	264	0.6	20.3			1,301	0.7
against the person	657	21,000	21,657	15.5		361	8,507	8,868	19.3	29.1			30,525	16.4
against the State's legal status	100	277	377	0.3		3	97	100	0.2	21.0			477	0.3
against the admin. of justice	149	4,314	4,463	3.2		55	540	595	1.3	11.8			5,058	2.7

typology of crimes	Italians				Foreigners					Overall total	%
	women	men	Total	%	women	Men	toal	%	%*		
public economy	8	476	484	0.3	0	8	8	0.0	1.6	492	0.3
Fines	56	3,506	3,562	2.5	17	484	501	1.1	12.3	4,063	2.2
foreigners' law	6	93	99	0.1	120	2,263	2,383	5.2	96.0	2,482	1.3
against feelings & piety for the deceased	29	1,137	1,166	0.8	7	86	93	0.2	7.4	1,259	0.7
other crimes	47	2,668	2,715	1.9	16	352	368	0.8	11.9	3,083	1.7
total crimes	3,785	136,060	139,845	100.0	2,144	43,923	46,067	100.0	24.8	185,912	100.0

Source: DAP – Ufficio per lo Sviluppo e la Gestione del Sistema Informativo Automatizzato – Sezione Statistica.

Note: If a number of different crimes, falling within one or more categories, are attributed to the same detainee, they will be counted several times, once for each offence. Hence, the general total turns out to be higher than the number of subjects (that is, 185,912 criminal offences for 59,060 detainees), see http://www.giustizia.it/statistiche/statistiche_dap/detderg54_reati.htm

As the Table shows, the percentage of total crimes ascribed to foreigners is lower than the percentage of foreigners themselves in the total number of detainees. The only crime figuring as committed mostly by foreigners is 'prostitution'. This corresponds to police practices – often conditioned by local mobilizations of 'zealous' citizens (see Becker, 1963) more or less racist – against street prostitution now practised mainly by foreigners, often victims of organized crime. However, many foreign prostitutes are victims of violence and sometimes murder by Italian and not just foreign pimps.[14]

The total number of crimes for which foreigners are charged constitute 23.6 per cent of the crimes attributed to the total prison population of 59,060 detainees; in other terms, on its own, this figure shows that the thesis seeking to attribute the increase in delinquency to immigrants is false. This is even more true when the most serious crimes (organized crime, murder, armed robbery) are considered. The ratio between crimes committed and the number of detainees is 4 for Italians and 2 for foreigners, who are hence imprisoned for committing fewer crimes than the Italians. The great majority of foreigners are either accused of minor crimes (dealing, theft, causing injuries) or of crimes that are typically attributed to immigrants (against public administration, for infringing the law on immigration); the criminal offence regarding unlawful weapons may just concern the possession of a knife. In other senses, if one observes the ratio between peop being reported and people being arrested, it surfaces that as the years pass, foreigners face an increasing possibility of being arrested rather than reported, whereas the opposite occurs for Italians, who – apart from serial repeat offenders – generally benefit from discounts on jail terms, alternative sentencing to prison etc. As is well known, the Bossi-Fini law[15] has further worsened this trend by formally and effectively turning the status of clandestine or irregular immigration into a criminal offence (that may even apply to people who have been in Italy regularly for years but have not been able to renew their permits, not because they have committed crimes, but because they can no longer find regular employment and accommodation; the second time that they are stopped without papers they go to prison, that is, they go on to have criminal offences and are destined to be expelled). The dogged pursuit of so-called *clandestini* (irregular immigrants) always depends on inputs from central government and from local authorities, but it is quite obvious that police forces 'turn even two blind eyes' when they have

---

14   On these aspects see Palidda (2001, 2009b); Dal Lago and Quadrelli (2003).

15   The 'Bossi-Fini' law passed on 30 July 30 2002 (Bossi is the leader of the Northern League and Fini was the leader of the right-wing party). The law emphasizes all aspects of prohibitionism and repression of immigration. Those aspects were already in the previous centre-left law passed on 6 March 1998. With the current government, Minister Maroni has increased the penalties for crimes typically attributed to immigrants even more. It is also now more difficult to achieve and maintain immigration regularity. On all these issues, see the website www.asgi.it

to deal with 'illegals'[16] who work silently in the underground economy for small company bosses who are well protected from the threat of controls, since they are either subcontractors for large construction businesses or provide cleaning and other services to banks, ministries, courts and, maybe, even in prefectures and city police headquarters.[17]

We can now observe criminalization rates, calculated considering foreign males in relation to the total number of regular male immigrants, to which I have added an estimate of irregular migrants (minors are not recorded by residence permits); as regards Italians, the calculation concerns males between 18 and 65 years of age (by law, minors cannot be held in prison, while it is very rare to find inmates who are over 65). It is then important to compare the detention rate for each nationality with the Italian rate (as we do for blacks and Latinos with respect to whites in the United States).

Almost 70 per cent of foreign detainees are made up of Moroccans, Tunisians, Albanians, Romanians, Algerians and Nigerians. The rate for Italian males is 197 (that is, 197 detainees for every 100,000 males between 18 and 65 years of age), while that for foreign males is 946 (for every 100,000 regulars + an estimate of irregulars); the ratio between the detention rate for foreigners and the rate for Italians is 5; four nationalities ('the bad guys') have a rate that is more than ten times higher than the Italian rate, whereas nine ('the good guys') of those taken into consideration display a rate which is less than or equal to that of Italians. Predictably, higher rates are likely to reproduce themselves although, in comparison with recent years, there has been an evident decrease in the detention rates of Albanians and Algerians. Moreover, in spite of the government and media campaigns inciting hatred against Romanians, they do not exhibit the highest rates. Conversely, the 'good guys' are generally the object of positive prejudice and are effectively better treated by police forces, also because they often live in milieus that are less visible to the public (as is the case with domestic workers). Generally, the majority of foreigners in prison is composed of youths who are charged with offences of theft, stolen goods and small-time drug dealing, often 'desperate' youths who have become deviant due to a lack of possibility of regular and stable social integration, either because they are intoxicated by the illusion of quick and

16   According to recent more reliable estimates (see Fondazione ISMU 2009) irregular immigrants in Italy are about 500,000–650,000 and they live mainly in Northern Italy where the Northern League party and Mr Berlusconi's party govern all local administrations. Both local and national police do not stop these immigrants because they are indispensable in theirs multiple possible roles: carers, workers or neo-slaves, caporals enslaving their countrymen and, in a small part, dealers, fences of stolen goods and 'workers' in other small illegal activities (in other words, clerical jobs especially in poorly paid, dangerous risky environments).

17   Moreover, remember the sensational case of the 'clandestine' Nigerian security guard employed for as long as 19 months as an armed guard in the UK Home Office (Corriere.it, 7 December 2007). Ridiculous but tragic for the victim: he was arrested and immediately expelled.

easy earnings, or because they had already slipped into delinquency in their home countries, particularly when these are marked by the sharp deterioration in their institutional structures (as is the case with Algeria, Nigeria, and other African and Middle Eastern countries) (see Palidda, 2001, 2008a, 2008b).

Table 13.6   Foreign detainees by leading nationalities in Italy (at 31 December 2008)

Country (% of women on total of permits)	Male detainees	Rate for males	Ratio, foreign rate/ Italian rate
Albania (44.7 % women)	2,582	1,099	6
Algeria (30.5 % women)	1,105	4,804	24
Bangladesh (32.4 % women)	32	58	0
Bosnia (43.9 % women)	162	810	4
China (47.3 % women)	306	340	2
Croatia (47.9 % women)	109	606	3
Ecuador (60.2 % women)	114	326	2
Egypt (29.5 % women)	379	632	3
Philippines (58.5 % women)	50	111	1
Ghana (43.7 % women)	137	685	3
India (40.2 % women)	88	220	1
Macedonia (42.4 % women)	106	193	1
Morocco (40.8 % women)	4,791	2,083	11
Moldova (66.4 % women)	207	767	4
Nigeria (57 % women)	790	3,950	20
Pakistan (30 % women)	120	300	2
Peru (60.7 % women)	152	434	2
Poland (70.2 % women)	194	554	3
Romania (52.9 % women)	2,485	777	4
Senegal (19.4 % women)	366	665	3
Sri Lanka (44.2 % women)	42	105	1
Tunisia (35.1 % women)	2,618	3,740	19
Ukraine (80.4 % women)	152	507	3
Total, foreign men	20,806	946	5
Italians	37,169	197	1

Source: produced by the author on the basis of DAP and ISTAT data.

According to a *cliché* that has also been supported by democratic experts,[18] irregular immigrants are supposed to be 'bad', whereas regular immigrants are 'good'. The basis for this assertion is that almost all the foreigners in prison do not possess a residence permit. In reality, this is a ridiculous claim, not just because any foreigner who ends up in jail loses his or her regular status, but also because research about the number of detainees who had a residence permit in the past has never been carried out, and it is predictable that irregular migrants are more likely to experience repressive policing and penal measures (starting from the offence of not returning to the home country after an expulsion injunction, or because they are suspected of other crimes).

A Question of *Terroni*[19]

As we have seen in previous contributions, in the United States the customary target for repressive and penal action is constituted by blacks and Latinos, in England by non-British citizens, in Germany, by foreigners, in France by foreigners and French of foreign origin, while Belgium and Holland are more or less similar situations to the French case. In Italy, next to foreigners, there is a perpetuation of the criminalization of southerners. They are often considered the alleged authors of certain crimes, especially on suspicion of membership in a Mafia-type organization. The following is what can be drawn from official statistics.

Table 13.7   Detainees by region of birth at the end of 2008

Region of birth	detained males	rates for males	ratio wrt average rate for 'virtuous'
Abruzzo	365	88.1	1.2
Basilicata	278	148.8	2.1
Calabria	2,717	430.4	6.1
Campania	9,184	501.2	7.1
Emilia R.	594	44.1	0.6
Friuli V. G.	225	57.4	0.8

18   According to ISTAT (the Italian National Institute of Statistics) the degree of deviance of the regulars would be only 2 per cent; the majority of crimes committed by foreigners is at 80 per cent due to their irregular condition.

19   *Terroni* (and before that *cafoni*) is the derogatory term historically used for the people of the south which refers to their rural, uncouth origin.

Region of birth	detained males	rates for males	ratio wrt average rate for 'virtuous'
Latium	2,316	132.4	1.9
Liguria	459	94.0	1.3
Lombardy	2,781	88.5	1.3
Marches	185	38.3	0.5
Molise	73	72.4	1.0
Piedmont	1,134	81.6	1.2
Apulia	4,024	311.9	4.4
Sardinia	1,387	247.6	3.5
Sicily	7,075	456.0	6.4
Tuscany	603	52.6	0.7
Trentino A. A.	182	56.3	0.8
Umbria	90	33.0	0.5
Valle d'Aosta	8	19.3	0.3
Veneto	845	53.7	0.8
Born abroad	21,076	958.0	13.5
National total	**55,601**	294.0	4.2
Italians	34,525	194.5	2.8

Source: elaborated by the author on the basis of data from www.giustizia.it

As the data from the previous Table showed, males born abroad are imprisoned 4.2 times more on average than Italians, but it must also be noted that those born in the *Mezzogiorno* are imprisoned 2–2.5 times more on average. One finds the highest rates of imprisonment in Campania, Calabria, Sicily, Apulia and Sardinia. By comparing the rates affecting people born in the southern regions (i.e. *terroni*) and people born abroad, with the 'virtuous rates' (i.e. lower than 100) affecting the remaining regions – Abruzzo, Basilicata, Emilia Romagna, Friuli, Lazio, Liguria, Lombardy, the Marches, Molise, Piedmont, Tuscany, Trentino, Umbria, Val d'Aosta and Veneto – one finds that the resulting ratios are quite high: those born abroad are imprisoned 13.5 times more than 'good Italians', while *terroni* are imprisoned from 3.5 to 7.1 times more. In the regions where the rate of imprisonment of natives is comparatively higher, the incarceration rate of foreigners is lower or equal to that of natives (which means that natives and foreigners are included in the same category as a priori suspects).

Table 13.8   Differences between 'virtuous' and 'rogue' regions of Italy

Regions of detention	Total	Born abroad	
Abruzzo	1,678	472	28.1 %
Basilicata	533	168	31.5 %
Calabria	2,286	674	29.5 %
Campania	7,185	981	13.7 %
Emilia R.	4,074	2,139	52.5 %
Friuli V. G.	741	439	59.2 %
Latium	5,366	2,107	39.3 %
Liguria	1,380	745	54.0 %
Lombardy	8,090	3,619	44.7 %
Marches	1,017	421	41.4 %
Molise	396	87	22.0 %
Piedmont	4,636	2,403	51.8 %
Apulia	3,556	727	20.4 %
Sardinia	2,132	912	42.8 %
Sicily	6,870	1,853	27.0 %
Tuscany	3,811	1,881	49.4 %
Trentino A. A.	339	187	55.2 %
Umbria	906	397	43.8 %
Valle D'Aosta	152	100	65.8 %
Veneto	2,979	1,870	62.8 %
National total	58,127	22,182	38.2 %

Source: www.giustizia.it

In as many as 13 regions, the proportion of foreign detainees is higher than the national average, and in eight they reach or exceed the 50 per cent threshold. 80 per cent of foreigners in prison are concentrated in seven regions (Piedmont, Lombardy, Veneto, Emilia, Tuscany, Latium and Sicily). It is worth noting than in Sicily there is a relatively high number of imprisoned foreigners for 'repeat offences' with respect to the injunction to leave and, perhaps, also because the

Mafia sometimes causes foreigners to be arrested to distract attention from itself and gain favour among the police forces.

Thus, it appears that the traditional paradigm of post-unitary Italy re-emerges again. According to nineteenth-century criminologists, like Lombroso and his acolytes, there could be no interpretative doubts: *terroni* are more criminal than 'civilized' Italians, and foreign *terroni* even more so (as was the case with 'blood-thirsty savages' from the colonies, as Lombrosians used to say and write – see Palidda, 2008a, 2008b). In effect, albeit not explicitly, even today, many (not just Lega Nord supporters, but even 'left-wing' northern supremacists[20]) subscribe to this prejudice and such construct appears to be confirmed by 'evidence' that seems indisputable: those imprisoned the most are born in mafia-ridden regions, in towns with the most delinquency and deterioration (territories deemed to be 'not very civilized'; furthermore, an interpretation of the book *Gomorra*[21] by the nordist people lends credit to the thesis according to which a southern deviant or delinquent must inevitably be an actual or potential member of a Mafia-style organization, while a majority of public opinion seems to think that all the ills of the Naples metropolitan area – from unauthorized waste dumps to the Camorra, up to the corruption of politicians – are entirely the Neapolitans' fault).

But are the imprisoned southerners really delinquents or criminals who are members of Mafia-like organizations? One would not say so from what emerges from the charges, even though they are sometimes made worse than they are (attempted theft or mugging being turned into attempted robbery)[22]; effectively, a large majority of foreigners and southerners arrested and imprisoned are mere deviants, or just suspected delinquents. In short, they belong to that share of the population facing high odds of being criminalized due to negative stereotyping, as well as government racism that develops into state racism through the acts of some police officers and magistrates.[23] It is obvious that southern deviants are

---

20   Beyond appearances, the majority of Italian intelligentsia – even that of southern origin now participating in the national mainstream – share the stigma of the South with a revival of negative stereotypes (amoral familism, propensity to lawlessness etc.). Hence the success of the Northern League, which collects votes even among older Italian immigrants of southern origin: the affirmation of their emancipation involves also the adherence to nordism, i.e. the superiority over the South and especially to obtain more privileges as 'nordist-padanian citizens' than the rest of Italians. The same is true of Italian immigrants well integrated in the countries of immigration, for example in France, many Italians are racist, *plus français que les Français* (more French than the French).

21   A critique from by a 'left' point of view of the famous book by Saviano is proposed by Dal Lago (2010), but also – implicitly – by Petrillo (2009).

22   According to statistics of the Dipartimento Amministrazione Penitenziaria (DAP) (see Table 12.4) convictions for crimes regarding criminal Mafia-like organizations are a small minority while most prisoners in southern Italy are charged with rape, robbery, assault, burglary, larceny / theft, motor vehicle theft and arson.

23   The literature on the practices of the police since the first Chicago school until Banton, Bittner, Goldstein, Reiner, Reiss and others has shown that discretion within police

liable to become workhands for Mafia rings, but it is likewise evident that this is a self-fulfilling prophecy if Mafia-like organizations are the only existing social institutions, which, in their own way 'take care of the people', and provide credible job offers in a 'market' where legitimate institutions have either melted away or have become corrupt and unlawful as well (widespread corruption in the South is a mix between neoliberal privatizations of public services and old nepotism linked to Mafias).

Recent examples of criminalization, particularly of Neapolitans, include the campaign against 'wild garbage' that systematically singled out the population as the uncivilized culprits, when it is precisely the population who rebelled against illegal dumping. The population has been clamouring for years for better waste management, while engaging in the separation of domestic waste for recycling, and vociferously complaining about the disposal of toxic waste in residential areas where people are facing a dramatic increase in death rates and illnesses resulting from environmental contamination by toxic wastes.[24]

A grotesque episode in 2008 concerned the hypermediatization of a falsely reported assault on a train in the Termini train station of Rome by Neapolitan football supporters, a falsification that was zealously reinforced even by interior minister Maroni and his police chief.[25]

On 31 August, as the first weekend of Italian football drew to a close, television news programmes and newspapers announced that a horde of Napoli *ultras* (soccer hooligans) had assaulted the 'Modigliani' Intercity train heading to Rome from Naples, devastating it, beating the ticket inspectors and holding hostage dozens of frightened passengers in the process. The only source for such alleged news: a statement by Trenitalia that spoke of an 'entirely vandalised train, substantial damage to 11 train cars, the emergency brake activated repeatedly, a first estimate of damages at 500,000 euros'. A review of the media coverage on television news programmes and newspaper headlines follows.

Tg1 TV news: 'Intercity for Rome, only football hooligans on board: 500,000 euros in damages'. Tg2: 'Chaos in Naples and Rome stations: Napoli supporters attack a train'. Tg3: 'Napoli supporters take over the train, hell breaks loose in Naples station, 300 passengers taken hostage, stations devastated'. Studio Aperto: 'Warfare, panic among passengers thrown out of the train, four railway workers injured'. *Corriere della Sera*: 'Ultras raid trains: damages and chaos'. *La Repubblica*: 'Ultras raid train, passengers thrown out by fans'. *Il Mattino*: 'Naples, ultras assault train'. *La Stampa*: 'Ultras destroy train'. *L'Unità*: 'The train of fear: an Intercity taken hostage by Napoli supporters'. *Il Giornale*: 'Napoli

---

powers can turn into discrimination and free will (sometimes 'to good ends' – see also Palidda 2000, 2010a and 2010b).

24   On this episode and in general about the criminalization of meridional people, see the excellent research undertaken by the team directed by Petrillo (2009).

25   Here, I draw on extracts from documents on football supporters collected by Tommaso Tintori for his PhD thesis at Dipt. (Disa) of Genoa University.

ultras 'steal' the train: there's the game, passengers thrown out' (followed by an editorial titled 'Football Gomorra').

Some TV reports even spoke of 'homemade bombs' exploded on arrival at Termini station. Then the government and the police, facing criticism for not having prevented something that was rather predictable, stated that the *ultras* were in fact disguised *camorristi* engaged in 'terrorism' (recall that charges of terrorism have also been brandished against Roman *ultras* after the disturbances – real ones – following the death of football fan Sandri after he was shot by a police officer miles away from any stadium). This fabrication also produced huge xerox-like headlines[26]: '200 previous offenders on the ultras' train'. 'Not hooligans, but camorristi and terrorists'. 'What are the judges doing?'. 'Zero tolerance'. 'Certainty of punishment'. The president of the Lega Calcio [Football League] Antonio Matarrese proposed to arrest a few thousand of them and hold them locked up in stadiums, like Pinochet did. Panorama: 'Maroni: zero tolerance against ultras'. 'Maroni: camorristi and delinquents among the ultras. Out of 3,096 Napoli fans who bought tickets for the game against AS Roma, 810 had police records and 27 were linked to the Camorra. This is what the interior minister, Roberto Maroni, said during a hearing to the Constitutional Affairs commission of the Senate.. the minister explained that 'there is the influence of the Camorra' on Napoli supporters. Corriere: 'This is not about organized supporters, it is about organized crime.. The words of interior minister Maroni found fertile ground. In Naples, organized crime means Camorra, so the chief of police Manganelli upped the ante: 'It is possible to say that there is the influence of organized crime behind the direction of the disturbances caused by Napoli fans.'. Six months later, not even one *ultrà* had been charged or arrested. In an investigative report titled 'La bufala campana' [*bufala* is a word used both to refer to high-grade mozzarella cheese from Campania made with water buffalo milk, and to signal a hoax or a spoof story], Rainews24 correspondent Enzo Cappucci, working on the conclusions reached by the prosecuting magistrate in charge of the case, Antonello Ardituro, showed that it was a matter of a lot of noise about nothing. No arrests, no wanton destruction. Only some instances of damage. No homemade bombs, at most some petards and fireworks. As for the injuries to ticket inspectors, there is no trace of them as yet: Rainews asked for their medical records, in vain. Of the 11 carriages that were 'vandalized', Trenitalia has only placed four at the investigators' disposal: the others are still travelling without any worries. And what about the '500,000 euros worth of damages'? There is no sign of them. The DIGOS [the political police directorate overseeing special operations] and Carabinieri talk of 80 damaged curtains, some cuts in seats, two broken glass partitions and a ripped out toilet (although it must be proven that it was the *ultras* who did this, considering the state in which Italian

---

26   All headlines and quotations are taken from the newspapers (see M. Travaglio, 'Tanto fumo, niente arresti', 5 October 2008 at: http://www.voglioscendere.ilcannocchiale. it/post/2047620.html) and above all by the report of RAINEWS24 available at : http://www. youtube.com/watch?v=LUItACXfyT4

trains are in even in the absence of *ultras*): things worth a few thousand euros, no more than that. And the 'assaults against the two stations?'. Another lie: 'Normal images of an ordinary Sunday arrival of soccer fans into another city'. Rainews 24 showed sequences of Verona fans leaving Naples a couple of years earlier, insulting police officers and Neapolitans amid the usual cloud of smoke bombs (at the time, however, this did not even merit a short article). Cappucci interviewed some eyewitnesses, including Tommaso Delli Paoli, secretary-general of the SIULP-CGIL police trade union: 'The ultras are no angels, but nothing of what was said actually happened. [It was] normal tension between ultras with tickets and documents who wanted to get to the stadium of Rome, and the Trenitalia staff who first blocked the train in the station and then again in the open countryside. I don't think they pulled the emergency brakes, since they were in a hurry to get to Rome. It appears that the train shown on television was not the real one.' Violence against train staff, ticket officers and passengers? Two Austrian sports journalists who were on the train in question as well, did not see 'any violence or clash. Destruction? No, the train was too full for people to move. The only fear was that of missing the game, as the train was not leaving.' What about the Camorra? And terrorism? Yes, there were a few dozen people with criminal records, so what? (see previous footnotes).

What was the cause of such alarm? Does the criminal offence of reporting false and misleading news liable to disrupt public order exist? Why did the interior minister and the head of police make such statements? And what about the falsehoods concerning the rebellion of Neapolitan citizens against the emergency construction of waste disposal landfills?

Everything occurs as if social history is repeating itself. The mind goes to the times of Hugo's France or Engels' England. A criminalized population or a population turned criminal can easily morph into the 'mass' or the 'mob' which power resorts to and manoeuvres in order to interiorize the discourse and categorizations of dominant actors. So it isthis kind of *lumpeproletariat*, these *classes dangereuses* which make part of the Southern population that are today called to mobilize against Roma gypsies, against African immigrants, or to display their hooligan enthusiasm for a charismatic leader.[27]

---

27 There are eloquent documentaries in this respect: 'Presa diretta' by Iacona (2009), and, more recently, 'Il Tempo delle Arance', http://www.vimeo.com/8812128, shot by InsuTv in Rosarno during the days (January 2010) of the pogroms and deportations of immigrant fruit-pickers in Calabria.

PART III
Particular Practices

Chapter 14

The Road to Racial Profiling Was Paved by Immigrants

Bernard E. Harcourt

The 'legal use of racial profiling' – it is hard to even utter these words.[1] Yet, for several decades now, at least since the mid-1970's, the highest court of the United States has condoned the use of ethnic or racial features in law enforcement. In explicit terms, the Supreme Court has allowed police officers to use the colour of someone's skin to justify a stop, to legitimate interrogation, to facilitate a police search.

To trace the genealogy of this sordid practice, one must begin on the back roads and interstate highways off the Mexican–American border – at the road blocks, INS checkpoints, and roving patrols policing immigrant border crossings. The road to racial profiling in the United States, it turns out, was paved on those dirt paths. There, the United States Supreme Court opened the door to racial profiling – and it did so at the most sensitive location, the place where ethnicity and appearance were at their most salient. Naturally, racial profiling has not stopped at the border. Today, it has spilled over into countless other areas of policing and social practice.

There is a saying in American that 'a chain is only as strong as its weakest link'. In the United States, the anti-discrimination chain was broken at the border – at the exact location where ordinary men and women so easily became despised. The consequences, tragically, were foreseeable and the repercussions are now long lasting. To begin the story, though, let's start at the trail head, in the Southern deserts, on the American border with Mexico.

---

1   In this chapter, 'racial profiling' is defined as the knowing use by the police of race as a factor in the decision to investigate a suspect, based on the assumption that persons of the designated race or ethnicity are more likely to be offenders. The term 'racial profiling' is of recent vintage. See generally Harcourt (2004); Skolnick and Caplovitz (2003) (discussing the history of the 'racial profiling' expression). There is today some controversy over the definition of the term 'racial profiling'. Some commentators argue that the term 'racial profiling' should be limited more narrowly to those cases where the police rely on race exclusively; others use the term when race is a significant factor among others in the decision to investigate. For discussions of the controversy, see, for example, Russell (2001); Alschuler (2002); Gross and Barnes (2002). The definition used in this chapter includes using race alone or as one factor among others in the decision to stop and search.

Patrolling the Mexican Border

As politicians became increasingly concerned with extralegal immigration in the mid-twentieth century, the INS Border Patrol – the agency in charge of patrolling the borders of the United States – refined its techniques for detecting immigrants travelling inland, narrowing its primary arsenal to three main devices: the fixed INS checkpoint, the temporary checkpoint and roving patrols. These three inland devices supplemented the line-watch agents stationed at the actual border, checking papers and guarding the entrances to the country.

Fixed INS checkpoints were placed on larger highways and interstates, about 50 to 100 miles from the actual border with Mexico. These checkpoints were essentially roadblocks that would bring northbound traffic down to a snail's pace, allowing Border Patrol agents to look into every passing car and detain motorists for short questioning and for the production of documents. The checkpoints were generally marked ahead with large black-on-yellow signs and flashing lights, and subsequent warnings as motorists got closer. At some of the checkpoints, a border patrol officer called a 'point agent' would visually screen all northbound traffic, which had come to a virtual, if not complete stop. Standing between the two lanes, the point agent would allow most motorists to proceed without any verbal inquiry or further inspection. But the point agent would select a number of motorists for further investigation, directing them to a secondary inspection site for questioning about the citizenship and immigration status of the motorists. Those further investigations would last on average three to five minutes – unless, of course, they led to arrest. At other checkpoints, Border Patrol officers might stop all northbound traffic for brief questioning. Local inhabitants who the officers recognized would be waived through, but all others would be stopped for interrogation.

'Temporary checkpoints' were set up in a similar way, but generally maintained on back roads where the traffic was less intense and in locations 'where the terrain allows an element of surprise. Operations at these temporary checkpoints are set up at irregular intervals and intermittently so as to confuse the potential violator.'[2] The third major technique, 'roving patrols', consisted of mobile Border Patrol tactical units that roamed the back roads near larger interstates to stop and search automobiles at points removed from the actual border. These 'roving patrols' would often work in combination with the fixed checkpoints to make sure that motorists were not trying to evade larger highways to avoid being stopped at a roadblock.

By the early 1970s, it had become routine for Border Patrol officers to use the appearance of Mexican ancestry as one factor – and sometimes as the only factor – in the decision to stop and investigate motorists. This is evidenced in the *Brignoni-Ponce* case itself, where the Border Patrol agents conceded in court that 'their only reason for [stopping Brignoni-Ponce] was that its three occupants

---

2   See INS Border Patrol Handbook at 9–3 (discussed in Baca, 368 F. Supp. at 406).

appeared to be of Mexican descent'.[3] In this sense, border policing in the 1970s reflected the larger turn to criminal profiling in law enforcement.

The Legal Landscape at the Border

The Supreme Court had addressed Border Patrol investigations on a number of occasions and set forth some contours of permissible police intervention. Stops, interrogations, and searches right at the border or its functional equivalent – say, an international flight landing at O'Hare in Chicago – were constitutionally permitted without warrant or probable cause, as a routine matter.[4] Fourth Amendment protections applied, however, in areas removed from the border – including areas *near* the Mexican-United States border.

In *Almeida-Sanchez v. United States* in 1973,[5] the Court had ruled that the Fourth Amendment precluded the Border Patrol from using 'roving patrols' to stop and search automobiles without a warrant or probable cause at any point removed from the actual border. Under *Almeida-Sanchez*, in the absence of a judicial warrant allowing roving patrols in a designated area, probable cause was therefore necessary before roving patrol agents could stop and search a vehicle in the general vicinity of the border. In *United States v. Ortiz*,[6] a companion case to *Brignoni-Ponce*, the Court extended the same requirements of probable cause or judicial warrant for any search conducted at a permanent INS checkpoint.

There were also legislative statutes purporting to regulate the conduct of Border Patrol agents. Congress had passed on these questions. Under the Immigration and Nationality Act, at least two provisions were on point. Section 287(a)(1) authorized any officer or employee of the INS 'to interrogate any alien or person believed to be an alien' without a warrant 'as to his right to be or to remain in the United States'.[7] And Section 287(a)(3) authorized any officer of the INS without a warrant 'within a reasonable distance from any external boundary of the United States, to board and search for aliens any vessel with the territorial waters of the United State and any railway car, aircraft, conveyance, or vehicle'.[8] Moreover, under federal regulations implemented by the INS after notice and public comment, the authority under Section 287(a)(3) could be exercised anywhere within 100 air miles of the border.[9]

Many questions, though, were left open. First, on the question of race and ethnicity, whether the appearance of Mexican ancestry was a constitutionally

---

3   422 U.S. at 875.
4   See, for example, Almeida Sanchez v. United States, 413 U.S. 266, 272 (1973).
5   413 U.S. 266 (1973).
6   422 U.S. 891 (1975).
7   8 U.S.C. Sec. 1357(a)(1).
8   8 U.S.C. Sec. 1357(a)(3).
9   CFR Sec. 287.1(a) (1975).

valid reason to stop, question or search anyone. Second, whether questioning under Section 287(a)(1) should be treated differently than searches under Section 287(a)(3). Third, whether differences in police practices – roving patrols versus fixed checkpoints versus temporary checkpoints – would make any difference in these equations. These rules and these questions would be put to the test first in the case of *Brignoni-Ponce*.

The *Brignoni-Ponce* Case

It was early morning on 11 March 1973 near the permanent INS checkpoint at San Clemente, 65 miles north of the Mexican border on Interstate 5 between San Diego and Los Angeles. The United States Border Patrol usually maintained a roadblock there, but due to inclement weather, the checkpoint was closed. Two INS Border Patrol agents were sitting in their patrol car by the side of the road, observing the northbound traffic. It was dark, so the officers used their headlights to inspect the passing cars. A car drove by. The three occupants appeared to be of Mexican descent, so the agents decided to investigate. In fact, the agents said later, that was the only reason they decided to investigate.[10] They pursued and interrogated. They discovered that the two passengers were in the country illegally, arrested all three, and charged the driver, Felix Humberto Brignoni-Ponce, with transporting two illegal immigrants in violation of the Immigration and Nationality Act.[11]

When the case reached the United States Supreme Court, on certiorari, the Court focused on the narrow question whether a roving Border Patrol agent could stop a motorist *based on race alone*. The government, the Court emphasized, conceded that the patrol officers were engaged in a roving patrol. It conceded that *Almeida-Sanchez* should apply retroactively to *Brignoni-Ponce*. And it conceded that the location of the stop was not at the border or its functional equivalent, but near the border. As such, the Court explained, 'The only issue presented for decision is whether a roving patrol may stop a vehicle in an area near the border and question its occupants when the only ground for suspicion is that the occupants appear to be of Mexican ancestry.'[12] In other words, whether being of Mexican ancestry satisfies the required 'founded suspicion'. By a unanimous vote, though with different reasoning, the Court declared that it did not.

Justice Powell wrote the principal court opinion for himself and Justices Brennan, Stewart, Marshall, and Rehnquist. Powell first easily dismissed the government's arguments from statutory authority, repeating cursorily that 'no Act of Congress can authorize a violation of the Constitution'.[13] The stops and questioning involve seizures and therefore trigger the demands of the Fourth

---

10   422 U.S. at 875.
11   422 U.S. at 874–5.
12   422 U.S. at 878.
13   422 U.S. at 877 (quoting Almeida-Sanchez, 413 U.S. at 272).

Amendment. On the constitutional analysis, Powell engaged in a traditional balancing of interests analysis, weighing the important governmental interest in having effective measures to police the border and prevent the illegal entry of Mexicans against the individual liberty interests of persons travelling in the border areas – the traditional 'balance between the public interest and the individual's right to personal security free from arbitrary interference by law officers'.[14] This is the traditional balancing approach that the Court has applied to assess the reasonableness of Fourth Amendment seizures.

Powell emphasized the limited nature of the stop. The intrusion, Powell said, is 'modest'. It lasts no more than a minute. There is no search (unless further evidence develops). All that is required, as the government explained and Powell reiterated, 'is a response to a brief question or two and possibly the production of a document evidencing a right to be in the United States'.[15] These conditions are similar, Powell suggested, to the limited intrusion of the pat-down search in *Terry v. Ohio* or the brief stop of a suspicions individual in *Adams v. Williams*. On the other side of the scale, the public's interest in preventing illegal immigration from Mexico, Powell asserted, was 'valid.'[16] 'The INS now suggests there may be as many as 10 or 12 million aliens illegally in the country,' Powell explained.[17] This has the potential of creating significant social and economic problems for citizens, as well as for the immigrants themselves.

Accordingly, building on *Terry* and *Adams*, Powell declared that Border Patrol agents may constitutionally conduct a limited stop to investigate without full-blown probable cause. All that is needed is that 'an officer's observations lead him reasonably to suspect that a particular vehicle may contain aliens who are illegally in the country'.[18] As in *Terry*, the scope of the police intervention had to be tailored to the more limited scope of reasonable suspicion. The Border Patrol agent could stop the vehicle briefly and investigate, but not engage in a full blown search unless other evidence developed: 'The officer may question the driver and passenger about their citizenship and immigration status, and he may ask them to explain suspicious circumstances, but any further detention or search must be based on consent or probable cause.'[19]

On the key question of racial profiling, Powell declared the Court unwilling to let Mexican ancestry *alone* substitute for reasonable suspicion. Mexican appearance, Powell declared for the Court, may be one 'relevant factor' but is not alone sufficient to support a police stop. 'Large numbers of native-born and naturalized citizens have the physical characteristics identified with Mexican ancestry, and

---

14 422 U.S. at 878.
15 422 U.S. at 880.
16 422 U.S. at 879.
17 422 U.S. at 878.
18 422 U.S. at 881.
19 422 U.S. at 881–2.

even in the border area a relatively small proportion of them are aliens.'[20] There are many factors that may be taken into account, Powell explained. Erratic driving behaviour, or obvious evasion from the police, certain station wagons with large compartments for hiding people, or cars that appear more heavily weighted down than they should. These are all factors that Border Patrol agents may consider.

In addition, Powell wrote, they should be allowed to consider Mexican appearance. 'The Government also points out that trained officers can recognize the characteristic appearance of persons who live in Mexico, relying on such factors as the mode of dress and haircut.'[21] This, Powell declares, is acceptable. 'In all situations the officer is entitled to assess the facts in light of his experience in detecting illegal entry and smuggling.'[22] But Mexican appearance *alone* would not suffice: 'The likelihood that any given person of Mexican ancestry is an alien is high enough to make Mexican appearance a relevant factor, but standing alone it does not justify stopping all Mexican-Americans to ask if they are aliens.'[23] The bottom line on race then is that it may be one factor, but not the only one.

The *Martinez-Fuerte* Case

The following term, the Supreme Court returned to the border, this time addressing the constitutionality of fixed immigration checkpoints. The case would resolve the open question whether the Border Patrol agents required any articulable suspicion to stop and question motorists at a roadblock within 100 miles of the Mexican border. Powell again would write the Court's opinion. Powell again would emphasize that ethnic appearance is relevant. But this time, he pulled the stops and allowed for wider police discretion. The result would be far reaching for racial profiling.

The cases arose from arrests made at two different permanent immigration checkpoints within 100 miles from the Mexican border, one in California, the other in Texas. Both checkpoints were marked in the traditional fashion with large black-on-yellow signs and flashing lights, and subsequent warning signs as motorists got closer. At the San Clemente checkpoint, the point agent visually screened all northbound traffic, but did not conduct questioning there. Instead the agent would select a number of motorists for further investigation at a secondary inspection site, where other agents would stop and question the motorists about their citizenship and immigration status. At the time of the arrests at the San Clemente checkpoint, a magistrate had issued a 'warrant of inspection' which authorized the Border Patrol to conduct roadblock operations at the site. At the Sarita checkpoint, Border Patrol officers would stop all northbound traffic for brief

---

20   422 U.S. at 886.
21   422 U.S. at 885.
22   422 U.S. at 885.
23   422 U.S. at 886–7.

questioning, with the exception of local residents who the officers recognized. Also, in contrast to the San Clemente checkpoint, there was no judicial warrant regarding the operations at Sarita.

When the case reached the Supreme Court, the Court held in a 7-to-2 decision that neither articulable suspicion nor a judicial warrant was necessary as a precondition for a search at an immigration roadblock. Justice Powell again wrote the opinion for the Court; only Justices Brennan and Marshall were in dissent.

Justice Powell began, again, by considering the balance of interests. Permanent checkpoints, the government had maintained before the Court, are 'the most important of the traffic-checking operations'.[24] And they are highly effective, Powell suggested. The San Clemente checkpoint, for instance, resulted in the apprehension of 17,000 illegal aliens in 1973 from a traffic of about 10 million cars. In contrast, the intrusion on liberty was relatively minor – in Powell's words, 'quite limited'.[25] All that was required was a 'brief detention of travelers', 'a response to a brief question or two' and 'possibly the production of a document evidencing a right to be in the United States'.[26] As a result, and because of the more limited expectation of privacy in cars as opposed to homes, Justice Powell concluded that no individualized suspicion at all is needed 'at reasonably located checkpoints'.[27]

More important for the larger issue of racial profiling, though, was the Court's treatment of the secondary inspection area at the San Clemente checkpoint. There, Powell was prepared to assume that the referrals were made on the basis of Mexican ancestry. Powell writes: 'even if it be assumed that such referrals are made largely on the basis of apparent Mexican ancestry, we perceive no constitutional violation'.[28] Powell then drops two odd footnotes. In the first, footnote 16, Powell suggests, relaying on a dubious statistical analysis,[29] that Border Patrol agents do not rely on Mexican ancestry *alone* to refer motorists to the secondary area; in the second, footnote 17, Powell suggests that 'to the to the extent that the Border Patrol relies on apparent Mexican ancestry at this checkpoint, see n. 16, *supra,* that reliance clearly is relevant to the law enforcement need to be served'.[30] But even if they do rely on the appearance of Mexican ancestry *entirely,* there is no Fourth Amendment problem. 'As the intrusion here is sufficiently minimal that no

---

24 428 U.S. at 556.

25 428 U.S. at 557.

26 428 U.S. at 558 (also quoting Brignoni-Ponce at 880).

27 428 U.S. at 562.

28 428 U.S. at 563.

29 Powell reasons that less than one per cent of motorists are stopped for questioning, but that between 13 and 18 per cent are likely to appear to have Mexican ancestry. From this, Powell concludes that the Border Patrol does not rely exclusively on apparent Mexican ancestry. Another equally plausible interpretation of the data is that the Border Patrol rely exclusively on apparent Mexican ancestry, but only have the resources to stop 1/16th of those persons.

30 428 U.S. 564 n.17.

particularized reason need exist to justify it, we think it follows that the Border Patrol officers must have wide discretion in selecting the motorists to be diverted for the brief questioning involved.'[31]

Justice Powell repeats in footnote 17 that the appearance of Mexican ancestry 'clearly is relevant to the law enforcement need to be served.'[32] *Brignoni-Ponce* only held that ethnic background *alone* does not create reasonable suspicion for roving patrols, not that ethnicity, ancestry or race are not relevant. And not that it could not be used *alone* as a basis for a stop and interrogation at a fixed checkpoint. There, there was no need for any reasonable suspicion at all, so the police could rely on race alone if they wanted to. The lack of a reasonableness requirement does not exclude reliance on race. Powell's discussion in *United States v. Martinez-Fuerte* was sufficiently cryptic that it allowed the issue to continue to percolate, to fester and wind its way through the lower courts.

Justice Brennan wrote a heated dissent, in which Justice Marshall joined. Brennan described the result as the 'defacement of Fourth Amendment protections',[33] declaring that 'Today's decision is the ninth this Term marking the continuing evisceration of Fourth Amendment protections against unreasonable searches and seizures.'[34] Most troubling to Brennan was the fact that the ruling would allow racial profiling. By requiring no standard whatsoever, the Court was giving the Border Patrol free rein to profile all persons of Mexican ancestry for secondary questioning and inspection. The limitation from *Brignoni-Ponce* would have no effect whatsoever. Brennan exclaimed:

> In abandoning any requirement of a minimum of reasonable suspicion, or even articulable suspicion, the Court in every practical sense renders meaningless, as applied to checkpoint stops, the *Brignoni-Ponce* holding that 'standing alone [Mexican appearance] does not justify stopping all Mexican-Americans to ask if they are aliens.' Since the objective is almost entirely the Mexican illegally in the country, checkpoint officials, uninhibited by any objective standards and therefore free to stop any or all motorists without explanation or excuse, wholly on whim, will perforce target motorists of Mexican appearance. The process will then inescapably discriminate against citizens of Mexican ancestry and Mexican aliens lawfully in this country for no other reason than that they unavoidably possess the same 'suspicious' physical and grooming characteristics of illegal Mexican aliens.[35]

---

31   428 U.S. at 563–4.
32   428 U.S. 564 n.17.
33   428 U.S. at 569 (Brennan, J., dissenting).
34   428 U.S. at 567 (Brennan, J., dissenting).
35   428 U.S. at 571–2 (Brennan, J., dissenting).

Brennan concluded: 'That law in this country should tolerate use of one's ancestry as probative of possible criminal conduct is repugnant under any circumstances.'[36] Tragically, Brennan was in a miniscule minority. Though repugnant, racial profiling was now constitutional.

The Immediate Implications for Policing and Immigration Policies

Brignoni-Ponce and *Martinez-Fuerte* had important and immediate consequences not just for Fourth Amendment jurisprudence, but also for border patrol and policing more generally. The decisions signalled a green light to criminal profiling – including racial profiling. The weakest link had been broken, and the chain would soon collapse. The Court had given the police a clear message that the use of a multiple factor profile, including as one factor race or ethnicity, was a constitutional and legitimate police technique.

At the national level, the DEA began implementing criminal profiling, especially the drug-courier profile, with vigour. The original experimental use of a drug-courier profile was deemed a success, and the program went nationwide after *Brignoni-Ponce* and *Martinez-Fuertes*. Between 1976 and 1986 there were in excess of 140 reported court decisions involving DEA stops of passengers at airports across the country based on the drug-courier profile.[37] Several scholars, David Cole in particular, have compiled lists of the drug-courier profile characteristics, which are often internally contradictory.[38] With time, however, the profiles only proliferated.[39]

Meanwhile, on the Mexican border, the political climate continued to heat up in the aftermath of the two cases. The 1980s and 90s saw renewed public concern and political rhetoric surrounding illegal immigration. In 1993, Democratic President William Clinton, under attack by Republicans, pledged his support to increased surveillance: 'In September 1993 the administration proclaimed Operation Hold-the-Line in El Paso, Texas ... an effort to curtail illegal entrants by deploying Border Agents at close intervals along the border itself, and in September 1994 Attorney General Janet Reno proclaimed the initiation of Operation Gatekeeper in San Diego'.[40] These were not just empty policy promises: 'The government increased the overall size of the Border Patrol by 51 percent from 1993 to 1995 bringing the number of agents to more than 4,500... . In mid-1995 Congress also approved a special $328 million enhancement for concentrated border enforcement.'[41] As Joseph Nevins suggests, this huge increase was due to political pressure generally

---

36 428 U.S. at 571 n.1 (Brennan, J., dissenting).
37 See 428 U.S. at 417 n.2, 417–18.
38 See, for example, Cole (1999); Becton (1987: 421).
39 Becton (1987: 433–4).
40 Nevins (2002: 271).
41 Nevins (2002: 271).

and specifically as a response to California's ballot initiative, proposition 187, also entitled 'SOS (Save our State)', which would deny medical and health services to illegal immigrants.

The Impact on Racial Profiling

The most significant implication of *Brignoni-Ponce* and *Martinez-Fuerte*, naturally, was that race or ethnicity, if relevant to the policing objective, could be used as one factor among others – and in some limited cases as the only factor – in determining whether there is sufficient reason to conduct investigation, such as a stop and questioning. In the process, the Court paved a constitutional path to racial profiling in the United States, constructing a four-part legal structure that frames consideration of the 'legal use' of race in policing. The constitutional structure is framed by four important legal distinctions:

First Legal Distinction: Race as a, but not the Factor

The Court's rulings in *Brignoni-Ponce* and *Martinez-Fuerte* effectively communicated that race is relevant to policing. In the Fourth Amendment context, race can legitimately be considered as a factor in the determination to stop an individual so long as the police independently have reasonable suspicion. Commentators most often cite *Brignoni-Ponce* for precisely the proposition that the Supreme Court has condoned the use of race as 'one factor' in making immigration stops.[42]

Martinez-Fuerte however had muddied the waters a bit, allowing the sole use of race where there was no need for any articulable reason. The Supreme Court offered little guidance in the years after *Brignoni-Ponce* and *Martinez-Fuerte*. The result has been some confusion among the lower federal courts. Most federal courts either ignore the race question or allow the use of race *sub judice*. But many other courts have simply sidestepped the race issue by relying on non-racial factors either to find or not find reasonable suspicion.[43] Still other lower federal courts have struck down the use of race under circumstances suggesting that race was one among several factors used to stop or search a suspect.[44] And one panel of the Ninth Circuit held, in an interesting opinion in the case of *United States v. Montero-Camargo*, that the appearance of Mexican ancestry is of little, or no

---

42   See, for example, Johnson (2003); Ramirez, Hoopes, and Lai Quinlan (2003); Carbado (2002).

43   See generally Gross and Barnes (2002: 735), discussing Derricott v State, 611 A2d 592 (Md Ct App 1992), and United States v Davis, 2001 US App LEXIS 10997 (2d Cir. 2001).

44   See United States v Laymon, 730 F Supp 332, 339 (D Colo 1990); United States v Nicholas, 448 F2d 622, 625 (8th Cir 1971).

probative value at INS checkpoints because the majority of people who pass through checkpoints are Hispanic.[45]

At the end of the day, though, there remains a loose legal distinction between using race exclusively and using race as one among other factors. The first use of race is practically unanimously condemned. The second use of race as one among other factors is slightly more controversial, but is generally avoided by focusing on the other factors that raise suspicion.[46]

Second Legal Distinction: Fourth vs. Fourteenth Amendment

Brignoni-Ponce and *Martinez-Fuerte* also communicated that Fourth Amendment analysis differs in kind from Equal Protection analysis, and, implicitly, that claims of racial bias should be addressed to the latter, not the former. It would take however another 20 years before the Court would make this explicit, in the case of *Whren v United States*.[47] In *Whren*, the Court declared that the Fourth Amendment does not concern itself with the subjective intentions of police officers, including their possible reliance on race, so long as they had reasonable suspicion or probable cause to justify the seizure – in that case, a traffic violation. Race claims should be addressed to the Equal Protection clause, not the Fourth Amendment.

This doctrinal framework of bifurcated Fourth and Fourteenth Amendment analysis has guided lawyers and lower courts. Most legal discussions of racial profiling today address each claim separately. Most constitutional scholars have criticized this practice and argued that notions of equal protection should inform our interpretation of the Fourth Amendment.[48] But the legal distinction has stuck and holds tightly today.

Third Legal Distinction: Eye-witness Identification

The third constitutional pillar of racial profiling analysis is focused on Equal Protection analysis. It draws a distinction between using race absent individualized suspicion about the particular suspect and using race where there is an eye-witness identification based on race. The first is generally associated with racial profiling: stopping a minority motorist because minority motorists are assumed to offend at higher rates. The second is what we generally associate with detective work: getting an identification from a witness and tracking down suspects who match that description. Most courts hold that the latter is not 'using race'. Often, the

---

45   United States v Montero-Camargo, 208 F3d 1122, 1131 (9th Cir 2000) (the Court affirmed the conviction because other grounds were sufficient).

46   See Banks (2001); Gross and Barnes (2002: 733).

47   517 US 806 (1996).

48   See, for example, Steiker (1994); Alschuler (2002); Thompson (1999); Rudovsky (2001: 348).

reason is that relying on an identification is a race-neutral policy: the content may be race-specific, but the policy itself is race neutral.[49]

Fourth Legal Distinction: Intent to Discriminate

The final pillar of racial profiling law in the United States draws on the Supreme Court's decisions in *McCleskey v Kemp*[50] and *United States v Armstrong*[51] – which extend the *Washington v Davis*[52] requirement that discrimination be proved by evidence of intentional bias on the part of a state actor to the criminal justice sphere. This sets up the final major legal distinction in the racial profiling context. It is the requirement that a successful equal protection challenge rest on evidence of intentional discrimination rather than on inference from unexplained disparate treatment.[53] Many commentators have criticized the actual intent requirement in the racial profiling context – as well as in other criminal justice contexts;[54] but it is in all likelihood a permanent fixture in this jurisprudence.

The result of these four pillars is that practically no federal constitutional challenges to racial profiling have prevailed since the *Brignoni-Ponce* case.[55] Federal challenges have either failed due to one or more of these legal distinctions[56] or have been settled out of court, primarily for injunctive relief.[57] Given the reality of contemporary policing – especially the fact that a police officer usually has a number of reasons why he or she may focus attention on one particular suspect – the Supreme Court's early decisions in *Brignoni-Ponce* and *Martinez-Fuerte*, allowing race or ethnicity to be considered as one among a number of factors in the decision to search, essentially paved the constitutional path to racial profiling.

The Practice of Racial Profiling

Let us fast forward to early morning on 8 March 1989. Braniff Flight 650, the red-eye from Los Angeles, had just landed at the Kansas City airport. DEA agent Carl Hicks and two local detectives were on the concourse, eyeing passengers as

---

49   See, for example (2d Cir 2000) (deeming race-neutral the state policy of 'investigat[ing] crimes by interviewing the victim, getting a description of the assailant, and seeking out persons who matched that description').

50   481 US 279 (1987).

51   517 US 456 (1996).

52   426 US 229 (1976).

53   See generally Rudovsky (2001: 322–9).

54   See, for example, Rudovsky (2001: 322–9); Alschuler (2002: 201–7); Gross and Barnes (2002: 741).

55   For a critique of these four legal distinctions and the four-part structure of constitutional analysis in the racial profiling context, see Harcourt (2004).

56   See, for example, Gross and Barnes (2002: 727).

57   See Gross and Barnes (2002: 727–8); Garrett (2001: 75–81, 98–105).

Bibliography

Abulafia, D. 1988. *Frederick II: A Medieval Emperor.* London: Allen Lane the Penguin Press.

Achim, V. 2004. *The Roma in Romanian History.* Budapest: CEU Press.

Adler, J.S. 2003. We've Got a Right to Fight; We're Married: Domestic Homicide in Chicago, 1875–1920. *Journal of Interdisciplinary History*, 34, 1, 27–48.

Aebi, M.F. and Delgrande, N. 2008. *Council of Europe Annual Penal Statistics. Space I, Survey 2006.* Strasbourg: Council of Europe.

Aebi, M.F. and Delgrande, N. 2009. *Council of Europe Annual Penal Statistics. Space I, Survey 2007.* Strasbourg: Council of Europe.

Agamben, G. 1998. *Homo Sacer: Sovereign Power and Bare Life.* Stanford, CA: Stanford University Press, 1998 (Spanish 1998. Valencia: Pre-Textos).

Agamben, G. 2005. *State of Exception.* Chicago: University of Chicago Press (Italian 2003. *Stato di eccezione.* Turin: Bollati Boringhieri)

Aguilera Reija, M. 2005. Situación jurídica de las extranjeras presas, in *Delitos y fronteras*, edited by M.T. Martín Palomo, M.J. Miranda López and C. Vega Solís. Madrid: Complutense, 253–70.

Agustin, L. 2007. *Sex at the Margins: Migration, Labour Markets and the Rescue Industry.* London: Zed Books.

Aierbe, P. 2006. The 'assault' by 'sub-Saharan immigrants' in the media. [Online]. Available at: http://www.statewatch.org/news/2006/jul/sos-migrants-media-peio-2006.pdf [accessed: 25 March 2010].

Ajami, F. 1992. *The Arab Predicament: Arab Political Thought and Practice since 1967.* London and New York: Cambridge University Press.

Ajami, F. 2003. Iraq and the Arab's Future. *Foreign Affairs*, 1, January–February.

Aktion Courage – Sos Racismus 1999. *Polizeiübergriffe gegen Ausländerinnen und Ausländer.* Bonn: Dokumentation.

Alain, C. 2001. L'impasse citoyenniste. Contribution à une critique du citoyennisme. [Online]. Available at: http://infokiosques.net/IMG/pdf/impasse_citoyenniste.pdf

Alasia, F. and Montaldi, D. 1961. *Milano Corea.* Turin: Einaudi.

Albera, D., Blok, A. and Bromberger, C. (eds) 2001. *L'anthropologie de la Mediterranée.* Paris: Maisonneuve et Larose.

Albini, U. and Maltese, E.V. (eds) 2004. *Bisanzio nella sua letteratura.* Milan: Garzanti.

Albrecht, H.J. 1994. *Strafzumessung bei schwerer Kriminalität.* Berlin: Duncker & Humblot.

Albrecht, H.J. 1997. Ethnic Minorities, Crime and Criminal Justice in Germany. *Crime and Justice, A Review of Research*, 21, 31–99 (first version in *Délit d'Immigration*, edited by S. Palidda. Brussels: European Community, 1996).

Albrecht, H.J. 2006. Illegalität, Kriminalität und Sicherheit, in *Illegalität. Grenzen und Möglichkeiten der Migrationspolitik*, edited by J. Alt and M. Bommes. Wiesbaden: VS Verlag, 60–80.

Albrecht, H.J. 2007. Trafficking in Humans and Human Rights, in *Sociology of Crime, Law and Deviance – Crime and Human Rights*, edited by S. Parmentier and E. Weitekamp, vol. 9. Amsterdam: Elsevier, 39–71.

Albrecht, P.A. and Pfeiffer, C. 1979. *Die Kriminalisierung junger Aunsländer. Befunde und Reaktionen sozialer Kontrollinstanzen*. Munich: Juventa.

Alschuler, A.W. 2002. Racial Profiling and the Constitution. *University of Chicago Legal Forum*, 163, 168–73 and n. 24.

Altheide, D. 2002. *Creating Fear: News and the Construction of Crisis*. Piscataway: Aldine Transaction.

Althusser, L. 1996. Du Capital à la philosophie de Marx, in L. Althusser, E. Balibar, R. Establet, P. Macherey and J. Rancière, *Lire le Capital*. Paris: Qaudrige and PUF, 1–79.

Anderson, B. 1983. *Imagined Communities: Reflections on the Origins and Spread of Nationalism*. London: Verso.

Andrijasevic, R. 2006a. How to Balance Rights and Responsibilities on Asylum at the EU's Southern Border of Italy and Libya. [Online]. Available at: http://www.statewatch.org/news/2006/may/andrijasevic-Libya-Lampedusa.pdf [accessed: 25 March 2010].

Andrijasevic, R. 2006b. Tra Lampedusa e la Libia. Storie di internamenti e deportazioni. *Conflitti Globali*, 4, 145–56.

Anhut, R. and Heitmeyer, W. 2000. Desintegration, Konflikt und Ethnisierung, in *Bedrohte Stadtgesellschaft. Soziale Desintegrationsprozesse und ethnisch-kulturelle Konfliktkonstellationen*, edited by W. Heitmeyer and R. Anhut. Munich: Weinheim, 17–75.

Anie, A., Daniel, N. and Others. 2005. An Exploration of Factors Affecting the Successful Dispersal of Asylum Seekers, *Home Office Online Report 50/05*.

Anitua, G.I. 2005. *Historias de los pensamientos criminológicos*. Buenos Aires: Del Puerto.

Appadurai, A. 1996. *Modernity at Large: Cultural Dimensions of Globalization*. Minneapolis and London: University of Minnesota Press.

Aradau, C. and van Munster, R. 2007. Governing Terrorism through Risk: Taking Precautions, (un)Knowing the Future. *European Journal of International Relations*, 13, 1.

Ararteko 2005. *Los cuerpos policiales dependientes de las administraciones públicas debn dotarse de códigos de conducta con relación al tratamiento de la información que proporcionan sobre la inmigración*. Vitoria: Gasteiz.

Arendt, H. 1958. *The Origins of Totalitarianism*. New York: Meridian.

Arrigoni, P. and Vitale T. 2008. Quale legalità? Rom e gagi a confronto. *Aggiornamenti Sociali*, 3, 183–94.

Asociación Pro Derechos Humanos De Andalucía 2008. *Informe Derechos Humanos en la Frontera Sur 2007*. [Online]. Available at: http://www.apdha. org/media/informeinmigra07.pdf [accessed: 25 March 2010].

Asúa Batarrita, A. 2002. La expulsión del extranjero como alternativa a la pena: incongruencias de la subordinación del derecho penal a las políticas de control de la inmigración, in *Inmigración y derecho penal. Bases para un debate*, edited by P. Laurenzo Copello. Valencia: Tirant lo Blanch, 17–96.

Aubusson de Cavarlay, B. 1996. Les statistiques de police: méthodes de production et conditions d'interprétation. *Mathématiques, informatique et sciences humaines*, 136, 39–61.

Aubusson de Cavarlay, B. 2006. La détention provisoire. Mise en perspective et lacunes des sources statistiques. *Questions pénales*, 3, 1–4.

Bade, K. 2006. Integration und Politik – aus der Geschichte lernen? *Aus Politik und Zeitgeschichte*, 40–41, 3–6.

Baier, D., Pfeiffer, C., Simonson, J. and Rabold, S. 2009. Jugendliche in Deutschland als Opfer und Täter von Gewalt. *Zeitschrift für Jugendkriminalrecht und Jugendhilfe*, 20, 2, 112–19.

Balibar, E. 2005. *Europe, Constitution, Frontière*. Bègles: Editions du Passant.

Balibar, E. and Wallerstein, I. 1991. *Race, Nation, Class: Ambiguous Identities*. London and New York: Verso.

Banks, R.R. 2001. Race-Based Suspect Selection and Colorblind Equal Protection Doctrine and Discourse. *UCLA Law Review*, 48, 1075, 1086–7.

Banton, M. 1964. *The Policeman in the Community*. London: Tavistock.

Banton, M. 1973. *Police–Community Relations.* London: Collins.

Banton, M. 1994. *Discrimination*. Buckingham: Open University Press.

Baratta, A. 1982. *Criminologia critica e critica del diritto penale*. Bologna: il Mulino (Spanish 1993. Siglo XXI, 4th edn, México City).

Barker, M. 1981. *The New Racism: Conservatives and the Ideology of the Tribe*. London: Junction Books.

Barsony, J. and Daroczi, A. 2008. *Pharrajimos: The Fate of the Roma during the Holocaust*. Amsterdam: IDEA.

Bateson, G. 1973. Culture Contact and Schismogenesis, in *Steps to an Ecology of Mind: Collected Essays in Anthropology, Psychiatry, Evolution and Epistemology*. Frogmore: Paladin.

Baucells i Lladós, J. 2005. El Derecho penal ante el fenómeno inmigratorio. *Revista de Derecho y Proceso Penal*, 13, 45–62.

Bauman, Z. 1989. *Modernity and the Holocaust.* Oxford: Blackwell.

Bauman, Z. 2000. *Liquid Modernity*. Cambridge: Polity Press (Spanish 2002. Buenos Aires: FCE).

Bauman, Z. 2004. *Wasted Lives: Modernity and its Outcasts*. Cambridge: Polity Press.

Bauman, Z. 2005. *Trabajo, consumismo y nuevos pobres*. Barcelona: Gedisa.

Bayerisches Staatsministerium für Arbeit und Sozialordnung 2008. *Familie und Frauen: Statistik Spätaussiedler und deren Angehörige 2007*, Munich.

Beck, U. 1998. *La sociedad del riesgo*. Barcelona: Paidós (English 1992. *Risk Society: Towards a New Modernity*. London: Sage).

Becker, G.S. 1974. Crime and Punishment: An Economic Approach, in *Essays in the Economics of Crime and Punishment*, edited by G.S. Becker and W.M. Landes. New York: Columbia University Press, 1–54.

Becker, H.S. 1963. *Outsiders: Studies in the Sociology of Deviance*. New York: Free Press (French 1985).

Becker, H.S. 1982. *Art Worlds*. Berkeley: University of California Press.

Beckett, K. 1997. *Making Crime Pay: Law and Order in Contemporary American Politics*. New York: Oxford University Press.

Becton, C.L. 1987. The Drug Courier Profile. *North Carolina Law Review*, 65, 417–80.

Bedoya, M.H. 2008. Dura lex sed lex, in *Informe Anual sobre el racismo en el Estado español 2008*, edited by Sos Racismo. Barcelona: Icaria Editorial.

Bergalli, R. (ed.) 2006. *Flujos migratorios y su (des)control*. Barcelona: Anthropos.

Berger, P. 1969. *A Rumor of Angels: Modern Society and the Rediscovery of the Supernatural*. Garden City, NY: Doubleday.

Berger, P. 1992. *A Far Glory: The Quest for Faith in an Age of Credulity*. New York: Free Press.

Berger, P.L. and Luckmann, T. 1966. *The Social Construction of Reality*. New York: Doubleday.

Bernadac, C. 1996 [1989]. *Sterminateli! Adolf Hitler contro i nomadi d'Europa*. Rome: Libritalia.

Bernardi, A. 2007. Le droit pénal, bouclier ou épée des différences culturelles, in *Les droits de l'homme, bouclier ou épée du droit pénal?* edited by Y. Cartuyvels, H. Dumont, F. Ost, M. van de Kerchove and S. Van Drooghenbroeck. Brussels: Publications des F.U.S.L./Bruylant, 497–551.

Bernardot, M. 2008. *Camps d'étrangers*. Bellecombe-en-Bauges: Éditions du Croquant.

Bietlot, M. 2003. Du disciplinaire au sécuritaire. *Multitudes*, 11. [Online]. Available at: http://multitudes.samizdat.net/article.php3?id_article=103 [accessed: 22 March 2005].

Bigo, D. 1996a. Circuler, refouler, enfermer, éloigner. *Cultures & Conflits*, 23, 3–7.

Bigo, D. 1996b. Frontiers, Identity and Security in Europe, an Agenda of Research. *Journal of Boundaries Studies*, 2.

Bigo, D. 1998a. Sécurité et immigration: vers une gouvernementalité par l'inquiétude? *Cultures & Conflits*, 31–2, 13–38.

Bigo, D. 1998b. L'immigration à la croisée des chemins sécuritaires. *Revue européenne des migrations internationales*, 1, 25–46.

Bigo, D. 2004. Identifier, catégoriser et contrôler. Police et logiques proactives, in *Pratiques et discours sécuritaires: la machine à punir*, edited by L. Bonelli and G. Sainati. Paris: L'esprit frappeur, 56–88.

Bigo, D. 2005. Globalised in(Security): the Field and the Ban-Optican, in *Translation, Philosophy and Colonial Difference, Traces: A Multilingual Series of Cultural Theory*, edited by J. Solomon and N. Sakai 4. [Online]. Available at: http://www.ces.fas.harvard.edu/conferences/muslims/Bigo.pdf.

Bigo, D., Bonelli, L. and Deltombe, T. (eds) 2009. *Au nom du 11 septembre. Les démocraties à l'épreuve de l'antiterrorisme*. Paris: La Découverte.

Bigo, D. and Guild, E. 2002. De Tampere à Séville, vers une ultra gouvernementalisation de la domination. *Cultures & Conflits*, 45, 5–25.

Bigo, D. and Guild, E. 2003. Le Visa Schengen: expression d'une stratégie de 'police' à distance. *Cultures & Conflits*, 49–50, 22–37.

Bigo, D. and Tsoukala, A. (eds) 2008. *Terror, Insecurity and Liberty: Illiberal Practices of Liberal Regimes after 9/11*. Abingdon: Routledge.

Binotto, M. and Martino, V. (eds) 2005. *Fuori luogo. L'immigrazione e i media italiani*. Cosenza: Pellegrini Eri-Rai.

Bittner, E. 1990. *Aspects of Police Work*. Boston: Northeastern University Press.

Blanc-Chaléard, M.C. 2000. Police et migrants jusqu'en 1945. *Vingtième Siècle*, 66, 154–6.

Blanc-Chaléard, M.C., Douki, C., Dyonet, N. and Millot, V., 2001. *Police et migrants. France 1667–1939*. Rennes: Presses universitaires de Rennes.

Bloch, A. 2000. A New Era or More of the Same? Asylum Policy in the UK. *Journal of Refugee Studies*, 13, 1.

Blondiaux, L. 1999. *La Fabrique de l'opinion. Une histoire sociale des sondages aux Etats-Unis et en France*. Paris: Belin.

Blumenberg, H. 1960. Paradigmen zu einer Metaphorologie. *Archiv für Begriffsgeschichte*, vol. VI, Bonn: Bouvier.

Blumstein, A. and Wallman, J. 2000. *The Crime Drop in America*. Cambridge: Cambridge University Press.

Bonelli, L. 2008. *La France a peur. Une histoire sociale de l'insécurité*. Paris: La Découverte.

Borrel, C. 2006. Enquêtes annuelles de recensement 2004 et 2005. Près de 5 millions d'immigrés à la mi-2004. *Insee Première*, 1098.

Boswell, C. 2003. *European Migration Policies in Flux: Changing Patterns of Inclusion and Exclusion*. Oxford: Blackwell.

Bosworth, M. 2007. Immigration Detention in Britain, in *Human Trafficking*, edited by M. Lee. Cullompton: Willan.

Bosworth, M. and Guild, M. 2008. Governing through Migration Control: Security and Citizenship in Britain. *British Journal of Criminology*, 48, 6, 703–19.

Boucher, M., 2001. Les représentations pusillanimes des quartiers d'habitat social, de la présence immigrée et de l'Islam en France, in *De l'égalité formelle à l'égalité réelle. La question de l'ethnicité dans les sociétés contemporaines*, edited by M. Boucher. Paris: L'Harmattan, 217–40.

Bourdieu, P. 1973. L'opinion publique n'existe pas. *Les Temps modernes*, 29 (318), 1292–1309.

Bourdieu, P. 1980. *Sociologie de l'Algérie*. Paris: PUF.

Bourdieu, P. 1986. La force du droit. *Actes de la recherche en sciences sociales*, 64, 1, 3–19.

Bourdieu, P. (ed.) 1993. *La misère du monde*. Paris: Seuil.

Bourdieu, P. 1997. *Méditations pascaliennes*. Paris: Seuil.

Bourgois, P. 2003. *In Search of Respect: Selling Crack in El Barrio*. Cambridge: Cambridge University Press.

Boursier, G. 1995. Lo sterminio degli zingari durante la seconda guerra mondiale. *Studi Storici*, 36, 2, 363–95.

Bowen, J. 2007. *Why the French Don't Like Headscarves: Islam, the State and Public Space*. Princeton: Princeton University Press.

Branca, P. 2003. *Moschee inquiete. Tradizionalisti, innovatori, fondamentalisti nella cultura islamica*. Bologna: Il Mulino.

Braudel, F. 1979. *Civilisation matérielle, economie et capitalisme (XV–XVIII siècle)*. Paris: Armand Colin.

Bravi, L. 2002. *Altre tracce sul sentiero per Auschwitz*. Rome: Cisu.

Bréhier, L. 1970a. *Les Institutions de l'empire byzantin*, 2nd edn. Paris: Albin Michel.

Bréhier, L. 1970b. *La civilization byzantine*, 2nd edn. Paris: Albin Michel.

Bribosia, E. and Rea, A. (eds) 2002. *Les nouvelles migrations. Un enjeu européen*. Brussels: Editions Complexe.

Brion, F. 2000. Des jeunes filles à sauver aux jeunes filles à mater: identité sociale et islamophobie, in *Voix et voies musulmanes de Belgique*, edited by U. Manço. Brussels: Publications des Facultés universitaires Saint-Louis, 117–46.

Brion, F. (ed.) 2004. *Féminité, minorité, islamité. Questions autour du hijâb*. Louvain-la-Neuve: Academia-Burylant.

Brion, F. 2005. L'inscription du débat français en Belgique, in *La politisation du voile. L'affaire en France, en Europe et dans le monde arabe*, edited by F. Lorcerie. Paris: L'Harmattan, 121–45.

Brodeur, J.P. 2003. *Les visages de la police. Pratiques et perceptions*. Montréal: Les Presses de l'Université de Montréal.

Brouwer, E., Catz, P., Guild, E. and Others. 2003. *Immigration, Asylum and Terrorism: A Changing Dynamic in European Law*. Nijmegen: Instituut voor Rechtssociologie, Centrum voor Migratierecht.

Brown, P. 1982. *Society and the Holy in Late Antiquity*. London: Faber & Faber.

Brubaker, R. 1996. *Nationalism Reframed: Nationhood and the National Question in the New Europe*. Cambridge: Cambridge University Press.

Brubaker, R. 2004. *Ethnicity without Groups*. Cambridge, MA: Harvard University Press.

Brubaker, R., Feischmidt, M., Fox, J. and Grancea, L. 2006. *Nationalist Politics and Everyday Ethnicity in a Transylvanian Town*. Princeton: Princeton University Press.

Brunello, P. (ed.) 1996. *L'urbanistica del disprezzo*. Rome: Manifestolibri.

Bruno, M. 2004. L'ennesimo sbarco di clandestini. La tematica dell'arrivo nella comunicazione italiana, in *Fuori luogo. L'immigrazione e i media italiani*, edited by M. Bigotto and V. Martino. Cosenza: Pellegrini Eri-Rai.

Bruno, M. 2008. *L'islam immaginato. Rappresentazioni e stereotipi nei media italiani*. Milan: Guerini e Associati.

Bureau of Justice Statistics 2007. *Capital Punishment 2006*. [Online]. Available at: http://www.ojp.usdoj.gov/bjs/pub/html/cp/2006/cp06st.htm

Burgio, A. 1998. *L'invenzione delle razze: studi su razzismo e revisionismo storico*. Rome: Manifestolibri.

Busch, H. 2000. *Andere Länder – ähnliche Sitten. Polizeiübergriffe und Kontrolle in Großbritannien und Frankreich*. Berlin: Cilip, 67, 49–53.

Calavita, K. 1998. Immigration, Law and Marginalization in a Global Economy: Notes from Spain. *Law and Society Review*, 32, 3, 529–66.

Campanini, M. 1999. *Islam e politica*. Bologna: Il Mulino.

Campanini, M. 2005. *Dizionario dell'islam. Religione, legge, storia, pensi*ero. Milan: Rizzoli.

Campesi, G., Re, L. and Torrente, G., 2009. *Dietro le sbarre e oltre*. Turin: L'Harmattan Italia.

Carbado, D.W. 2002. (E)racing the Fourth Amendment. *Michigan Law Review*, 100, 946, 997–1000.

Cardini, F. 1991. *La vera storia della Lega lombarda*. Milan: Mondadori.

Caritas (ed.) 2010. *Immigrazione Dossier Statistico*. Rome: Edizioni Idos.

Cartledge, P. 1996. La nascita degli opliti e l'organizzazione militare, in *I Greci*, editd by S. Settis, Turin: Einaudi, Vol. II, 1, 681–714.

Castel, R. 1991. From Dangerousness to Risk, in *The Foucault Effect*, edited by G. Burchell, C. Gordon and P. Miller. Chicago: University of Chicago Press.

Castel, R. 1999. *Les métamorphoses de la question sociale. Une chronique du sal*ariat. Paris: Fayard.

Castel, R. 2007. *La discrimination négative*. Paris: Seuil.

Castles, D. and Miller, D. 2009. *The Age of Migrations*, 4th edn. London: Palgrave Macmillan.

Catani, M. and Palidda, S. (eds) 1987. *Le rôle du mouvement associatif dans l'évolution des communautés immigrées*. Paris: FAS, D.P.M.-Min. de la Solidarité.

Cavadino, M. and Dignan, J. 2006. *Penal Systems: A Comparative Approach*. London: Sage.

CDMG 1998. Problems Arising in Connection with the International Mobility of the Roma in Europe. Report of European Council on Migration. Brussels.

CEAR 2009. *Situación de los centros de Internamiento para extranjeros en España*. [Online]. Available at: http://www.cear.es/informes/Informe-CEAR-situacion-CIE.pdf [accessed: 25 March 2010].

Cesari, J. 1997. *Faut-il avoir peur de l'Islam?* Paris: Presses de Sciences Po.

Ceyhan, A. 2004. Sécurité, frontières et surveillance aux États-Unis après le 11 septembre 2001. Surveillance politique: regards croisés. *Cultures & Conflits*, 53, 113–45. [www.conflits.org/index1005.html].

Champagne, P. 1990. *Faire l'opinion. Le nouveau jeu politique*. Paris: Minuit.

Chandler, D. 1966. *The Campaigns of Napoleon*. London: Macmillan.

Chevalier, L. 1984. *Classes laborieuses et classes dangereuses*. Paris: Hachette.

Christie, N. 1986a. Suitable Enemies, in *Abolitionism: Toward a non-Repressive Approach to Crime*, edited by H. Bianchi and R. Van Swaaningen. Amsterdam: Free University Press, 42–54.

Christie, N. 1986b. The Ideal Victim, in *From Crime Policy to Victim Policy: Reorienting the Justice System*, edited by E. Fattah. London: Macmillan.

Christie, N. 1993. *Crime Control as Industry: Towards Gulags Western Style*. New York: Routledge (Spanish 1993. Buenos Aires: Del Puerto).

Christie, N. 1998. El Derecho Penal y la societad civil. Peligros de la sobrecriminalización, in *XX Jornadas Internacionales de Derecho Penal*, edited by Various Authors. Bogotá: Univ. Externado de Colombia.

Christie, N. 2004. *A Suitable Amount of Crime*. London: Routledge (Spanish 2004. Buenos Aires: Del Puerto).

Ciccarelli, R. 2005. Samuel Huntington e la nuova America. *Conflitti globali*, 1, 5, 182–7.

Ciccarelli, R. 2006a. Guerra ai pirati del XXI secolo. *Conflitti globali*, 4, 97–106.

Ciccarelli, R. 2006b. Intervista a Gilles Kepel. *Conflitti globali*, 3, 82–92.

Cid Moliné, J. and Larrauri Pijoan, E. 2001. *Teorías criminológicas*. Barcelona: Bosch.

Cimade 2004. Les prétoires de la misère. Observation citoyenne du Tribunal correctionnel de Montpellier, *Causes Communes*. Paris: Cimade.

Cimade 2007. *Centres et locaux de rétention administrative. Rapport 2006*. Paris: Cimade.

Cimade 2008. *Centres et locaux de rétention administrative. Rapport 2007*. Paris: Cimade.

Cittalia-Fondazione Anci ricerche 2009. *Oltre le ordinanze. I sindaci e la sicurezza urbana*, rapporto di ricerca.

Clark, C. and Campbell, E. 2000. Gypsy Invasion: A Critical Analysis of Newspaper Reaction to Czech and Slovak Asylum-Seekers in Britain. *Journal of the Gypsy Lore Society*, 10, 1, 23–48.

Clark, N. 2003. George Soros, a Profile. *New Statesman*, 2 June.

Clifford, J. 1997. *Routes: Travel and Translation in the Late 20th Century*. Cambridge, MA: Harvard University Press.

Clochard, O. 2010. Les camps d'étrangers, symbole d'une politique. [Online]. Available at: http://blog.mondediplo.net/2010–06–01-Les-camps-d-etrangers-symbole-d-une-politique-forum

CNCDH 2004. *Étude sur les étrangers détenus*. Paris: Commission Nationale Consultative des Droits de l'Homme.

CNCDH 2008a. *Étude sur les étrangers détenus*. Paris: Commission Nationale Consultative des Droits de l'Homme.

CNCDH 2008b. *La lutte contre le racisme et la xénophobie: rapport d'activité 2007*. Paris: La Documentation française.

Cohen, R. 1994. *Frontiers of Identity: The British and the Others*. New York: Longman.

Cohen, S. 1972. *Folk Devils and Moral Panics: The Creation of the Mods and Rockers*. London: McGibbon & Kee.

Cohen, S. 2002. *Folk Devils and Moral Panics: Creation of Mods and Rockers*, 3rd edn. London: Routledge.

Colacicchi, P. 2008. Ethnic Profiling and Discrimination against Roma in Italy: New Developments in a Deep-Rooted Tradition. *Roma Rights*, 2, 35–44. [Online]. Available at: http://www.errc.org/db/03/B8/m000003B8.pdf

Cole, D. 1999. *No Equal Justice: Race and Class in the American Criminal Justice System*. New York: New Press.

Cole, D. 2003. *Enemy Aliens: Double Standards and Constitutional Freedoms in the War on Terror*. New York: New Press.

Colley, L. 2002. *Captives: Britain, Empire and the World, 1600–1850*. London: Jonathan Cape.

Comnena, A. 1969. *The Alexiad*, edited and translated by E.R.A. Sewter. Harmondsworth: Penguin.

Consejo Económico y Social 2007. *Memoria Anual 2006*. Madrid: CES.

Council of Europe 2009. Report by Thomas Hammarberg, Commissioner for Human Rights of the Council of Europe, following his visit to Italy on 13–15 January 2009. [Online]. Available at: https://wcd.coe.int/ViewDoc.jsp?id=1428427 [accessed 9 March 2010].

Cour des Comptes 2004. *L'accueil des immigrants et l'intégration des populations issues de l'immigration*. Paris: Cour des Comptes.

Currle, E. 2007. Migration in Europa. Daten und Hintergründe. Stuttgart 2004. *Statistisches Bundesamt: Bevölkerung und Erwerbstätigkeit*, 252, 55–8.

Cuttitta, P. 2007. Le monde-frontiére. Le contrôle de l'immigration dans l'espace globalisé. *Cultures & Conflits*, 68, 61–84.

Dal Lago, A. 1983. *L'ordine infranto. Max Weber e la crisi del razionalismo*. Milan: Unicopli.

Dal Lago, A. (ed.) 1998. *Lo straniero e il nemico*. Genoa: Costa & Nolan.

Dal Lago, A. 1999a. *Non-persone. L'esclusione dei migranti in una società globale*. Milan: Feltrinelli (2nd edn 2004; English 2009. *Non-Persons: The Exclusion of Migrants in a Global Society*. Milan: Ipoc Press].

Dal Lago, A. 1999b. La tautologia della paura. *Rassegna Italiana di Sociologia*, 1, 5–42.

Dal Lago, A. 2001. *Descrizione di una battaglia. I rituali del calico*, 2nd edn. Bologna: Il Mulino.

Dal Lago, A. 2003. *Polizia globale. Guerra e conflitti dopo l'11 settembre*. Verona: Ombre corte.

Dal Lago, A. 2004b. Controllo sociale e nuove forme di devianza. *Questione giustizia*, 2, 3.

Dal Lago, A. 2005a. Fronti e frontiere. Note sulla militarizzazione della contiguità. *Conflitti globali*, 2, 7–15.

Dal Lago, A. 2005b. La sociologia di fronte alla globalizzazione, in *Invito allo studio della società*, edited by P.P. Giglioli. Bologna: Il Mulino, 211–34.

Dal Lago, A. 2005c. La guerra-mondo. *Conflitti globali*, 1, 11–31.

Dal Lago, A. 2006. Esistono davvero i conflitti tra culture? Una riflessione storico-metodologica in *Multiculturalismo*, edited by C. Galli. Bologna: Il Mulino, 45–80.

Dal Lago, A. and Molinari, A. (eds) 2002. *Giovani senza tempo. Il mito della giovinezza nella società globale*. Verona: Ombre corte.

Dal Lago, A. and Palidda, S. (eds) 2010. *Conflict, Security and the Reshaping of Society: The Civilisation of War*. London: Routledge.

Dal Lago, A. and Quadrelli, E. 2003. *La città e le ombre. Crimini, criminali e cittadini*. Milan: Feltrinelli.

Daniel, N. 1979. *The Arabs and Medieval Europe*. London and New York: Longman (Italian 1981. *Gli Arabi e l'Europa nel Medioevo*. Bologna: Il Mulino).

Dassetto, F. and Bastenier, A. 1984. *L'islam transplanté: vie et organisation des minorités musulmanes en Belgique*. Anvers: EPO.

Dassetto, F. Bastenier, A. and El-Achy, A. 1987. *Medias-u-akbar: confrontations autour d'une manifestation*. Louvain-la-Neuve: Ciaco.

Davis, A.Y. 2003. *Are Prisons Obsolete?* New York: Seven Stories Press.

De André, F. 1999. *Tutte le canzoni*. Turin: Einaudi.

De Genova, N. 2002. Migrant 'Illegality' and Deportability in Everyday Life. *Annual Review of Anthropology*, 31, 419–47.

De Giorgi, A. 2000. *Zero Tolleranza*. Rome: DeriveApprodi.

De Giorgi, A. 2006. *Re-Thinking the Political Economy of Punishment: Perspectives on Post-Fordism and Penal Politics*. Aldershot: Ashgate.

De Giorgi, A. (forthcoming). Immigration Control, Post-Fordism, and Less Eligibility: A Materialist Critique of the Criminalization of Immigration across Europe. *Punishment & Society*.

De Lucas, J. 2005. Nuevas estrategias de estigmatización. El Derecho, frente a los inmigrantes, in *Mutaciones de Leviatán. Legitimación de los nuevos modelos penales*, edited by G. Portilla Contreras. Madrid: Univ. Internacional Andalucía/Akal, 205–20.

Deleuze, G. 1995. *Conversaciones*. Valencia: Pre-Textos.

Deleuze, G. and Guattari, F. 2004. *A Thousand Plateaus*. London and New York: Continuum.

Delgado Ruiz, M. 2010. Gli studi sulle migrazioni in Spagna. Un bilancio e una certa riflessione, in *Ambiguità e business sui migranti*, edited by Salvatore Palidda. Messina: Mesogea.

Dell, F., Legendre, N. and Ponthieux, S. 2003. La pauvreté chez les enfants, *Insee Première*, no. 896.

Deltombe, T. 2005. *L'Islam imaginaire. La construction médiatique de l'islamophobie en France*. Paris: La Découverte.

Der Polizeipräsident in Berlin (ed.) 2007. *Polizeiliche Kriminalstatistik 2004 Berlin*. Berlin.

Diodoro Siculo 2004. *Biblioteca storica*, edited by G. Cordiano and M. Zorat. Milan: RCS Libri.

Dombey, D. and Kuper, S., 2007. Britons 'More Suspicious' of Muslims, *Financial Times*, 20 August.

Donziger, S. (ed.) 1996. *The Real War on Crime*. New York: Harper.

Dougherty, J.E. 2004. *Illegals: The Imminent Threat Posed by our Unsecured U.S.–Mexico Border*. Nashville: WND Books.

Douglas, M. 1996. *Rischio e colpa*. Bologna: Il Mulino (English 1966. *Purity and Danger: An Analysis of Concepts of Pollution and Taboo*. London: Routledge and Kegan Paul).

Douglas, M. and Wildawsky A. 1982. *Risk and Culture: An Essay on the Selection of Technical and Environmental Dangers*. Berkeley and Los Angeles: University of California Press.

Dumont, L. 1983. *Essais sur l'individualisme. Une perspective anthropologique sur l'idèologie moderne*. Paris: Seuil.

Dundes Renteln, A., 2004. *The Cultural Defense*. New York: Oxford University Press.

Durkheim, E. 1912. *Les formes élémentaires de la vie réligieuse. Le systhème totémique en Australie*. Paris: Alcan (Italian 1963).

Duroselle, J.B. and Serra, E. (eds) 1978. *L'immigrazione italiana in Francia prima del 1914*. Milan: Angeli.

Ehrlich, I. 1974. Participation in Illegitimate Acitivities: An Economic Analysis, in *Essays in the Economics of Crime and Punishment*, edited by G.S. Becker and W.M. Landes. New York: Columbia University Press, 68–134.

Eichenhofer, E. (ed.) 1999. *Migration und Illegalität*. Osnabrück: Universitätsverlag Rasch.

Eisenberg, A. and Spinner-Halev, J. (eds) 2005. *Minorities Within Minorities: Equality, Rights and Diversity*. Cambridge: Cambridge University Press.

Elias, N. 1969. *Über den Prozess der Zivilisation I. Wandlungen des Verhaltens in den Weltlichen Oberschichten des Abendlandes*. Frankfurt: Suhrkamp.

Elias, N. and Dunning, E. 1986. *Quest for Excitement: Sport and Leisure in the Civilizing Process*. Oxford: Basil Blackwell.

Enzmann, D. and Wetzels, P. 2000. Gewaltkriminalität junger Deutscher und Ausländer. *Kölner Zeitschrift für Soziologie und Sozialpsychologie*, 52, 146–52.

ERPC 2008. *Discrimination against Roma in Europe*, Factsheet/Background press release, European Roma Policy Coalition. Brussels: ERPC.

ERRC 2000. *Campland: Racial segregation of Roma in Italy*. Budapest: ERRC.

Escobar, R. 2007. *Metamorfosi della paura*. Bologna: Il Mulino.

Esser, F. 1999. Medienwirkung und fremdenfeindliche Straftaten. Eine Langzeitanalyse von 1991 bis 1996, in *Von 'Antisemitismus' bis 'Xenophobie'. Rechtsextreme Medien in Deutschland*, edited by Bundesprüfstelle für Jugendgefährdende Schriften. Bonn, 49–55.

Eurobarometer 2007. *Discrimination in the European Union*. Brussels: Eurobarometer, 263 (special issue).

Eurobarometer 2008. *Discrimination in the European Union*. Brussels: Eurobarometer, 296 (special issue).

European Commission against Racism and Intolerance (ECRI) 2002. Second Report on Italy adopted on 22 June 2001. Strasbourg: ECRI.

European Commission against Racism and Intolerance (ECRI) 2004. Third Report on Germany adopted on 5 December 2003. Strasbourg: ECRI.

European Commission against Racism and Intolerance (ECRI) 2006. Third Report on Spain. [Online]. Available at: http://www.coe.int/t/e/human_rights/ecri/1%2Decri/2%2Dcountry%2Dby%2Dcountry_approach/spain/Spain%20third%20report%20-%20cri06–4.pdf [accessed: 25 March 2010].

European Commission against Racism and Intolerance (ECRI) 2006. Third Report on Italy adopted on 16 December 2005. Strasbourg: ECRI.

European Commission 2008. *Community Instruments and Policies for Roma Inclusion*, COM_2008_420 CSWD 27[1].6.08. Brussels: European Commission.

European Council 2008. *Presidency Conclusions on inclusion of the Roma*, 8 December 2008. Brussels: European Union, par. 50.

European Parliament 2007. *Conditions des ressortissants de pays tiers retenus dans des centres (camps de détention, centres ouverts ainsi que des zones de transit) au sein des 25 Etats membres de l'Union Européenne*. Strasbourg: European Parliament.

European Parliament 2008. *Resolution on a European Strategy on the Roma*, adopted on 31 January 2008, P6_TA2008) 0035. Strasbourg: European Parliament.

Fallaci, O. 2004. *La trilogia*. Milan: Rizzoli.

Farell, J.A. 2004. Bush Courting Hispanics. *Denver Post*, 8 January, A1. 8.

Faria, J.E. 2001. *El Derecho en la economía globalizada*. Madrid: Trotta.

Farinelli, F. 2003. *Geografia. Un'introduzione ai modelli del mondo*. Turin: Einaudi.

Faso, G. 2008. *Lessico del razzismo democratico. Le parole che escludono*. Rome: Derive & Approdi.

Fassin, D. (ed.) 2010. *Les nouvelles frontières de la société française*. Paris: La Découverte.

Fassin, D. and Fassin, E. (eds) 2008. *De la question sociale à la question raciale? Représenter la société française*. Paris: La Découverte.

Fassin, E. 2009. De discours volontaristes en faux débats. L'immigration, un 'problème' si commode, *Le Monde Diplomatique*, 22 November. [Online]. Available at: http://www.monde-diplomatique.fr/2009/11/FASSIN/18386

Feeley, M. and Simon, J. 1992. The New Penology: Notes on the Emerging Strategy of Correction and its Implications. *Criminology*, 4, 449–74.

Feeley, M. and Simon, J. 1994. Actuarial Justice: The Emerging New Criminal Law, in *The Futures of Criminology*, edited by D. Nelken. London: Sage, 173–201.

Feltes, T. 2006. Legitime und illegitime Gewaltanwendung durch die Polizei, in *Gewalt. Beschreibungen, Analysen, Prävention*, edited by W. Heitmeyer and M. Schröttle. Bonn: Bundeszentrale für politische Bildung, 539–56.

Ferrajoli, L. 1989. *Diritto e ragione. Teoria del garantismo penale*. Rome and Bari: Laterza.

Fishman, M. 1978. Crime Waves as Ideology. *Social Problems*, 25, 5, 531–43.

Fishman, M. 1980. *Manufacturing the News*. Austin: University of Texas Press.

Flori, J. 1999. *Richard Coeur de Lion. Le Roi-chevalier*. Paris: Payot.

Flori, J. 2001. La guerre sainte. La formation de l'idée de croisade dans l'Occident Chrétien. Paris: Aubier.

Foblets, M.-C. 1998. Cultural Delicts: The Repercussion of Cultural Conflicts on Delinquent Behaviour. Reflections on the Contribution of Legal Anthropology to a Contemporary Debate. *European Journal of Crime, Criminal Law and Criminal Justice*, 6, 3, 187–207.

Fofi, G. 1964. *L'immigrazione meridionale a Torino*. Milan: Feltrinelli.

Fondazione ISMU (ed.) 2009. *Quindicesimo rapporto sulle migrazioni 2009*. Milan: Franco Angeli.

Forbes, I. and Mead, G., 1992. *Measure for Measure: A Comparative Analysis of Measures to Combat Racial Discrimination in the Member States of the European Community*. Southampton: University of Southampton.

Forrai, E. 2006. The Political Economy of Exclusion: Unemployment, Poverty and Excess Deaths amongst Roma Men in Hungary, report presented at the seminar 'Welfare State(s): Equality or Recognition?', Roskilde University, 21–22 August.

Foucault, M. 1966. *Les mots et les choses. Une archéologie des sciences humaines*. Paris: Gallimard.

Foucault, M. 1969. *L'archéologie du savoir*. Paris: Gallimard. (English 2002. *The Archaeology of Knowledge*. London: Routledge).

Foucault, M. 1970. *L'ordre du discourse*. Paris: Gallimard. (English 1980. The Order of Discourse, in R. Young (ed.) *Untying the Text: A Poststructuralist Reader*. Boston: Routlege and Kegan Paul, 48–78).

Foucault, M. 1975. *Surveiller et punir. Naissance de la prison*. Paris: Gallimard.

Foucault, M. 1994. *Dits & Ecrits*, III. Paris: Gallimard.

Foucault, M. 1995. *La verdad y las formas jurídicas*, 4th edn. Barcelona: Gedisa.

Foucault, M. 1997. *Il faut défendre la société. Cours du Collège de France 1975–1976*. Paris: Hautes Études (Spanish 2000. Buenos Aires: FCE).

Foucault, M. 2004a. *Sécurité, territoire, population. Cours au Collège de France, 1977–1978*. Paris: Gallimard and Seuil (English 2007. *Security, Territory,*

Population: Lectures at the College de France, 1977–78. Basingstoke: Palgrave Macmillan).

Foucault, M. 2004b. *Naissance de la biopolitique. Cours au Collège de France, 1978–1979.* Paris: Gallimard and Seuil.

Foucault, M. 2008. *Le gouvernement de soi et des autres.* Paris: Hautes Études, Gallimard and Seuil.

Fowler, R. 1991. *Language in the News: Discourse and Ideology in the Press.* London and New York: Routledge.

Frampton, M.L., López I.H. and Simon J. (eds) 2008. *After the War on Crime.* New York: New York University Press.

Franzina, E. and Stella, G.A. 2002. Brutta gente. Il razzismo anti-italiano, in *Storia dell'emigrazione italiana. Arrivi*, edited by P. Bevilacqua, A. De Clementi and E. Franzina. Rome: Donzelli, 283–312.

Franzke, B. 1993. Polizei und Ausländer. *Kriminalistik*, 615–18.

Fraser, A. 1992. *The Gypsies.* Oxford: Blackwell.

Frean, A. 2009. Security Flaws Halt Work on ContactPoint Child Database, *The Times*, 24 March.

Friedlander, H. 1995. *The Origins of Nazi Genocide.* London: University of North Carolina Press.

Fuentes Osorio, J.L., 2005. Los medios de comunicación y el derecho penal, *Revista electrónica de ciencia penal y criminología*, 7, 7/16. [Online]. Available at http://criminet.ugr.es/recpc/07/recpc07–16.pdf

Fukuyama, F. 1992. *The End of History and the Last Man.* New York: Free Press.

Fukuyama, F. 2004. *State-Building: Governance and the World Order in the 21st Century.* Ithaca, NY: Cornell University Press.

Gabrielli, F. (ed.) 1987. *Storici arabi delle crociate.* Turin: Einaudi.

Galli, C. (ed.) 2006. *Multiculturalismo.* Bologna: il Mulino.

Galvagno, D. 1974. in *Cenni storici sulle misure di prevenzione nell'Italia 'liberale'*, edited by I. Mereu. Proceedings of the IX Conference on 'Enrico De Nicola', hosted by the Centro nazionale di prevenzione e difesa sociale, Alghero, Italy, 26-28 April.

García España, E. and Pérez Jiménez, F. 2005. *Seguridad ciudadana y actividades policiales*, El Monte. Málaga: IAIC/Fund.

García Vázquez, S. 2005. El estatuto jurídico constitucional del extranjero en España, unpublished PhD thesis, University of Coruña.

García Vázquez, S. 2007. *El estatuto jurídico-constitucional del extranjero en España.* Valencia: Tirant Lo Blanch.

García-Pablos de Molina, A. 1999. *Tratado de Criminología.* Valencia: Tirant lo Blanch.

Garrett, B. (2001). Remedying Racial Profiling. *Columbia Human Rights Law Review, 33*, 141–8.

Garfinkel, H. 1956. Conditions of Successful Degradation Ceremonies. *American Journal of Sociology*, 61, 420–4.

Garlan, Y. 1972. *La guerre dans l'antiquité.* Paris: Nathan.

Garland, D. 1996. The Limits of the Sovereign State: Strategies of Crime Control in Contemporary Society. *British Journal of Criminology*, 36, 4, 445–71.

Garland, D. (ed.) 2001a. *Mass Imprisonment: Social Causes and Consequences*. London and New York: Sage.

Garland, D. 2001b. *The Culture of Control: Crime and Social Order in Contemporary Society*. Chicago: University of Chicago Press (Spanish 2005. Barcelona: Gedisa).

Gastaut, Y. 2000. *L'immigration et l'opinion en France sous la Ve République*. Paris: Seuil.

Geertz, C. 1973. *The Interpretation of Cultures*. New York: Basic Books.

Geisser, V. 2003. *La nouvelle islamophobie*. Paris: La Découverte.

Geißler, R. and Marißen, N. 1990. Kriminalität und Kriminalisierung junger Ausländer. Die tickende soziale Zeitbombe – ein Artefakt der Kriminalstatistik. *Kölner Zeitschrift für Soziologie und Sozialpsychologie*, 42, 663–87.

Gesemann, F. 2003. Ist egal ob man Aunsländer ist oder so – jeder Mensch braucht die Polizei – Die Polizei in der Wahrnehmung junger Migranten, in *Die Ethnisierung von Alltagskonflikten*, edited by A. Groenemeyer and J. Mansel. Opladen: Leske and Budrich, 203–28.

Gesemann, F. 2004. *Junge Zuwanderer und Kriminalität in Berlin. Bestandsaufnahme – Ursachenanalyse – Präventionsmaßnahmen*. Berlin: Der Beauftragte des Senats von Berlin für Integration und Migration, 67–8.

Gèze, F. 2006. Les intégristes de la République et les émeutes de novembre. *Mouvements*, 44, 88–100.

Gibbon, E. 1973. *History of the Decline and Fall of Roman Empire* (Italian. Turin: Einaudi, 3 vols).

Gibney, M. 2004. *The Ethics and Politics of Asylum: Liberal Democracy and the Response to Refugees*. Cambridge: Cambridge University Press.

Gibson, M. 2002. *Born to Crime: Cesare Lombroso and the Origins of Biological Criminology*. Westport, CT: Praeger.

Giglioli, P.P. and Ravaioli, P. 2004. Bisogna davvero dimenticare il concetto di cultura? Replica ai colleghi antropologi. *Rassegna italiana di sociologia*, 45, 2, 267–98.

Gil Araújo, S. 2005. Muros alrededor de 'el Muro'. Prácticas y discursos en torno a la inmigración en el proceso de construcción de la política migratoria comunitaria, in *Delitos y fronteras*, edited by M.T. Martín Palomo, M.J. Miranda López and C. Vega Solís. Madrid: Complutense, 113–38.

Gilmore, R. 2007. *Golden Gulag: Prisons, Surplus, Crisis, and Opposition in Globalizing California*. Berkeley: University of California Press.

Ginsberg, B. 1986. *The Captive Public: How Mass Opinion Promotes State Power*. New York: Basic Books.

Glaze, L.E. and Bonczar, T.P. 2007. *Bureau of Justice Statistics Bulletin*. Washington, DC: Department of Justice.

Glaze, L.E. and Bonczar, T.P. 2008. *Probation and Parole in the United States*. Washington, DC: Bureau of Justice Statistics.

Goffman, E. 1986. *Stigma: Notes on the Management of Spoiled Identity*. New York: Simon & Schuster.

Goldberg, A. and Sauer, M. 2003. *Konstanz und Wandel der Lebenssituation türkischstämmiger Migranten in Nordrhein-Westfalen*. (Zusammenfassung der fünften Mehrthemenbefragung 2003 im Auftrag des Ministeriums für Gesundheit, Soziales, Frauen und Familie des Landes Nordrhein-Westfalen). Duisburg: Stiftung Zentrum für Türkeistudien-Universität Duisburg-Essen.

Gomolla, M. and Radtke, F.O. 2002. *Institutionnelle Diskriminierung. Die Herstellung ethnischer Differenz in der Schule*. Opladen: Leske and Budrich.

Goode, E. and Ben-Yehuda, N. 1994a. *Moral Panics: The Social Construction of Deviance*. Oxford: Blackwell; 2009. 2nd edn. Chichester: Wiley-Blackwell.

Goode, E. and Ben-Yehuda, N. 1994b. Moral Panics: Culture, Politics, and Social Construction. *Annual Review of Sociology*, 20, 149–71.

Goodey, J. (ed.) 2006. Ethnic Profiling, Criminal (In) Justice and Minority Populations. *Critical Criminology*, special issue, 14, 3.

Graham, K. and Wells, S. 2003. Somebody's Gonna Get Their Head Kicked in Tonight. Aggression among Young Males in Bars – A Question of Values? *British Journal of Criminology*, 43, 546–66.

Greger, R. 1987. Strafzumessung bei Vergewaltigung. *Monatsschrift für Kriminologie und Strafrechtsreform*, 70, 261–77.

Groenemeyer, A. and Mansel, J. (eds) 2003. *Die Ethnisierung von Alltagskonflikten*. Opladen: Leske and Budrich.

Gross, S.R. and Barnes, K.Y. 2002. Road Work: Racial Profiling and Drug Interdiction on the Highway. *Michigan Law Review* 101, 651, 738 and nn 278–82.

Guet, M. 2005. *What is anti-Gypsyism/anti-Tsiganism/Romaphobia?*, report presented at the seminar on anti-discrimination organised by the Hungarian Presidency of the 'Decade for Roma Inclusion', Budapest. [Online]. Available at: http://www.osce.org/item/23161.html

Guglielmo, R. and Waters, T.W. 2005. Migrating towards Minority Status: Shifting European Policy towards Roma. *Journal of Common Market Studies*, 43, 4, 763–86.

Guild, E. 2005. L'Etat d'exception, le juge, l'étranger et les droits de l'Homme: trois défis des Cours britanniques. *Cultures & Conflits*, 58, 183–204.

Guild, E. 2006. *Constitutional Challenge to the European Arrest Warrant*. Oisterwijk: Wolf Legal Publishers.

Guild, E. 2008. Les étrangers en Europe, victimes collatérales de la guerre contre le terrorisme, in *Au nom du 11 septembre. Les démocraties à l'épreuve du terrorisme*, edited by D. Bigo, L. Bonelli and T. Deltombe. Paris: La Découverte, 139–50.

Guild, E. and Bigo, D. 2005. Polizia a distanza. Le frontiere mobili e i confini di carta. *Conflitti Globali*, 2, 58–77.

Guillén, F. and Vallés, L. 2003. Inmigrante e inseguridad: ¿un problema de delincuencia o de victimización?, in *La seguridad en la sociedad del riesgo. Un debate abierto*, edited by C.Agra and Others. Barcelona: Atelier, 303–25.

Guillonneau, M., Kensey, A. and Portas, C. 1999. Détenus étrangers. *Cahiers de démographie pénitentiaire*, 6, 1–4.

Güller, N. 1999. La criminalité des Turcs en Allemagne, in *Crimes et cultures* edited by J.M. Bessette. Paris: L'Harmattan, 237–52.

Gutman, A. (ed.) 1994. *Multiculturalism: Examining the Politics of Recognition.* Princeton: Princeton University Press.

Guy, W. 2001. *Between Past and Future: The Roma of Central and Eastern Europe.* Hatfield: University of Hertfordshire Press.

Guy, W. 2009. EU Initiatives on Roma: Limitations and Ways Forward, in *Romani Politics in Contemporary Europe,* edited by N. Trehan and N. Sigona. Basingstoke: Palgrave Macmillan.

Hall, S. 1966. When Was the Post-Colonial?, in *The Post-Colonial Question*, edited by I. Chambers and L. Curti. London: Routledge, 242–60.

Hall, S., Critcher, C., Jefferson, T., Clarke, J. and Roberts, B., 1978. *Policing the Crisis: Mugging, the State and Law and Order.* London: Macmillan.

Halm, D. and Sauer, M. 2006. Parallelgesellschaft und ethnische Schichtung. *Aus Politik und Zeitgeschichte*, 1–2, 18–24.

Hamood, S. 2006. *African Transit Migration through Libya to Europe: The Human Cost.* Cairo: American University in Cairo.

Hancock, I. 1987. *The Pariah Syndrome: An Account of Gypsy Slavery and Persecution.* Ann Arbor: Karoma Publishers.

Hancock, I. 1995. Responses to the Porrajmos (The Romani Holocaust), in *Is the Holocaust Unique?* edited by A. Rosenbaum. Boulder: Westview Press, 39–64.

Hannerz, U. 1992. *Cultural Complexity: Studies in the Social Organization of Meaning.* New York: Columbia University Press.

Hanon, J.P. 2006. Militari. Dal campo di battaglia alla Guerra al terrorismo. *Conflitti globali*, 3, 33–43.

Hanson, V.D. 1989. *The Western Way of War.* New York: Knopf.

Hanson, V.D. 1999. *The Wars of the Ancient Greeks.* London: Cassell.

Hanson, V.D. 2001. Carnage and Culture: Landmark Battles in the Rise of Western Power. New York: Doubleday.

Harcourt, B.E. 2001. *Illusion of Order: The False Promise of Broken Windows Policing.* Cambridge, MA: Harvard University Press.

Harcourt, B.E. 2004. Rethinking Racial Profiling. *University of Chicago Law Review*, 71, 1275, 1276, 2.

Harcourt, B.E. 2007. *Against Prediction: Profiling, Policing and Punishing in an Actuarial Age.* Chicago: University of Chicago Press.

Harvey, D. 2005. *A Brief History of Neoliberalism.* Oxford: Oxford University Press.

Hayes, B. and Rowlands, M. 2008. Coming for the Kids: Big Brother and the Pied Pipers of Surveillance. *Statewatch Bulletin*, 18, 2 April–June.

Hazard, A. 2008. Les étrangers dans les statistiques pénitentiaires. *Cahiers de démographie pénitentiaire*, 25, 1–4.

Heilmann, E. 2007. Sorvegliare (a distanza) e prevenire. Verso una nuova economia della visibilità, *Conflitti globali*, 5, 24–36.

Heitmeyer, W. 1995. *Gewalt*. Munich: Weinheim.

Hermant, D. and Bigo, D. 2001. Les politiques de lutte contre le terrorisme, in *European Democracies against Terrorism: Governmental Policies and Intergovernmental Cooperation*, edited by F. Reinares. Aldershot: Ashgate.

Herodotus 2000. *Le storie*, Libro II, *L'Egitto*, edited by A.B. Lloyd. Milan: Fondazione Lorenzo Valla / Arnoldo Mondadori.

Hesse, M. 1966. *Models and Analogies in Science*. Notre Dame: University of Notre Dame Press.

Hillyard, P. 1993. *Suspect Communities: People's Experience of the Prevention of Terrorism Acts in Britain*. London: Pluto Press.

Hillyard, P. 2005. The War on Terror: Lessons from Ireland, in *The War on Freedom and Democracy*, edited by T. Bunyan. London: European Civil Liberties Network, 5–11.

Home Office 1998. *Fairer, Faster and Firmer: A Modern Approach to Immigration and Asylum*. London: Home Office, Cm 4018.

Home Office 2005a. *Controlling Our Borders: Making Migration Work for Britain. Five Year Strategy for Asylum and Immigration*. London: Home Office, Cm 6472.

Home Office 2005b. *Integration Matters: A National Strategy for Refugee Integration*. London: Home Office.

Home Office 2006. *Race and the Criminal Justice System: overview 2004–2005*. [Online]. Available at http://www.statewatch.org/news/2006/mar/s95race05overview.pdf

Home Office 2007a. Press Release, Asylum figures lowest since 1993, February 23. [Online.] Available at http://www.homeoffice.gov.uk/about-us/news/asylum-quarter-report?version.

Home Office 2007b. *Control of Immigration: Statistics United Kingdom 2006*, London, Home Office, Cm 7197.

Hopkins, K. 1983. *Death and Renewal*. Cambridge: Cambridge University Press.

House of Commons 2005. Debate on Immigration, Nationality and Asylum Bill, 5 July, 2005. [Online]. Available at: http://www.publications.parliament.uk/pa/cm200506/cmhansrd/vo050705/debindx/50705-x.htm [accessed 24 January 2008].

Human Rights Watch 2002a. Discretion Without Bounds: The Arbitrary Application of Spanish Immigration Law. [Online]. Available at http://www.hrw.org/reports/2002/spain2/

Human Rights Watch 2002b. The Other Face of the Canary Islands: Rights Violations against Migrants and Asylum Seekers. [Online]. Available at: http://www.hrw.org/reports/2002/spain/

Huntington, S.P. 1993. The Clash of Civilizations? *Foreign Affairs*, 72, 3, 22–49.

Huntington, S.P. 1996. *The Clash of Civilizations and the Remaking of World Order*. New York: Simon & Schuster.

Huntington, S.P. 2004. *Who are We? The Challenges to America's National Identity*. New York: Simon & Schuster.

Huysmans, J. 2006. *The Politics of Insecurity: Fear, Migration and Asylum in the EU*. London: Routledge.

Innenministerium Baden-Württemberg 2005. *Schusswaffengebrauch der Polizei*, Stuttgart, Pressestelle Innenministerium.

INSEE 2005. *Les immigrés en France*. Paris: Insee.

International Labour Organization 2009. *Report of the Committee of Experts on the Application of Conventions and Recommendations*. [Online]. Available at: http://www.ilo.org/global/What_we_do/Officialmeetings/ilc/ILCSessions/98thSession/ReportssubmittedtotheConference/lang--en/docName--WCMS_103484/index.htm [accessed 9 March 2010].

Irwin, J., Schiraldi, V. and Ziedenberg, J. 1999. *America's One Million Nonviolent Prisoners*. Washington, DC: Justice Policy Institute.

ISPO 2008. *Italiani, rom e sinti a confronto. Una ricerca quali-quantitativa*, report presented on occasion of the European Conference on Population, Rome, 22–23 January. Rome: Ministero degli Interni.

ISTAT 2004. *Settore Famiglia e società, La sicurezza dei cittadini. Reati, vittime, percezione della sicurezza e sistemi di protezione*. Multi-purpose inquiry on families, 'Sicurezza dei cittadini' Year 2002. [Online]. Available at: http://www.istat.it/dati/catalogo/20040915_00/

Jackson, P.I. 1997. Minorities, Crime and Criminal Justice in France, in *Minorities, Migrants and Crime: Diversity and Similarity across Europe and the United States*, edited by I.H. Marshall. London: Sage, 130–50.

Jameson, F. and Miyoshi, M. (eds) 1999. *The Cultures of Globalization*. Durham, NC and London: Duke University Press.

Jaroka, L. 2009. The Politician Jaroka on the Situation of the Roma. *Die Tageszeitung*, 28 March.

Jaschke, H.-G. 1997. *Öffentliche Sicherheit im Kulturkonflikt*. Frankfurt: Campus Verlag.

Jobard, F. 2006. Police, justice et discriminations raciales, in *De la question sociale à la question raciale*, edited by D. Fassin and E. Fassin. Paris: La Découverte, 219–37.

Jobard, F. 2007. L'usage de la force par la police, in *Traité de la sécurité intérieure*, edited by M. Cusson, F. Lemieux and B. Dupont. Lausanne: Polytechniques et Universitaires Romandes, 530–40.

Jobard, F. and Lévy, R. 2009. *Police et minorités visibles: les contrôles d'identité à Paris*, Open Society Institute, New York. [Online]. Available at: http://www. laurent-muchielli.org/public/Les_controles_d_identite.pdf

Jobard, F. and Nevanen, S. 2007. La couleur du jugement. Les discriminations dans les décisions judiciaires en matière d'infractions à agents de la force publique (1965–2005). *Revue française de sociologie*, 48, 2, 243–72.

Johnson, K.R. 2003. September 11 and Mexican Immigrants: Collateral Damage Comes Home. *De Paul Law Review*, 52, 849–68.

Joxe, A. 2005. Il lavoro dell'Impero e la regolazione democratica della violenza globale. *Conflitti globali*, 1, 70–79.

Joxe, A. 2010. The Barbarization of Peace: The Neo-Conservative Transformation of War and Perspectives, in *Conflict, Security and the Reshaping of Society: The Civilization of War*, edited by A. Dal Lago and S. Palidda. London and New York: Routledge, 37–56.

Kaminski, A. 1982. *Konzentrationslager 1896 bis heute*. Stuttgart: Kohlhammer.

Kantorowicz, E. 1923. *Kaiser Friedrich der Zweite*. Berlin: Georg Bondi (Italian 1988. *Federico II imperatore*, 2nd edn. Milan: Garzanti).

Kensey, A. 2007. *Prison et récidive*. Paris: Armand Colin.

Kertesi, G. 2005. *The Employment of the Roma in the End of the 20th Century*. Budapest Working Papers on the Labour Market, 4. [Online]. Available at: http://www.econ.core.hu/doc/bwp/bwp/Bwp0504.pdf

Kitsuse, J.I. and Cicourel, A.V. 1963. A Note of the Uses of Official Statistics. *Social Problems*, 11, 2, 131–9.

Kobelinsky, C. and Makaremi, C. (eds) 2009. *Enfermés dehors. Enquêtes sur le confinement des étrangers*. Bellecombe-en-Bauge: Editions du Croquant.

Kotek, J. and Rigoulot, P. 2000. *Le siècle des camps*. Paris: J-C. Lattès.

Kovats, M. 2003. The Politics of Roma Identity: Between Nationalism and Destitution. *Open Democracy*, 29 July. [Online]. Available at: http://www. opendemocracy.net/people.../article_1399.jsp

Kroeber, A.L. and Kluckhohn, C. 1952. *Culture: A Critical Review of Concepts and Definitions*. New York: Vintage Books.

Kroeber, A.L. and Parsons, T. 1958. The Concept of Culture and of Social System. *American Sociological Review*, 23, 582–3.

Kubink, M. 1993. *Veständnis und Bedeutung von Ausländerkriminalität. Eine Analyse der Konstitution sozialer Probleme*. Pfaffenweiler: Centaurus.

Kunda, G. 1992. *Engineering Culture: Control and Commitment in a High-Tech Corporation*. Philadelphia: Temple University Press.

Kymlicka, W. 1995. *Multicultural Citizenship: A Liberal Theory of Minority Rights*. Oxford: Clarendon Press (French 2001).

Landes, D.S. 1999. *The Wealth and Poverty of Nations*. New York: Norton.

Langewiesche, W. 2004. *The Outlaw Sea: A World of Freedom, Chaos and Crime*. New York: North Point Press.

Larrauri, E. 2000. *La herencia de la criminología crítica*, 3rd edn. Madrid: Siglo XXI.

Laurens, S. 2006. *Hauts fonctionnaires et immigration en France (1962–1981). Socio-histoire d'une domination à distance.* Paris: Ecole des Hautes Etudes en Sciences Sociales Phd in sociology.

Le Bohec, Y. 1989. *L'armé romaine sous le Haut-Empire.* Paris: Picard.

Le Cour Grandmaison, O. 2005. *Coloniser. Exterminer. Sur la guerre et l'Etat colonial.* Paris: Fayard.

Leca, J. 1991. La citoyenneté entre la nation et la société civile, in *Citoyenneté et nationalité. Perspectives en France et au Québec*, edited by D. Colas, C. Emeri and J. Zylberberg. Paris: PUF, 479–505.

Legoux, L. 1995. *La crise de l'asile politique en France.* Paris: Ceped.

Lessana, C. 1998. Loi Debré: la fabrique de l'immigré. *Cultures & Conflits*, 29–30, 125–41 and 31–2, 141–58.

Lessing, G.E. 1986 [1779]. *Nathan der Weise. Ein Dramatisches Gedicht in fünf Aufzügen.* Stuttgart: Reclam.

Lévy, R. 1987. *Du suspect au coupable. Le travail de police judiciaire.* Paris and Geneva : Méridiens Klincsieck-Médecine et Hygiène.

Lévy, R., Goris, I. and Jobard, F. 2009. *Police et minorités visibles: les contrôles d'identité à Paris.* New York: Open Society Justice Initiative.

Lévy, R. and Zauberman, R. 1998. La police et les minorités visibles: les contradictions de l'idéal républicain, in *Politique, police et justice au bord du futur*, edited by Y. Cartuyvels, F. Digneffe, A. Pirès and P. Robert. Paris: L'Harmattan, 287–300.

Lévy, R. and Zauberman, R. 2003. Police, Minorities and the French Republican Ideal. *Criminology*, 41, 4, 1065–1100.

Lévy-Bruhl, L. 1910. *Les fonctions mentales dans les sociétés inférieures* (Italian 1970. *Psiche e società primitive*. Rome: Newton Compton).

Lewis, B. 1982. *The Muslim Discovery of Europe.* London: Weidenfeld and Nicolson.

Lewis, B. 1995. *Cultures in Conflict: Christians, Muslims and Jews in the Age of Discovery.* Oxford and New York: Oxford University Press.

Lewis, B. 2003. *The Crisis of Islam: Holy War and Unholy Terror.* London: Weidenfeld & Nicolson.

Liberti, S. 2008. *A Sud di Lampedusa.* Rome: Minimumfax.

Liegeois, J.P. and Gheorghe, N. 1995. *Roma/Gypsies*: *A European Minority.* London: Minority Rights Group International.

Linebaugh, P. and Rediker, M. 2000. *The Many-headed Hydra: Sailors, Slaves, Commoners and the Hidden History of the Revolutionary Atlantic.* Boston: Beacon Press.

Lister, R. 1998. Vocabularies of Citizenship and Gender: The UK. *Critical Social Policy*, 13, 3, 301–31.

Lochak, D. 2006. L'intégration comme injonction. Enjeux idéologiques et politiques liés à l'immigration. *Cultures & Conflits*, 64, 129–47.

Lochak, D. 2007. *Face aux migrants: État de droit ou état de siège?* Paris: Textuel.

Loisy De, A. 2005. *Bienvenue en France! Six mois d'enquête clandestine dans la zone d'attente de Roissy*. Paris: Le Cherche Midi.

Lombroso, C. 2006 [1879]. *L'uomo delinquente*. Milan: Hoepli.

Loury, G. 2008. *Race, Incarceration, and American Values*. Cambridge, MA: MIT Press.

Lüdemann, C. 1992. Zur 'Ansteckung Wirkung' von Gewalt gegenüber Ausländern – Anwendung eines Schwellenwert Models kollektiven Verhaltens. *Soziale Probleme*, 3, 137–53.

Luff, J. and Gerum, M. 1995. *Ausländer als Opfer von Straftaten*. Munich: Bayerische Landes-Kriminalamt.

Lynch, J.P. and Simon, R.J. 1999. A Comparative Assessment of Criminal Involvement among Immigrants and Natives across Seven Nations. *International Criminal Justice Review*, 9, 1–17.

MacKeith, J. (ed.) 2004. The Psychiatric Problems of Detainees Under the 2001 Anti-Terrorism, Crime and Security Act, 13 October. [Online]. Available at: http://www.statewatch.org/news/2004/nov/belmarsh-mh.pdf

Macpherson, C.B. 1962. *The Political Economy of Possessive Individualism: Hobbes to Locke*. Oxford: Oxford University Press.

Malinowski, B. 1922. *Argonauts of the Western Pacific: An Account of Native Enterprise and Adventure in the Archipelagoes of Melanesian New Guinea*. London: G. Routledge (Italian 1973).

Malinowski, B. 1944. *A Scientific Theory of Culture and Other Essays*. Chapel Hill, NC: University of North Carolina Press (Italian 1971).

Malloch, M.S. and Stanley, E. 2005. The Detention of Asylum Seekers in the UK: Representing Risk, Managing the Dangerous. *Punishment & Society*, 7, 1, 53–71.

Manço, U. and Brion, F. 1999. *Muslim Voices in the European Union: Belgian Country Report*, Centre d'Etudes Sociologiques. Brussels: Facultés universitaires Saint-Louis.

Maneri, M. 1995. Stampa quotidiana e senso comune nella costruzione sociale dell'immigrato, Phd dissertation, Trento.

Maneri, M. 1998. Lo straniero consensuale. La devianza degli immigrati come circolarità di pratiche e discorsi, in *Lo straniero e il nemico. Materiali per l'etnografia contemporanea*, edited by A. Dal Lago. Genoa: Costa & Nolan, 236–74.

Maneri, M. 2001. Il panico morale come dispositivo di trasformazione dell'insicurezza. *Rassegna Italiana di Sociologia*, 1, 5–40.

Maneri, M. 2003. La construction d'un sens commun sur l'immigration en Italie. Les 'gens' dans le discours médiatique et politique. *La revue internationale et stratégique*, 50, 95–104.

Manning, P. 2001. *News and News Sources: A Critical Introduction*. London: Sage.

Manuel II Paléologue 1966. *Entretien avec un Musulman*. Paris: Les Sources Chrètiennes.

Manza, J. and Uggen, C. 2008. *Locked Out: Felon Disenfranchisement and American Democracy*. Oxford: Oxford University Press.

Maoluf, A. 1999. *Le crociate viste dagli arabi*. Turin: Sei.

Marcus, G. E. and Fischer, M.J. 1986. *Anthropology as a Cultural Critique: An Experimental Moment in the Human Sciences*. Chicago: University of Chicago Press.

Márquez Lepe, E. 2005. La construcción retórica del extranjero inmigrante en el discurso político español, in *Delitos y fronteras*, edited by M.T. Martín Palomo, M.J. Miranda López and C. Vega Solís. Madrid: Complutense, 183–216.

Martínez Veiga, U. 2001. El Ejido, un experimento del capitalismo moderno. *Archipiélago*, 48, 81–5.

Marushiakova, E. and Popov, V. 2001. New Ethnic Identities in the Balkans: The Case of the Egyptians. *Facta Universitatis, Philosophy and Sociology,* 2, 8, 465–77.

Mary, F.L. and Tournier, P. 1998. La répression pénale de la délinquance des étrangers en France. *Information – Prison – Justice*, 84.

Matelly, J.H. and Mouhanna, C. 2007. *Police: des chiffres et des doutes. Regard critique sur les statistiques de la délinquance*. Paris: Michalon.

Matera, V. 2004. Presentazione a Pensare la cultura. *Rassegna italiana di sociologia*, I.

Matras, Y. 2000. Romani Migrations in the Post-Conflict Era: Their Historical and Political Significance. *Cambridge Review of International Affairs*, 13, 2, 32–50.

Matthews, R. 2003. *Pagando tiempo*. Barcelona: Bellaterra.

Mauer, M. 2002. Mass Imprisonment and the Disappearing Voters, in *Invisible Punishment: The Collateral Consequences of Mass Imprisonment*, edited by M. Mauer and M. Chesney-Lynd. New York: The New Press, 50–58.

Mauer, M. 2006. *Race to Incarcerate*. New York: The New Press.

Mauer, M. and Chesney-Lynd, M. (eds) 2002. *Invisible Punishment: The Collateral Consequences of Mass Imprisonment*. New York: The New Press.

Mauer, M. and King, R.S. 2007. *Uneven Justice: State Rates of Incarceration by Race and Ethnicity*. Washington DC: The Sentencing Project.

Mauger, G. 2006. L'émeute de novembre 2005. Une révolte protopolitique. Paris: Éditions du Croquant.

Mauger, G. 2009. *La sociologie de la délinquance juvénile*. Paris: La Découverte.

Mauss, M. 1999 [1950]. Essai sur le don, in *Sociologie et anthropologie*. Paris: PUF.

McCarthy, K.F. and Vernez, G. *Immigration in a Changing Economy: California's Experience. Questions and Answers*. [Online]. Available at: http://www.rand.org/pubs/monograph_reports/MR854.1/

Mayer, N. 1999. *Ces Français qui votent Le Pen*. Paris: Flammarion.

Mead, G.H. 1918. The Psychology of Punitive Justice. *American Journal of Sociology*, 23, 577–602.

Melossi, D. 1989. An Introduction: Fifty Years Later. Punishment and Social Structure in Comparative Analysis. *Crime, Law & Social Change*, 13, 4, 311.

Melossi, D. 2002. *Stato, controllo sociale, devianza*. Milan: Bruno Mondadori.

Melossi, D. (ed.) 2003. Symposium on Migration, Punishment and Social Control in Europe. *Punishment and Society*, 4, 371–462.

Mermaz, L. 2001. *Les geôles de la République*. Paris: Stock.

Mereu, I. 1979. *Storia dell'intolleranza in Europa: sospettare e punire. Il sospetto e l'Inquisizione romana nell'epoca di Galilei. Milan:* Mondadori.

Mezzadra, S. 2005. *Derecho de fuga. Migraciones, ciudadanía y globalización.* Madrid: Traficantes de Sueños.

Mezzadra, S. (ed.) 2004. *I confini della libertà. Per un'analisi politica delle migrazioni contemporanee*. Rome: Derive & Approdi.

Mezzadra, S. and Rahola, F. (2006) The Postcolonial Condition. *Postcolonial Text*, 2, 1. [Online]. Available at: http://postcolonial.org/index.php/pct/article/view/393/819

Migreurop 2009. *Atlas des migrants en Europe. Géographie critique des politiques migratoires*. Paris: Armand Colin.

Miller, W.B. 1979. Die Kultur der Unterschicht als Entstehungsmilieu für Bandendelinquenz, in *Kriminalsoziologie*, 3rd edn, edited by F. Sack and R. König. Frankfurt: Suhrkamp, 339–59.

Milza, P. 1978. L'intégration des Italiens dans le mouvement ouvrier français à la fin du XIXe et au début du XXe siècle; le cas de la région marseillaise, in *L'emigrazione italiana in Francia prima del 1914*, edited by J.B. Duroselle and E. Serra. Milan: Angeli, 171–207.

Ministère de la Justice 2008. *L'administration pénitentiaire en chiffres*. Paris: Ministère de la Justice.

Ministerio del Interior 2007. *Anuario estadístico del Ministerio del Interior 2006*. [Online]. Available at: http://www.mir.es/MIR/PublicacionesArchivo/publicaciones/catalogo/anuarios/anuario_2006_web.pdf [accessed: 25 March 2010].

Ministerio del Interior 2008. *Balance de la lucha contra la inmigración ilegal*. [Online]. Available at: http://www.mir.es/DGRIS/DGRIS_Galeria_de_Imagenes/notas_prensa/2008/bal_lucha_inmigracion_ilegal_2007_mir.pdf

Ministerio del Interior 2009. *Anuario estadístico del Ministerio del Interior 2008*. [Online]. Available at: http://www.mir.es/MIR/PublicacionesArchivo/publicaciones/catalogo/anuarios/Anuario_Estaxstico2008.pdf [accessed: 25 March 2010].

Ministerio del Interior 2010. *Balance de la lucha contra la inmigración ilegal 2009*. [Online]. Available at: http://www.mir.es/DGRIS/Balances/Balance_2008/pdf/bal_lucha_inmigracion_ilegal_2008.pdf. [accessed: 25 March 2010].

Miró Miquel, G. 2005. La política criminal del problema droga. Etapas del problema y consecuencias de las soluciones adoptadas, in *Política Criminal y Sistema Penal. Viejas y nuevas racionalidades punitivas,* edited by I. Rivera Beiras. Barcelona: Anthropos, 303–17.

Moccia, S. 1997. *La perenne emergenza. Tendenze nel sistema penale*. Naples: Esi.

Momigliano, A. 1984. *Sui fondamenti della storia antica*. Turin: Einaudi.

Monclús Masó, M. 2002. La 'gestión' penal de la inmigración: otra excepción al Estado de Derecho. *Panóptico*, 3, 174–9.

Monclús Masó, M. 2005. Hacia una política criminal diferenciada para los extranjeros: la consolidación de la expulsión como sanción penal especial, in *Política Criminal y Sistema Penal. Viejas y nuevas racionalidades punitivas*, edited by I. Rivera Beiras. Barcelona: Anthropos, 330–47.

Morelli, A. 2004. *Gli italiani del Belgio. Storia e storie di due secoli*. Foligno: Editoriale Umbra.

Morice, A. and Rodier, C. 2010. Comment l'Union européenne enferme ses voisins. *Le Monde Diplomatique*, June, 12–13.

Morris, N. and Russell, B. 2008. More than 1,000 Children Jailed for Breaching Asbos. *Independent*, 25 August.

Mosconi, G. 2005. Inmigración, seguridad y cárcel en Italia (en la perspectiva de la guerra global), in *Política criminal de la guerra*, edited by R. Bergalli and I. Rivera Beiras. Barcelona: Anthropos, 144–72.

Mosher, C.J., Miethe, T.D. and Phillips, D.M. 2001. *Mismeasure of Crime*. Thousand Oaks, CA: Sage.

Moulier Boutang, Y. 1998. *De l'esclavage au salariat: économie historique du salariat bridé*. Paris: PUF.

Moulier Boutang, Y. 2002. Migrazioni internazionali e criminalità organizzata: cambiare seriamente opinione e pratiche, in *I crimini della globalizzazione*, edited by M.A. Pirrone and S. Vaccaro. Trieste: Asterios.

Mucchielli, L. 2002. *Violences et insécurité. Fantasmes et réalités dans le débat français*. Paris: La Découverte, 2nd edn.

Mucchielli, L. 2003. Délinquance et immigration en France: un regard sociologique. *Criminologie*, 2, 27–55.

Mucchielli, L. 2005. *Le scandale des 'tournantes'. Dérives médiatiques et contre-enquête sociologique*. Paris: La Découverte.

Mucchielli, L. 2006. Immigration et délinquance: fantasmes et réalités, in *La république mise à nu par son immigration*, edited by N. Guénif-Souilamas. Paris: La Fabrique, 39–61.

Mucchielli, L. (ed.) 2008a. *La frénésie sécuritaire*. Paris: La Découverte.

Mucchielli, L. 2008b. Le 'nouveau management de la sécurité' à l'épreuve: délinquance et activité policière sous le ministère Sarkozy (2002–2007), *Champ pénal / Penal Field*. [Online]. Available at: http://champpenal.revues.org/document3663.html

Mucchielli, L. 2008c. Une société plus violente ? Analyse sociohistorique de l'évolution des violences interpersonnelles en France depuis les années 1970. *Déviance et société*, 2, 115–46.

Muller, B.J. 2004. (Dis)Qualified Bodies: Securitisation, Citizenship and Identity Management. *Citizenship Studies*, 8, 3, 279–94.

Müller, J. 2000. Jugendkonflikte und Gewalt mit ethnisch-kulturellem Hintergrund, in *Bedrohte Stadtgesellschaft. Soziale Desintegrationsprozesse und ethnisch-kulturelle Konfliktkonstellationen*, edited by W. Heitmeyer and R. Anhut. Munich: Weinheim, 257–305.

Musti, D. 2004. *Storia greca*. Rome and Bari: Laterza.

Naplava, T. 2002. *Delinquenz bei einheimischen und immigrierten Jugendlichen im Vergleich. Sekundäranalyse von Schülerbefragungen der Jahre 1995–2000*. Freiburg: MPI.

Nell, L.M. 2004. Conceptualising the Emergence of Immigrants' Transnational Communities, *Migration Letters*, 1, 50–56.

Nevins, J. 2002. *Operation Gatekeeper: The Rise of the 'Illegal Alien' and the Making of the U.S.–Mexico Boundary*. New York: Routledge.

Nicolae, V. 2008. Anti-Gypsyism – a definition', European Grassroots Organisation, Bucharest: ERGO. [Online]. Available at: http://www.ergonetwork.org/antigypsyism.htm

Noiriel, G. 1988. *Le creuset français. Histoire de l'immigration, XIXe–XXe siècles*. Paris: Seuil.

Noiriel, G. 1991. *La tyrannie du national. Le droit d'asile en Europe (1793–1993)*. Paris: Calmann-Levy (new version: *Réfugié et sans-papiers. La République française face au droit d'asile. XIXe–XXe siècle*. Paris: Hachette, 1999).

Noiriel, G. 2001. *Etat, nation et immigration. Vers une histoire du pouvoir*. Paris: Belin.

Noiriel, G. 2007. *Immigration, antisémitisme et racisme en France (XIXe–XXe siècles). Discours publics, humiliations privées*. Paris: Fayard.

Norris, C. and Amstrong, G. 1999. *The Maximum Surveillance Society: The Rise of CCTV*. Oxford: Berg.

Norris, C., Moran, J. and Armstrong, G. (eds) 1998. *Surveillance, CCTV and Social Control*. Aldershot: Ashgate.

Oberwittler, D. and Köllisch, T. 2004. Nicht die Jugendgewalt, sondern deren polizeiliche Registrierung hat zugenommen – Ergebnisse einer Vergleichsstudie nach 25 Jahren. *Neue Kriminalpolitik*, 144–7.

Oberwittler, D., Blank, T., Köllisch, T. and Naplava, T. 2001. *Soziale Lebenslagen und Delinquenz von Jugendlichen*. Freiburg: MPI and OFS.

Observatori del Sistema Penal i els Drets Humans 2004. *Primer informe sobre los procedimientos administrativos de detención, internamiento y expulsión de extranjeros en Catalunya*. Barcelona: Virus.

Ocqueteau, F. 2004. *Polices entre Etat et marché*. Paris: Presses de Sciences Po.

Oficina económica del Presidente 2006. *Inmigración y economía española*. [Online]. Available at: http://www.la-moncloa.es/NR/rdonlyres/62B6B50E-AE7B-455A-85A5-600EF4EA9281/80515/InmigracionYEconomia Espaniola12Nov.pdf [accessed: 10 March 2008].

Ohlemacher, T. 1998. Fremdenfeindlichkeit und Rechtsextremismus. Mediale Berichterstattung, Bevölkerungmeinung und deren Wechselwirkung mit fremdenfeindlichen Gewalttaten 1991–1997, *Soziale Welt*, 49, 319–32.

Open Society Justice Initiative 2007. *'I Can Stop and Search Whoever I Want': Police Stops of Ethnic Minorities in Bulgaria, Hungary and Spain*. New York: Open Society Justice Initiative.

Oppermann, A. 1987. Straffällige junge Ausländer. Kriminalitätsbelastung und soziale Bedingungen. *Bewährungshilfe*, 34, 83–95.

Osservatorio di Pavia 2002. L'agenda dei telegiornali sulle notizie di criminalità e immigrazione: un confronto fra il 2000 e il 2001. [Online]. Available at: http://www.osservatorio.it/download/criminalita.pdf [accessed 9 March 2010].

Osservatorio di Pavia 2009. Sicurezza e media. [Online]. Available at: http://www.osservatorio.it/download/Criminalita2009.pdf [accessed 9 March 2010].

Pager, D. 2008. The Republican Ideal ? National Minorities and the Criminal Justice System in Contemporary France. *Punishment and Society*, 4, 375–400.

Palidda, S. (ed.) 1996. *Délit d'immigration*. Brussels: European Community.

Palidda, S. 1999. Polizia e immigrati: un'analisi etnografica. *Rassegna Italiana di Sociologia*, XL, 1, 77–114.

Palidda, S. 2000. *Polizia postmoderna. Etnografia del nuovo controllo sociale*. Milan: Feltrinelli.

Palidda, S. 2001. *Devianza e vittimizzazione tra i migranti*. Milan: ISMU-Angeli.

Palidda, S. 2005. The New Management of Migrations. *History and Anthropology*, 16, 1, 63–74.

Palidda, S. 2007. Missions militaires italiennes à l'étranger: la prolifération des hybrides. *Cultures & Conflits*, 67, Autumn. [Online]. Available at: http://conflits.revues.org/index3126.html [accessed: 2 April 2010].

Palidda, S. 2007. Politiche della paura e declino dell'agire pubblico. *Conflitti globali*, 5, 13–23 (English 2009. Policy of Fear and Decline of Political Sphere, in *Warlike Outlines of the Securitarian State: Life Control and Persons' Exclusion*, edited by G. Rodríguez, C. Fernández Bessa, I. Rivera Beiras and H.C. Silveira Gorski. Barcelona: OSPDH-Università di Barcelona, 67–81.

Palidda, S. 2008a. *Mobilità umane. Introduzione alla sociologia delle migrazioni*. Milan: Raffaelo Cortina.

Palidda, S. 2008b. Appunti di ricerca sulle violenze delle polizie al G8 di Genova. *Studi sulla questione criminale* – new series of *Dei delitti e delle pene*, 3, 1, 33–50.

Palidda, S. 2009a. Insertion, Integration and Rejection of Immigration in Italy, in *Illiberal Liberal States: Immigration, Citizenship and Integration in the EU*, edited by E. Guild and S. Carrera. Farnham: Ashgate, 357–72.

Palidda, S. 2009b. The Criminalization and Victimization of Immigrants: A Critical Perspective, in *Immigration, Crime and Justice*, Vol. 13 *Sociology of Crime, Law and Deviance*, edited by William McDonald. Bingley : Emerald/ JAI Press, 313–26.

Palidda, S. 2009c. Repenser la police et les contrôles par rapport à Foucault, in *Carceral Notebooks*, edited by B.E. Harcourt, 4, 175–86.

Palidda S. (ed.) 2010a. *Il discorso ambiguo sulle migrazioni*. Messina: Mesogea.

Palidda, S. 2010b. Violences policières e violences des pouvoirs en Italie, in *La violence politique en Europe*, edited by Crettiez X. and Mucchielli L. Paris: La Découverte, 251–69.

Palidda, S. 2010c. Revolution in Police Affairs, in *Conflict, Security and the Reshaping of Society: The Civilisation of War*, edited by A. Dal Lago and S. Palidda. London: Routledge, 118–28.

Pandolfi, M. 2002. Moral entrepreneurs, souverainetés mouvantes et barbelés. La biopolitique dans les Balkans postcommunistes. *Anthropologie et Sociétés* 26, 1, 40–41.

Pandolfi, M. and Fassin, D. 2008. *States of Emergency: Anthropology of Humanitarian Intervention*. New York: Zone Books.

Papastergiadis, N. 1999. *The Turbulence of Migrations: Globalization, Deterritorialization and Hybridity*. Cambridge: Polity Press.

Parekh, B. 1996. Minority Practices and Principles of Toleration. *International Migration Review*, 30, 251–84.

Parenti, C. 2000. *Lockdown America: Police and Prisons in the Age of Crisis*. New York: Verso.

Parsons, T. 1937. *The Structure of Social Action*. New York: McGraw-Hill (Italian 1968. *La truttura dell'azione sociale*. Bologna: Il Mulino).

Partner, P. 1998. *God of Battles: Holy Wars of Christanity and Islam*. Princeton: Princeton University Press.

Partner, P. 2003. *Corsairs and Crusaders*. Princeton: Princeton University Press.

Pavarini, M. (ed.) 2002. *Codice commentato dell'esecuzione penale*, vols I, II, III. Turin: Utet.

Pavarini, M. 2006. La neutralizzazione degli uomini inaffidabili. La nuova disciplina della recidiva e altro ancora sulla guerra alle Unpersonen. *Studi sulla questione criminale*, I, 2, 7–29.

Paye, J.C. 2005. *La fine dello stato di diritto*. Rome: Manifesto libri.

Pease, D.E. 2000. US Imperialism: Global Dominance without Colonies, in *A Companion to Postcolonial Studies*, edited by H. Schwarz and S. Ray. Oxford: Blackwell, 203–20.

Peirce, G. 2005. A Stampede against Justice. *Guardian*, 8 March.

Pepicelli, R. 2004. *2010: un nuovo ordine Mediterraneo?* Messina: Mesogea.

Pereda, C., Actis, W. and De Prada, M.A. 2005. *Inmigración y vivienda en España*. Madrid: Ministerio Trabajo y Asuntos Sociales.

Pérez Cepeda, A.I. 2006. El Código Penal de la seguridad: una involución en la Política criminal de signo reaccionario, in *La tensión entre libertad y seguridad. Una aproximación sociojurídica*, edited by M.J. Bernuz Beneitez and A.I. Pérez Cepeda. Logroño: Univiversidad La Rioja, 223–44.

Pérez Cepeda, A.I. 2007. *La seguridad como fundamento de la deriva del Derecho Penal postmoderno*. Madrid: Iustel.

Pertusi, A. 1976. *La caduta di Costantinopoli*, Vol I. *Le testimonianze dei contemporanei*, vol II: *L'eco nel mondo*. Milan: Fondazione Lorenzo Valla/ Arnoldo Mondadori.

Petraccone, C. 2000. *Le due civiltà Settentrionali e meridionali nella storia d'Italia.* Bari and Rome: Laterza.

Petrillo, A. (ed.) 2009. *Biopolitica di un rifiuto. Le rivolte anti-discarica a Napoli e in Campania.* Verona: Ombre corte.

Petti, G. 2004. *Il male minore.* Verona: Ombrecorte.

Petti, G. 2010. Enemies–Criminals: The Law and Courts against Global Terrorism, in *Conflict, Security and the Reshaping of Society: The Civilisation of War*, edited by A. Dal Lago and S. Palidda. London: Routledge, 138–50.

Piasere, L. 1991. *Popoli delle discariche.* Rome: CISU.

Piasere, L. 2006. *I rom d'Europa. Una storia moderna.* Bari and Rome: Laterza.

Portes, A. and DeWind J. (eds) 2008. *Rethinking Migration: New Theoretical and Empirical Perspectives.* New York: Berghahn.

Portilla Contreras, G. 2005. El Derecho Penal de la 'Seguridad'. Una secuela inevitable de la desaparición del Estado Social, in *Guerra global permanente. La nueva cultura de la inseguridad*, edited by J.A. Brandariz and J. Pastor. Madrid: Los libros de la Catarata, 52–70.

Pratt, A. and Valverde, M. 2002. From Deserving Victims to 'Masters of Confusion': Redefining Refugees in the 1990s. *Canadian Journal of Sociology*, 27, 2, 135–61.

Pratt, J. 1998. Toward the Decivilizing of Punishment? *Social & Legal Studies*, 7, 4, 487–515.

Pretel, O. 2006. Las fronteras intrametropolitanas, in *Fronteras interiores y exteriores*, edited by Various Authors. *Contrapoder*, 51–60.

Pritchett, W.K. 1971–85. *Greek States at War.* Berkeley: University of California Press, 4 vols.

Prontera, F. 1996. Il Mediterraneo come quadro della storia greca, in *I Greci*, edited by S. Settis. Turin: Einaudi, Vol. II, 1.

Quassoli, F. 1999. Immigrazione uguale criminalità: rappresentazioni di senso comune e pratiche degli operatori del diritto. *Rassegna italiana di sociologia*, 1, 43–76.

Rahola, F. 2003. *Zone definitivamente temporanee. I luoghi dell'umanità in eccesso.* Verone: Ombre corte.

Rahola, F. 2007. La forme-camp. Pour une genealogie des lieux de transit et d'internement du présent. *Cultures & Conflits*, 68, 31–51.

Ramirez, D.A., Hoopes, J. and Quinlan, T.L. 2003. Defining Racial Profiling in a Post-September 11 World. *American Criminal Law Review*, 40, 1195, 1204–6.

Ratzel, F. 1923. *Politische Geographie.* Munich and Berlin: R. Oldenbourg.

Re, L. 2006. *Carcere e globalizzazione. Il boom penitenziario negli Stati Uniti e in Europa.* Bari: Laterza.

Rechea Alberola, C., Fernández Molina, E. and Benítez Jiménez, M.J. 2005. La visión de la seguridad en la prensa. Una valoración del tratamiento que realizan los medios de prensa sobre la delincuencia y la inseguridad ciudadana.

[Online]. Available at: http://www.uned.es/investigacion/publicaciones/ Cuadernillo_Abril05.pdf [accessed: 25 March 2010].

Refugee Council UK 2007. *Briefing: The New Asylum Model*. [Online]. Available at: http://www.refugeecouncil.org.uk/NR/rdonlyres/BAD3EAD5-5267-4038 -9B16-E99362400DCD/0/Newasylummodel.pdf

Reiner, R. 1997. Media Made Criminality: The Representation of Crime in the Mass Media, in *The Oxford Handbook of Criminology*, edited by M. Maguire, R. Morgan and R. Reiner. Oxford: Oxford University Press, 189–232.

Rey, H. 1996. *La peur des banlieues*. Paris: Presses de Sciences-Po.

Reyniers, A. 1999. *Evaluation of Gypsy Populations and of Their Movements in Central and Eastern Europe and in Some OECD Countries, Focusing on the Issues of Migration, Application for Asylum, Demography and Employment*. Paris: OCDE.

Ricci, G. 2002. *Ossessione turca*. Bologna: Il Mulino.

Rigo, E. 2004. Aux frontières de l'Europe. Citoyennetés post-coloniales dans l'Europe élargie. *Multitudes*, 19, 73–84.

Rigo, E. 2007. *Europa di confine*. Rome: Meltemi.

Ringhold, D., Orenstein, M.A. and Wilkens, E. 2003. *Roma in an Expanding Europe: Breaking the Poverty Cycle*. Washington, DC: World Bank.

Rios Corbacho, J.M. 2006. Regulación juridical de la extranjería: situación actual, in *Sistema Penal y exclusion de extranjeros*, edited by L.R. Ruiz Rodríguez. Albacete: Bomarzo.

Ríos Martin, J.C. and Cabrera P.J. 1998. *Mil Voces Presas*. Madrid: Univ. Pontificia de Comillas.

Robert, P. 2005. *La sociologie du crime*. Paris: La Découverte.

Robert, P., Aubusson de Cavarlay, B., Pottier, M.-L. and Tournier, P. (eds) 1985. *Les comptes du crime, les délinquances en France et leurs mesures*. Paris: Sycomore.

Robert, P., Aubusson de Cavarlay, B., Pottier, M.-L. and Tournier, P. 1994. *Les comptes du crime. Les délinquance en France et leur mesure*. Paris: l'Harmattan.

Robert, P., Pottier, M.-L. and Zauberman, R. 2003. Les enquêtes de victimation et la connaissance de la délinquance. *Bulletin de méthodologie statistique*, 80, 5–24.

Robert, P., Zauberman, R., Névanen, S. and Didier, E. 2008. L'évolution de la délinquance d'après les enquêtes de victimation, France, 1984–2005. *Déviance et Société*, 4, 435–71.

Robin, C. 2004. *Fear: The History of a Political Idea*. Oxford: Oxford University Press (Italian 2005. Milan: Università Bocconi).

Robinson, V., Anderson, R. and Musterd, S. (eds) 2003. *Spreading the Burden? A Review of Policies to Disperse Asylum Seekers and Refugees*. Bristol: Policy Press.

Rodier, C. and Terray, E. (eds) 2008. *Immigration: fantasmes et réalités*. Paris: La Découverte.

Rodríguez, E. 2003. *El gobierno imposible.* Madrid: Traficantes de Sueños.

Romano, S. 1918. *Corso di diritto coloniale.* Rome: Athenaeum.

Ronchey, S. 2002. *Lo Stato bizantino.* Turin: Einaudi.

Rostovzeef, M. 1926. *The Social and Economic History of the Roman Empire.* Oxford: Oxford University Press (Italian 2003. *Storia economica e sociale dell'Impero romano.* Milan: Sansoni).

Rudovsky, D. (2001) Law Enforcement by Stereotypes and Serendipity: Racial Profiling and Stops and Searches Without Cause. *University of Pennsylvania Journal of Constitutional Law*, 3, 296–366.

Ruggiero, V. 2000. *Crime and Markets.* Oxford: Oxford University Press.

Ruiz Rodríguez, L.R. 2006. Extranjeros en prisión. Una marginación reiterada, in *Sistema Penal y exclusión de extranjeros,* edited by L.R. Ruiz Rodríguez. Albacete: Bomarzo, 181–93.

Runciman, S. 1951. *A History of the Crusades.* Cambridge: Cambridge University Press (Italian 1966. *Storia delle crociate*, 2 vols. Turin: Einaudi).

Russell, K.K. 2001. Racial Profiling: A Status Report of the Legal, Legislative, and Empirical Literature. *Rutgers Race & Law Review*, 3, 61, 65–8.

Sachverständigenrat für Zuwanderung und Integration 2004. *Migration und Integration – Erfahrungen nutzen, Neus Wagen.* Berlin: Jahresgutachten.

Said, E. 1985. *Orientalism.* New York: Columbia University Press (Italian 2001, 2nd edn. *Orientalismo.* Milan: Feltrinelli).

Said, E. 2000. *Reflections on Exile and other Literary and Cultural Essays.* London: Granta Books.

Saint-Saëns, I. 2004. Des Camps en Europe aux camps de l'Europe. *Multitudes*, 19, 61–72.

Sanna, C. 2006. L'islamico, l'extracomunitario e il clandestino. La rappresentazione della popolazione migrante nei quotidiani italiani prima e dopo l'11 settembre. Florence, PhD thesis.

Sartori, G. 2000. *Pluralismo, multiculturalismo e estranei. Saggio sulla società multietnica.* Milan: Rizzoli.

Sarzotti, C. (ed.) 2007. *Processi di selezione del crimine. Procure della Repubblica e organizzazione giudiziaria.* Milan: Giuffrè.

Sasse, G. 2006. Minority Rights in Central and Eastern Europe before and after EU Enlargement, report presented at the 'Ethnic mobilization in the New Europe' workshop, Brussels, 21–22 April.

Sassen, S. 2007. *A Sociology of Globalization.* New York: Norton.

Sayad, A. 1991. *L'immigration ou les paradoxes de l'alterité.* Brussels: Editions Universitaires et De Boeck.

Sayad, A. 1999. *La double absence. Des illusions de l'emigré aux souffrances de l'immigré.* Paris: Seuil (English 2004. *The Suffering of the Immigrant.* Cambridge: Polity Press.

Sayad, A. 2002. *Histoire et recherche identitaire.* Paris: Bouchène.

Scheingold, S. 1984. *The Politics of Law and Order: Street Crime and Public Policy.* New York: Longman.

Scheingold, S.A. 1991. *The Politics of Street Crime: Criminal Process and Cultural Obsession*. Philadelphia: Temple University Press.

Schlesinger, P. 1990. Rethinking the Sociology of Journalism: Source Strategies and the Limits of Media Centrism, *in Public Communication: The New Imperatives*, edited by M. Ferguson. London: Sage, 61–83.

Schneider, F.G. 2004. *The Size of the Shadow Economies of 145 Countries all over the World: First Results over the Period 1999 to 2003* (December). IZA Discussion Paper No. 1431. [Online]. Available at SSRN: http://ssrn.com/abstract=636661

Schuster, L. 2003. *The Use and Abuse of Political Asylum in Britain and Germany*. London: Frank Cass.

Schutz, A. 1979. *Saggi sociologici*. Turin: Utet.

Schwarz, H. and Ray, S. (eds) 2000. *A Companion to Postcolonial Studies*. Oxford: Blackwell.

Scull, A.T. 1977. *Decarceration: Community Treatment and the Deviant*. Englewood Cliffs, NJ: Prentice Hall.

Secretaría General de Instituciones Penitenciarias 2009. *Estadísticas mensuales. Noviembre 2009* [Online]. Available at: http://www.mir.es/INSTPENI/Gestion/Estadisticas_mensuales/2009/11/index.html [accessed 1 February 2010].

Secrétariat général du Comité interministériel de contrôle de l'immigration 2007. *Les orientations de la politique de l'immigration*. Paris: La Documentation française.

Sellin, T. 1984. *Conflits de culture et criminalité* (French trans. by Y. Marx). Paris: Editions Pédone.

Sennett, R. 2000. *The Corrosion of Character: The Personal Consequences of Work in the New Capitalism*. New York: Norton.

Servicio de Estudios de Caixa Catalunya 2006. *Informe semestral I/2006. Economía española y contexto internacional*. [Online]. Available at: http://www.caixacat.es/caixacat/es/ccpublic/particulars/publica/pdf/iee0706e0.pdf [accessed: 10 March 2008].

Shepherd, J. 2009. New Children's Database Faces Criticism. *Guardian*, 26 January.

Sigona, N. 2003. How Can a 'Nomad' be a Refugee? Kosovo Roma and Labelling Policy in Italy. *Sociology*, 37, 1, 69–80.

Sigona N. (ed.) 2006. Political Participation and Media Representation of Roma and Sinti in Italy, Report for OSCE/ODIHR, Varsaw. [Online]. Available at: http://www.osservazione.org/documenti/osce_italy.pdf

Sigona, N. 2008a. Sono il nemico pubblico n.1? *Reset*, 107, 87–8.

Sigona N. (ed.) 2008b. *The 'Latest' Public Enemy: Romanian Roma In Italy. The Case Studies of Milan, Bologna, Rome and Naples*, Draft Final Report. [Online]. Available at: http://www.osservazione.org/documenti/OSCE_publicenemy.pdf

Sigona, N. and Monasta, L. 2006. *Cittadinanze Imperfette. Rapporto sulla discriminazione razziale di rom e sinti in Italia*. Santa Maria Capua Vetere: Spartaco.

Sigona, N. and Trehan, N. 2009. *Romani Politics in Contemporary Europe: Poverty, Ethnic Mobilization and the Neoliberal Order*. London: Palgrave Macmillan.

Silveira Gorski, H.C. 1996. La exclusión del otro extranjero y la democracia de las diferencias, in *En el límite de los derechos*, edited by Various Authors. Madrid: Trotta, 133–63.

Silveira Gorski, H.C. 2002. Los Centros de Internamiento de Extranjeros y el futuro del Estado de derecho. *Mientras Tanto*, 83, 93–102.

Silveira Gorski, H.C. 2003. Inmigración y derecho: la institucionalización de un sistema dual de ciudadanía, in *Sistema penal y Problemas sociales*, edited by R. Bergalli. Valencia: Tirant lo Blanch, 539–76.

Simmel, G. 1908. *Soziologie*. Berlin: Duncker & Humblot (Italian 1989. *Sociologia*: Milan:, Comunità).

Simon, J. 1997. *Governing Through Crime, in The Crime Conundrum: Essays on Criminal Justice*, edited by L. Friedman and L. Fisher. Boulder, CO: Westview Press.

Simon, J. 2007. *Governing through Crime: How the War on Crime Transformed American Democracy and Created a Culture of Fear*. New York: Oxford University Press.

Simon, J. 2008. From the New Deal to the Crime Deal, in *After the War on Crime: Race, Democracy and a New Reconstruction*, edited by J. Simon, I. Haney-López and M.L. Frampton. New York: New York University Press, 48–60.

Simoni, A. 2008. I decreti emergenza nomadi: il nuovo volto di un vecchio problema. *Diritto, Immigrazione e Cittadinanza*, 10, 3–4, 44–56.

Skolnick, J.H. and Caplovitz, A. 2003. Guns, Drugs, and Profiling: Ways to Target Guns and Minimize Racial Profiling, in *Guns, Crime, and Punishment in America*, edited by B.E. Harcourt. New York: New York University Press, 249–79.

Slama, S. 2008. Politique d'immigration: un laboratoire de la frénésie sécuritaire, in *La frénésie sécuritaire. Retour à l'ordre et nouveau contrôle social*, edited by L. Mucchielli. Paris: La Découverte, 64–76.

Sobotka, E. 2003. Romani Migrations in the 1990s: Perspectives on Dynamic, Interpretation and Policy. *Romani Studies*, 13, 2, 79–121.

Soguk, N. and Whitehall, G. 1999. Wandering Grounds: Transversality, Territoriality and Movement. *Millennium: Journal of International Studies*, 128, 3.

Sperry, P. 2005. When the Profile Fits the Crime. *New York Times*, 28 July. [Online]. Available at: http://www.nytimes.com/2005/07/28/opinion/28sperry.html

Spire, A. 2005. *Etrangers à la carte*. Paris: Grasset.

Statewatch 2005a. The Prevention of Terrorism Act 2005. *Statewatch* bulletin, 15, 1, 21–2.

Statewatch 2005b. Criminalising Headgear, 15, 2, 9.

Statewatch 2008a. 'Mosquito' Told to Buzz Off, 18, 1, 3.

Statewatch 2008b. November supplement. Available at: http://www2.ohchr.org/
    english/bodies/crc/docs/AdvanceVersions/CRC.C.GBR.CO.4.pdf

Statewatch 2009. 'Terrorist' lists: monitoring proscription, designation and asset-
    freezing – Update March 2009. [Online]. Available at: http://www.statewatch.
    org/news/2009/mar/sw-terrorist-list-observatory-update-march-2009.pdf

Statistisches Bundesamt. *Stand und Entwicklung der Erwerbstätigkeit*, Wiesbaden.
    2004, 2005, 2006, 2007, 2008.

Statistisches Bundesamt 2004. *Strukturdaten uns Integrationsindikatoren über die
    ausländische Bevölkerung in Deutschland 2002*. Wiesbaden.

Statistisches Bundesamt: Bevölkerung und Erwerbstätigkeit 2008. *Bevölkerung
    mit Migrationshintergrund – Ergebnisse des Mikrozensus 2007*. Wiesbaden.

Steiker, C.S. 1994. Second Thoughts about First Principles. *Harvard Law Review*,
    107, 820, 844.

Stella, G.A. and Franzina, E. 2003. Brutta gente. Il razzismo anti-italiano, in *Storia
    dell'Emigrazione Italiana. Arrivi*, edited by P. Bevilacqua, A. De Clementi
    and E. Franzina. Rome: Donzelli.

Steinhilper, U. 1986. *Definitions– und Entscheidungsprozesse bei sexuell
    motivierten Gewaltdelikten*. Konstanz: Universitätsverlag Konstanz.

Stigler, G.J. 1974. The Optimum Enforcement of Laws, in *Essays in the Economics
    of Crime and Punishment*, edited by G.S. Becker and W.M. Landes. New York:
    Columbia University Press, 55–67.

Stora, B. 1991. *La gangrène et l'oubli. La mémoire de la Guerre d'Algérie*. Paris:
    La Découverte.

Stora, B. 1992. *Ils venaient d'Algérie. L'immigration algérienne en France (1912–
    1992)*. Paris: Fayard.

Sudbury, J. (ed.) 2005. *Global Lockdown: Race, Gender, and the Prison Industrial
    Complex*. New York: Routledge.

Surette, R. 1998. *Media, Crime, and Criminal Justice: Images and Realities*.
    London: Wadsworth.

Swarns, R.L. 2004. U.S. to Give Border Patrol Agents the Power to Deport Illegal
    Aliens. *New York Times*, A1, 11 August.

Taguieff, P.A. 1987. *La force du préjugé. Essai sur le racisme et ses doubles*.
    Paris: La Découverte (English 2001. *The Force of Prejudice: On Racism and
    Its Doubles*. Minneapolis: University of Minnesota Press)

Tavares, C. and Thomas, G., 2008. Statistics in Focus. *Population and Social
    Conditions*, 19, Brussels: Eurostat.

Taylor, C. 1992. *Multiculturalism and 'The Politics of Recognition'*. Princeton:
    Princeton University Press.

Ter Wal, J. 2002. Italy, in *Racism and Cultural Diversity in the Mass Media: An
    Overview of Research and Examples of Good Practice in the EU Member
    States, 1995–2000*, edited by European Monitory Centre on Racism and
    Xenophobia. Wien, 239–72.

Tesser, L. 2003. The Geopolitics of Tolerance: Minority Rights under EU Expansion in East-Central Europe. *East European Politics and Societies*, 17, 3, 483–532.

Tévanian, P. and Tessot, S. 2002. *Dictionnaire de la lepénisation des esprits*. Paris: L'Esprit Frappeur.

Thomas, H. 2010. *Les Vulnérables. La démocratie contre les pauvres*. Bellecombe-en-Bauge: Editions du Croquant.

Thompson, A.C. 1999. Stopping the Usual Suspects: Race and the Fourth Amendment. *New York University Law Review*, 74, 956, 961.

Tiberj, V. 2008. *La crispation hexagonale. France fermée contre France plurielle, 2001–2007*. Paris: Plon.

Tiemann, S. 2004. *Die Integration islamischer Migranten in Deutschland und Frankreich – ein Situationsvergleich ausgewählter Bevölkerungsgruppen*. Berlin.

Tillmann, K.J., Holler-Nowitzki, B., Holtappels, H.G., Meier, U. and Popp, U. 2000. *Schülergewalt als Schulproblem. Verursachende Bedingungen, Erscheinungsformen und pädagogische Handlungsperspektiven*. Munich: Weinheim.

Todorov, T. 1989. *Nous et les autres. La réflexion française sur la diversité humaine*. Paris: Seuil.

Tonry, M. (ed.) 1997. Ethnicity, Crime, and Immigration: Comparative and Cross-National Perspectives. *Crime and Justice. A Review of Research*, 21.

Tonry, M. 2004. *Thinking About Crime: Sense and Sensibility in American Penal Culture*. New York: Oxford University Press.

Topfer, E. 2008. Searching for Needles in an Ever Expanding Haystack: Cross-Border DNA Data Exchange in the Wake of the Prum Treaty. *Statewatch*, 18, 3, 14–17.

Tournier, P. 1997. Nationality, Crime and Criminal Justice in France, in Ethnicity, Crime, and Immigration. Comparative and Cross-National Perspectives, *Crime and Justice. A Review of Research*, 21, edited by M. Tonry. Chicago: University of Chicago Press, 523–51 [first version 1996, in *Délit d'immigration*, edited by S. Palidda. Brussels: European Community].

Tournier, P. and Robert, P. 1991. *Étrangers et délinquance. Les chiffres du débat*. Paris: L'Harmattan.

Travis, A. 2009. The Return of the Asbo. *Guardian*, 29 September.

Tsoukala, A. 2000. La criminalisation des immigrés en Europe. Syndicat de la Magistrature and French League of Human Rights Meeting, 'La pénalisation de la pauvreté', Montpellier, 26 May.

Tsoukala, A. 2002. Le traitement médiatique de la criminalité étrangère en Europe. *Déviance et Société*, 1, 61–82.

Tsoukala, A. (forthcoming) The Administrative Detention of Foreigners in France: An Expanding Network of Exclusionary Spaces, in *Civil Society, State and the Police in India and France*, edited by A. Mehra A. and R. Lévy. New Jersey: Pearson Education.

Turcan, R. 1989. *Les cultes orientaux dans le monde romain*. Paris: Les belles lettres.

UNDP 2002. *Roma in Central and Eastern Europe: Avoiding the Dependency Trap*, UNDP/ILO Regional Human Development Report. Bratislava: UNDP.

United Nations 2008. Report of the Committee on the Elimination of Racial Discrimination: Seventy-second session (18 February–7 March 2008), Seventy-third session (28 July–15 August 2008), General Assembly, Official Records, Sixty-third session, Supplement No. 18 (A/63/18).

UNHCR 2006. Draft Directive on Temporary Protection in the Event of a Mass Influx, Geneva, September.

Unnever, J.D. and Hembroff, L.A. 1988. The Prediction of Racial/Ethnic Sentencing Disparities: An Expectation States Approach. *Journal of Research in Crime and Delinquency*, 25, 53–82.

Valluy, J. 2005. Vrai ou faux réfugiés ? Espaces Temps (Réfléchir les sciences sociales). *Les Cahiers*, 89/90, 96–103.

Valluy, J. 2006. Les politiques européennes de l'immigration et de l'asile sous tension: entre logique des quotas et logique anti-migratoire. *Cahiers du CEMMM*, 8, 33–41.

Valluy, J. 2009. *Rejet des exilés. Le grand retournement du droit de l'asile*. Bellecombe-en-Bauge: Editions du Croquant.

Van Baar, H. 2008. The Way Out of Amnesia? Europeisation and the Recognition of the Roma's Past and Present. *Third Text*, 22, 3, 373–85.

Van Baar, H. 2009. Contesting Neo-liberal Practices in Central and Eastern Europe: Romani Minority Governance between Activation and Activism, unpublished paper presented at the conference 'Multi-Disciplinary and Cross-National Approaches to Romany Studies – a Model for Europe', 22 June – 10 July, Budapest: Central European University.

Van Broeck, J. 2001. Cultural Defence and Culturally Motivated Crimes (Cultural Offences). *European Journal of Crime, Criminal Law and Criminal Justice*, 9, 1, 1–32.

Various Authors 1970. *The Cambridge History of Islam, vol. II: The Further Islamic Lands – Islamic Societies and Civilizations*. London and New York: Cambridge University Press.

Various Authors 1981. *Le génie d'oc et l'homme méditerranéen*. Marseille: Rivages.

Various Authors 2002. *L'histoire familiale des détenus*. Paris: Insee, collection Insee Synthèses.

Various Authors 2006. Internamenti. CPT e altri campi. *Conflitti globali*, 4.

Vassallo Paleologo, F. 2009. La Guantanamo d'Europa?, in *Razzismo democratico*, edited by S. Palidda. Milan: Agenzia X, 200–213.

Vaux Defouletier, F. 1990 [1970]. *Mille anni di storia degli zingari*. Milan: Jaca Books.

Vermeersch, P. 2006. *The Romani Movement: Minority Politics and Ethnic Mobilization in Contemporary Central Europe*. Oxford and New York: Berghahn Books.

Vermeersch, P. 2010. Between Europeanisation and Discrimination: The Roma as a Special Focus of EU Policy, in Refugee Studies Centre, Romani Mobilities in Europe: Multidisciplinary Perspectives Conference Papers, University of Oxford, 200–210.

Veyne, P. 1975. *Le pain et le cirque. Sociologie historique d'un pluralisme politique*. Paris: Seuil.

Veyne, P. 1978. *Comment on écrit l'histoire*. Paris: Seuil.

Veyne, P. 1998. *Foucault: la storia, il nichilismo e la morale*, edited by M. Guareschi. Verona: Ombre corte.

Viet, V. 2004. *Histoire des Français venus d'ailleurs, de 1850 à nos jours*. Paris: Perrin.

Wacquant, L. 1999a. *Les prisons de la misère*. Paris: Raisons d'Agir (English 2009. University of Minnesota Press. Spanish 2000. Madrid: Alianza).

Wacquant, L. 1999b. Suitable Enemies: Foreigners and Immigrants in the Prisons of Europe, *Punishment and Society*, 1, 2, 215–22.

Wacquant, L. 2005a. Race as Civic Felony. *International Social Science Journal*, 183, 127–42.

Wacquant, L. 2005b. The Great Penal Leap Backward: Incarceration in America from Nixon to Clinton, in *The New Punitiveness: Trends, Theories, Perspectives*, edited by J. Pratt and Others. Cullompton: Willan, 3–26.

Wacquant, L. 2008. The Place of the Prison in the New Government of Poverty, in *After the War on Crime*, edited by M.L. Frampton, I.H. López and J. Simon. New York: New York University Press.

Wacquant, L. 2009a. *Punishing the Poor: The Neoliberal Government of Social Insecurity*. Durham, NC: Duke University Press (French 2004. Agone).

Wacquant, L. 2009b. *Prisons of Poverty*. Minneapolis: Minnesota University Press.

Wagman, D. 2006. *Perfil racial en España: Investigaciones y recomendaciones*. [Online]. Available at: http:// www.ecln.org/link.asp?linkid=530 [accessed: 10 March 2008].

Weber, C. 1995. *Simulating Sovereignty: Intervention, the State and Symbolic Exchange*. Cambridge: Cambridge University Press.

Weber, L. and Bowling, B. 2004. Policing Migration: A Framework for Investigating the Regulation of Global Mobility. *Policing and Society* 14, 3, 195–212.

Weber, M. 1920. *Gesammelte Aufsätze zur Religionssoziologie*. Tübingen: J.C.B. Mohr (Italian 1982. *Sociologia della religione*. Milan: Comunità).

Weber, M. 1922. *Wirtschaft und Gesellschaft*. Tübingen: J.C.B. Mohr (Italian 1999. *Economia e società*. Turin: Comunità, vol. IV).

Weber, M. 1958. *Gesammelte Politische Schriften*. Tübingen: J.C.B. Mohr (Italian 1999. *Scritti politici*. Rome: Donzelli).

Weber, M. 1988. Energetische Kulturtheorien, in *Gesammelte Schriften zur Wissenschaftslehre*. Tübingen: J.C.B. Mohr.

Weil, P. 1991. *La France et ses étrangers. L'aventure d'une politique de l'immigration, 1938–1991*. Paris: Calmann-Lévy.

Welch, M. and Schuster L. 2005. Detention of Asylum Seekers in the UK and USA: Deciphering Noisy and Quiet Constructions. *Punishment and Society*, 7, 397–417.

Wells, C.M. 1992. *The Roman Empire*, second edn. London: Fontana Press.

West, H.C. and Sabol W.J. 2008. *Prisoners in 2007*. Bureau of Justice Statistics, U.S. Department of Justice, Office of Justice Programs, December, NCJ 224280.

Western, B. 2006. *Punishment and Inequality in America*. New York: Russell Sage Foundation.

Wheatcroft, A. 2004. *Infidels: A History of the Conflict Between Christendom and Islam*. Harmondsworth: Penguin.

Wilson, W.J. 1987. *The Truly Disadvantaged: The Inner City, the Underclass, and Public Policy*. Chicago: University of Chicago Press.

Winter, B. 1994. Women, the Law, and Cultural Relativism in France: The Case of Excision. *Signs. Journal of Women in Culture and Society*, 19/4, 939–72.

Wolf, E.R. 1997. *Europe and the Peoples without History*, 2nd edn. Berkeley: University of California Press.

Wolfensohn, J.D. and Soros, G. 2003. *Why The Roma Matter in Eur*ope. Report presented at the Conference on Roma in an Expanding Europe: Challenges for the Future, Budapest, 30 June–1 July.

Worthington, A. 2007. *The Guantanamo Files: Stories of the 774 Detainees in America's Illegal Prison*. London: Pluto Press.

Xenophon 2002. *Elleniche*, edited by G. Daverio Rocchi. Milan: Biblioteca Universale Rizzoli.

Young, J. 1988. *Risk of Crime and Fear of Crime: The Politics of Victimisation Studies*. [Online]. Available at: http://www.malcolmread.co.uk/JockYoung/RISK.htm [accessed: 1 April 2010].

Young, J. 2003. *La sociedad 'excluyente'*. Madrid: Marcial Pons.

Zauberman, R. (ed.) 2009. *Victimisation and Insecurity in Europe: A Review of Surveys and their Use*. Criminologische Studies. Brussels: VUBPress.

Zimring, F. 2008. *The Great American Crime Decline*. Oxford: Oxford University Press.

Žižek, S. 2005. *Bienvenidos al desierto de lo real*. Madrid: Akal.

Zorzella, N. 2008. I nuovi poteri dei sindaci nel 'pacchetto sicurezza' e la loro ricaduta sugli stranieri. *Diritto, Immigrazione e Cittadinanza*, 3–4, 57–73.

Index

statistics 215–27, **216**, **217**, **218**,
    219–20, **222–3**, **226**, 227–30,
    227–8, **229**
refugees in 107n1
Roma in 90, 93n38, 120, 122–3, 124,
    125, 126, 127, 215, 233
Romanians in 24, 90, 127, 219, 225,
    226
southerners of 227–33, **227–8**, **229**
Tunisians in 225, **226**

Kosovo 124, 125, 131

language
    and government policies 84–5
    and media discourse 84–93
Latinos
    in Italy 24
    in USA 6, 26, 29, 134, **134**, **135**, 137,
        138
Latvia 25
Lega Nord 2n6, 19, 53–4, 83, 214n7, **220n**,
    220–21, 230n20
Lévy, R. 4n13, 155, 166, 175
Lombroso, Cesare 81, 119–20, 230

Macedonia 124, 125, 128
Macedonians **226**
Maghrebis 6, 28
    and France 111, 151, **152**, 158n30, 166,
        167, 175
    in Italy 53, 90
Malta 25
Maroni, Roberto 214, 220–21, 224n15,
    231, 232
Martinez-Fuerte case 242–5, 246, 247,
    248, 251
media discourse 77–84, 231–3
    and language 84–93, **86**
Mexicans
    entering USA 237–45, 250
        Brignoni-Ponce case 238, 240–42,
            244, 251
        Martinez-Fuerte case 242–5, 251
minors 254–60
Moldovans **226**
Montenegro 124, 125
Moroccans 5, 74, 147n2, 225, **226**

Muslims 11, 75
    in Belgium 69–72, 74
    and Christians 41–3, 55–6
    in France 148–9
    in Germany 178
    in Italy **86**, 86–7
    and media discourse **86**, 86–7
    in UK 261
    in US 251

National Front (France) 112–13, 148, 173
neoconservatism 2–4, 6, 135–6
neoliberalism 2–4, 6
    and cultural defence and cultural
        offence 65–8, 75
    in Europe 121, 131
    and punitive governance 143–4
    in US 135–6, 143–4
Netherlands, the 9, 26, **27**, 107n1, 116,
    227
New York 4n13
New York Police Department 4n13
Nigerians 225, **226**
Noiriel, G. 10n30, 17n48, 147n1, 173
North Africans 24
Northern League (Italy), *see* Lega Nord
Norway 26, **27**

Obama, Barack 144
Organization for Security and Co-operation
    in Europe 124, 127
Ottoman Empire 42–3, 55–6

Pakistanis **226**
Palestinians 11
Peruvians **226**
Poles 184, **226**
police 4n13, 13–14
    corruption, abuse and violence 16–19,
        215
    crime-solving rates 28
    in France 17, 174–5, 215n10
        crime statistics 154–60, **156**, **157**,
            160, 162–3, **163**, 173–4
    in Germany 17, 187–9, 195
        crime statistics 185–6, 194
    in Italy 17, 18n52, 19, 215
        crime statistics 215, **216**

Advances in Criminology

Full series list

Pervasive Prevention
A Feminist Reading of the Rise of
the Security Society
Tamar Pitch

Children's Rights and the Minimum
Age of Criminal Responsibility
A Global Perspective
Don Cipriani

Hate on the Net:
Extremist Sites, Neo-fascism On-line,
Electronic Jihad
Antonio Roversi

Decisions to Imprison:
Court Decision-Making Inside
and Outside the Law
Rasmus H. Wandall

The Policing of Transnational Protest
*Edited by Donatella della Porta,
Abby Peterson and Herbert Reiter*

Migration, Culture Conflict, Crime
and Terrorism
*Edited by Joshua D. Freilich and
Rob T. Guerette*

Re-Thinking the Political Economy
of Punishment:
Perspectives on Post-Fordism
and Penal Politics
Alessandro De Giorgi

Deleuze and Environmental Damage:
Violence of the Text
Mark Halsey

Globalization and Regulatory Character:
Regulatory Reform after the Kader Toy
Factory Fire
Fiona Haines

Family Violence and Police Response:
Learning From Research, Policy and
Practice in European Countries
*Edited by Wilma Smeenk and
Marijke Malsch*

Crime and Culture:
An Historical Perspective
*Edited by Amy Gilman Srebnick and
René Lévy*

Power, Discourse and Resistance:
A Genealogy of the Strangeways Prison
Riot
Eamonn Carrabine

Hard Lessons:
Reflections on Governance and Crime
Control in Late Modernity
Richard Hil and Gordon Tait

Becoming Delinquent: British and
European Youth, 1650–1950
Edited by Pamela Cox and Heather Shore

Migration, Culture Conflict and Crime
*Edited by Joshua D. Freilich, Graeme
Newman, S. Giora Shoham and
Moshe Addad*

Critique and Radical Discourses on Crime
George Pavlich

0 1341 1380724 9